India, Global Powers and West Asia

Political and Economic Dynamics

India, Global Powers and West Asia

Political and Economic Dynamics

Edited by

Anwar Alam
Director, Centre for West Asian Studies,
Jamia Millia Islamia, New Delhi.

New Century Publications
New Delhi, India

NEW CENTURY PUBLICATIONS
4800/24, Bharat Ram Road,
Ansari Road, Daryaganj,
New Delhi – 110 002 (India)

Tel.: 011-2324 7798, 4358 7398, 6539 6605
Fax: 011-4101 7798
E-mail: indiatax@vsnl.com • info@newcenturypublications.com
www.newcenturypublications.com

Editorial office:
LG–7, Aakarshan Bhawan,
4754-57/23, Ansari Road, Daryaganj,
New Delhi – 110 002

Tel.: 011-4356 0919

First Published: **2011**

ISBN: **978-81-7708-261-6**

Published by New Century Publications and printed at Salasar Imaging Systems, New Delhi.

Designs: Patch Creative Unit, New Delhi.

PRINTED IN INDIA

The Book

India's economic interests and its self imagination as an emerging global power have assumed a higher priority in defining India's foreign policy and security goals since early 1990s. This has guided the Indian policy makers to intensify its engagements with Iran, Saudi Arabia, Israel and other GCC countries—around which Indian foreign policy in the region revolves today in the political and economic sense of the term. This book deals with evolving political and economic dynamics and interactions of India with global and regional powers in West Asia, with particular focus on Persian Gulf in the post-Cold War period. It examines India's multi-dimensional relations with global powers such as USA, Russia, China and regional powers and organisations like Iran, Israel, Turkey and Gulf Cooperation Council (GCC) respectively.

Editor's Profile

Anwar Alam is currently Professor and Director, Centre for West Asian Studies, Jamia Millia Islamia, New Delhi. He has served as a Lecturer in the Department of Political Science, Aligarh Muslim University (AMU), and Assistant and Associate Professor at the Centre for West Asian and African Studies, School of International Studies, Jawaharlal Nehru University (JNU), New Delhi. He has been awarded the ICSSR Doctoral Fellowship (1991), International Visitor Programme (Islamic) Scholarship, USA, (2002), Indo-French Social Scientist Exchange Programme Fellowship (2003) and Alexandor Von Humboldt Post Doctoral Fellowship (2004-2006). He has been Visiting Fellow at Maison des Sciences de l'Homme (MSH), Paris, France (March-April 2005), Centre for Citizenship and Ethnicity, Department of Sociology, University of Bristol, Bristol, UK (May-June 2005) and at International Institute for the Study of Islam in the Modern World (ISIM), Leiden, Netherlands (July-August 2005). He has authored 4 books, *Religion and State: A Comparative Study of Contemporary Egypt, Iran and Saudi Arabia* (1998); *India and West Asia in the Era of Globalisation* (edited, 2008); *Iran and Post- 9/11 World Order* (edited, 2009) and *Contemporary West Asia* (edited, 2010). Besides, he has contributed several articles in national and international referred journals and chapters in edited books. His areas of research interest include International Politics, Political Theory, Religion and Politics, Political Islam, Globalisation and Muslim Society.

Contents

Contributors

Berdal Aral is an Associate Professor at the Department of International Relations, Fatih University, Istanbul, Turkey. He received his BA in the International Relations from Ankara University in 1985 and conducted his postgraduate studies, first, at the University of Kent where he wrote a thesis under the title, "Freedom of Movement for Workers between Turkey and the EEC" in February 1990. He then took up a PhD programme at the University of Glasgow where he wrote a thesis entitled "Turkey and International Society from a Critical Legal Perspective" which was accepted in September 1994. He is the author of *Uluslararası Hukukta Meşru Müdafaa Hakkı* (Self-Defence in International Law), published in 1999. He has written numerous articles on international law, human rights and Turkish foreign policy some of which have appeared in international journals and other publications. He has also joined a number of international and national conferences where he presented papers on human rights and international law. Dr. Aral is fluent in English, with some knowledge of French.

Faisal Ahmed is an Assistant Professor of International Business and Strategy and Program Director of International Business Program at Asia-Pacific Institute of Management, New Delhi. He is also Joint Co-ordinator of International Academic Exchange Program, France. He holds Master of International Business Management degree from Aligarh and Ph.D. in Economics from Udaipur. He has contributed more than twenty five research papers and is invited by premier universities, think tanks and chambers of commerce as speaker and expert panelist. His research interests include regional integration, trade policy, GCC and geopolitics and areas of consulting interests are international business facilitations and public diplomacy.

Javed Ahmad Khan is currently an Associate Professor at the Centre for West Asian Studies, Jamia Millia Islamia, New Delhi. His publications include: *Iraq Reconstruction–The Arabs Response to an Imperial Design* (2008), *India's Energy Security and the Arabian Gulf: Oil and Gas Market in Decontrolled Regime* (2005), *Islamic Banking in India-Scope and Challenges* (edited, 2003), *India and West Asia: Emerging Markets in the Liberalization Era* (1999) and *Islamic Economics and Finance: A Bibliography* (compiled, 1995). His areas of research include: Indo-Gulf economic relations and Islamic finance.

K.M. Sajad Ibrahim is an Assistant Professor in the Department of Political Science, University of Kerala, India. He has authored a book, *Palestinian Distress: The Ambiguity of Former Soviet Policy* (2007) and contributed more than 15 research articles in reputed journals including EPW, India Quarterly etc. His area of research includes West Asian politics, status of Indian Muslims, environment issues, election studies etc.

M. Mahtab Alam Rizvi is an Associate Fellow at the Institute for Defence Studies and Analyses (IDSA), New Delhi. He has done his Masters and Ph. D in Political Science, from A.M.U., Aligarh. He has written a number of articles in various reputed national and international journals. Some of his recent publications are *US Sanctions on Iran and their Impact on India,* Issue Brief, June 21, 2010, IDSA, New Delhi; *Iraq Desperate to Appease Iran Without Losing the US*, Strategic Analysis, Routledge Publication, Vol. 32, No. 6, November-December 2008; *An Assessment of Iran's Chemical and Biological Weapons*, CBW Magazine: Journal on Chemical and Biological Weapons, Vol. 2, No. 4, July-September 2009, Institute for Defence Studies & Analyses (IDSA), New Delhi, 2009. He focuses on political developments and energy security issues in Iran and the Gulf Region.

N. Janardhan is a UAE-based political analyst. He was formerly Programme Manager, Gulf-Asia Relations, at the Gulf Research Center in Dubai. His research areas include democracy, media, labour and international relations in the Gulf region, which are reflected in nearly 500 published articles in newspapers and several academic chapters. His book, *Boom Amid Gloom: The Spirit of Possibility in 21st Century Gulf,* is scheduled to be published by Ithaca Press (UK) soon.

Pankaj Kumar is an Assistant Professor in the Department of Political Science, Shyamlal College (Evening), University of Delhi, Delhi. He secured his M. Phil and Ph.D from the Centre for Canadian, US and Latin American Studies, School of International Studies, Jawaharlal Nehru University, New Delhi.

P. R. Kumaraswamy is currently professor and chairperson at Centre for West Asian Studies, School of International Studies, Jawaharlal Nehru University, New Delhi. He teaches contemporary Middle East. During 1991-99, he was a Research Fellow at the Harry S. Truman Research Institute for the Advancement of Peace, The Hebrew University of Jerusalem. His publications include *India's Israel Policy* (New York, Columbia University Press, 2010) and *Historical Dictionary of the Arab-Israeli Conflict*, (Scarecrow, 2006).

Pranav Kumar is currently an Assistant Professor, Department of Governance and Development Studies (GaDS), Hawassa University, Hawassa, SNNPR, Ethiopia. He has done his M. Phil and Ph.D from School of International Studies, Jawaharlal Nehru University, New Delhi.

Prasanta Kumar Pradhan is an Associate Fellow at the Institute for Defence Studies & Analyses, New Delhi. He did his Ph.D on "Human Rights in Islam: The Case of Saudi

Arabia" from the Centre for West Asian and African Studies, School of International Studies, Jawaharlal Nehru University, New Delhi. His areas of research are foreign policy, security and strategic issues in the Gulf region and West Asia.

Introduction:

India, Changing Global Power Structure and West Asia

By Anwar Alam

India is today at the cross roads. The sustained economic growth of India since early 1990s has convinced many in India and elsewhere about its rising status as a global power. Whether or not the current rate of growth and developmental indicators will translate into India actually acquiring the status of global power—its aspirations are unquestioned. It was this nationalist aspiration—in conjunction with other factors—that influenced the Indian leadership to play an independent and vocal role in the international arena right from its birth as an independent nation-state. As a result India spearheaded the Non-Alignment Movement at a time when the majority of post-colonial states preferred to align with one or other power bloc. The economic resurgence of the past two decades has further intensified its traditional aspiration of being recognized as a global power. Its demand for restructuring of the United Nations, particularly the issue of expansion of permanent members of the security council and its own candidature for the same, its enhanced mobility in the corridor of Western power structure, the Second Pokhran Nuclear Test (1998), its role in the formation of IBSA (India-Brazil-South Africa) and BRIC (Brazil-Russia-India-China) and other initiatives are indicative of its search for a greater role in the world affairs. The dominant section of Indian middle class, its knowledge industry and ruling elites have already started imagining and re-positioning India's stand that should be seen in congruence with the leading voices of the world.

Indian government, unlike in the past, has become very sensitive to the idea of power-politics and utilization of each opportunity that comes its way in the changed international power structure following the dissolution of erstwhile Soviet

Union and decline of Communist ideology and movement at global level. The phased liberalization of Indian economy and changes in the international power structure in the wake of disintegration on 'Soviet Empire' pushed successive Indian governments to reorient the thrust of Indian foreign policy first in accordance with the demands and expectations of US-led unipolar capitalist world order, and then with emerging multipolar world order. The Pax-Americana of early and mid-90s gradually paved the way for a multipolar world order—that was further intensified after 9/11 and US's invasion of Afghanistan and Iraq in 2001 and 2003 respectively.

The rise of Asian Powers—especially India and China—has certainly jolted the American aspiration of transforming the twenty first century into American century. In this context Fareed Zakaria has rightly noted: "On every dimension other than military power—industrial, financial, social, cultural—the distribution of power is shifting, moving away from U.S. dominance. That however does not suggest that we are entering an anti-American world; but that we are moving into a post-American world—one defined and directed from many places and by many people. [1] Former British Prime Minister, Tony Blair, has also observed that "In the next two decades China and India will undergo industrialisation four times the size of the United States and at five times the speed...For the first time in many centuries, power is moving East." Blair further added that "In this new world, we must clear a path to partnership, not stand off against each other competing for power. The world…cannot afford a return to the 20th century struggles for hegemony". [2] Further, the case of US invasion of Afghanistan and Iraq clearly demonstrates that military power, however strong, is in itself insufficient to obtain the political objectives of a war. The capacity of weaker opponents to impose high costs through asymmetric war fighting is enough to make even the strongest military power think carefully before embarking on a military option. Moreover, with increasing global interdependence, it appears that the various powers are striving for greater accommodation of interests and better management of contradictions, despite having divergent security and strategic perspectives.

By all accounts, the world is moving rapidly towards multipolarity and nation states including India are increasingly managing their bilateral and multilateral relations on the basis of a realpolitik assessment rather than ideology alone in this emerging multipolar world. As India struggles to become a responsible global power, it faces enormous challenges in terms of harmonizing its relationship with multiple competing global and regional power structures in the world. The end of the Cold War has freed India to pursue a simultaneous improvement in its relations with all the major powers, including the United States, Europe, Japan, China and Russia. Today, India is in the enviable position of having stable relations with all major military and economic powers. As Pranab Mukherjee, India's current Finance Minister, has aptly remarked, "We are no longer bound by the Cold War paradigm where good relations with one power automatically entailed negative consequences with its rivals." As a swing state being courted by all other major powers, India has to perform a balancing act. In other words, the challenge before Indian diplomacy is now to strike a balance among the competing global and regional powers and developing the diplomatic art of 'cooperating and competing' with these powers. Nowhere is this challenge more visible than in the region of West Asia, particularly in the Persian Gulf—a geographical mass that Indian government has called 'our extended neighborhood' and whose political stability is extremely important for the growth of Indian economy and its emergence as global power.

India's economic interests and its self imagination as an emerging global power have assumed a higher priority in defining India's foreign policy and security goals since early 1990s. This has guided the Indian policy makers to intensify its relationship with Iran, Saudi Arabia and Israel—the three states around which Indian foreign policy in the region revolves today in the political sense of the term. India's foreign policy postures towards Iran and Israel have been subject to much controversy in recent years. It was with reference to these two states that critics have accused successive Indian governments of abandoning its independent foreign policy. The critics saw in India's three successive negative vote against Iran in IAEA on latter's nuclear issue (2004, 2005 and 2009) and its 'perceived' lukewarm attitude towards the Iran-Pakistan-India (IPI) Pipe Line Project and growing defence and military ties with Israel as nothing but sort of surrendering its independent foreign policy in order to gain the favourable attention of Western nations, particularly the United States. While there may be a grain of truth in the critic's perception, what is interesting to note here is that India has been able to maintain its growing ties with all three states despite the mutually antagonistic relations that exist among them and the prevailing negative attitude of US and Israel towards Iran—all these must be factored in India's relations with these West Asian countries.

United States will continue to cast a shadow over Indian foreign policy in the years to come, especially if the conflict between US and Iran gets intensified. However it is equally important to stress that Indo-Iran relations are not hostage to Indo-US relations. Given the current rate of growth of Indian economy and its rising demand for energy products, India needs them both. The Indian policy makers have demonstrated their capability of maintaining 'a diplomatic balance' between the two which in part derived from its own understanding of emerging multipolar world order and mutuality of interest that binds India and USA as well as India and Iran together at the present international conjecture. Despite Iran expressing strong reservations over India's negative vote against her in IAEA, the trade volume between the two has increased from mere US$ 2 billion to US$14 billion (and US$ 32 billion via third country) today since the Delhi Declaration in 2003. India's energy needs are a major factor in India's deepening ties with

Iran. In January 2005, the Gas Authority of India Ltd (GAIL) signed a 30-year deal with the National Iranian Gas Export Corporation for the transfer of as much as 7.5 m tons of liquefied natural gas (LNG) to India per year. The deal, worth an estimated US$ 50 billion, will also entail Indian involvement in the development of Iranian gas fields.

India currently imports 16 per cent of crude oil from Iran out of its total oil import. It needs to be noted here that it is not merely energy-driven needs or historical-civilizational ties between India and Iran, or Iran's geo-strategic location (Iran controls Strait of Harmuz from where the bulk of oil tankers and other shipments passes) that propels India to maintain close ties with it; but also a political recognition of the growing influence of Iran in West Asia and Central Asia. By all accounts, Iran has emerged as one of the strongest power in the region following the US's invasion of Afghanistan and Iraq in 2001 and 2003 respectively. Its prestige, influence and domination have increased tremendously in the several quarters of the Arab World and Central Asia. It is capable of disrupting the political stability in the region, particularly in the Persian Gulf countries where India has vital economic stake. The American failure in Afghanistan and Iraq has led to a rethink within certain sections of American establishment towards seeking the support of Iran in stabilizing Iraq and Afghanistan. The Indian government cannot be oblivious to this emerging political reality and therefore Iran will continue to occupy a strategic position in India's foreign relations. For this reason India has never shared the US' and Israel's projection of 'Islamic' Iran as a 'rogue state', a threat to peace and stability of region, neither endorsed the Western suspicion about Iranian intention to misuse nuclear technology for making nuclear bomb under the garb of right to use nuclear technology for peaceful energy purposes. It does not buy either the US's perspective on the 'War on Terror' and its approach to dealing with religious (read Islamic) extremism/ terrorism in the region.

On the nuclear issue the successive governments of India have consistently maintained that within the structure of rights and obligations of NPT, Iran has the legitimate right to use nuclear technology for peaceful civilian purposes. Its three consecutive votes against Iran in the Board of Directors meeting of IAEA were guided by the following pragmatic national considerations: First, it was intended to convey a message to the West, particularly United States, that India is a reliable partner; second, to secure and operationalize the Indo-US Civil Nuclear Deal in order to end the 'nuclear isolation of India' that was imposed since its Pokhran nuclear Test in 1974 and to fulfill its energy requirements; third, to manage the non-nuclear proliferation lobby in the United States; fourth, to share the concern of Arab Gulf countries who have strong misgivings about Iranian nuclear programme; and finally, India's wariness over having another nuclear power state in its neighbour. The crux of the matter in this regard is not only that the Indian economy is strongly linked with the economy of Western nations and Arab Gulf countries but its future growth as global power is contingent upon the support, goodwill and recognition of these two regions, particularly the West. Further, the 'Chinese factor' binds US-India relations in future. Despite growing commercial and trade relations between India and China, China along with Pakistan is considered a 'hostile nation', which forces India to seek United States' support to manage these external threats in future. It was this set of considerations that forced the Indian governments to vote against Iran in the meetings of IAEA's Board of Director.

However, these negative votes of India were, unlike the West, not intended to punish Iran for its 'wrong doing'. This partly also explains why India displayed its reservation to the recent UN economic sanctions (2010) against Iran and decided to work out 'creative mechanism' [3] to mitigate the impact of sanctions on Indian economy and insulates the Indian companies from the same. These included joining a consortium with companies from Russia, China, and/or Kuwait, making it difficult to single out single countries or firms, and creating new corporate entities with no financial ties to the US or EU, to insulate them from any retaliation from the West. Other 'creative mechanism' recommended by Ministry of External Affairs in this regard are: (1) A Rupee-Rial arrangement for settling bilateral trade to avoid a ban on Indian banks from access to the US or EU financial system, (2) An arrangement to open letters of credit in Rial, as suggested by the Iranians at the 16th session of the India-Iran Joint Commission, (3) Investment by Indian firms through joint ventures in mining, fertilizer, food processing, pharmaceuticals and automobile projects that are not currently sanctioned and (4) Opening of warehouses for fast-moving Indian products in Iranian Free Trade Zone with a mechanism to provide insurance cover for political and economic risks. In a speech on 5th July 2010 at an India-Iran strategic dialogue in New Delhi, the Indian Foreign Secretary Nirupama Rao said, "We are justifiably concerned that the extra-territorial nature of certain unilateral sanctions recently imposed by individual countries, with their restrictions on investment by third countries in Iran's energy sector, can have a direct and adverse impact on Indian companies and more importantly, on our energy security and our attempts to meet the development needs of our people."

Similarly, the perception that India is unwilling to formalize the IPI pipeline gas project due to US pressure is not correct. One cannot rule out the implications of US role which might have affected the culmination of the deal, but for Indian governments the issue of pricing of gas, the cost and security of pipelines and the cost of distributive pipelines throughout the territory of India are crucial for finalizing this deal. Given the history of bad faith between India and Pakistan and in the present context of terrorism which is threatening the Pakistani state it is near impossible for any Indian government to mortgage a vital part of its security in the hand of Pakistan by concluding this agreement. The Iranian government is fully aware of these concerns and apprehensions of Indian government and therefore remains open to negotiations without ever blaming the Indian government for not formalizing the deal. Further, Iran knows well that given its international isolation, a cordial relationship with India at this juncture provides legitimacy to Iranian government, a booming market for Iranian hydrocarbon products, and access to cheap and quality higher educational opportunities in India for Iranian middle class who can no more afford the cost of education in the West due to its failing economy. Good relations with a nation close to western power structure at present conjecture could be useful for mediation between Iran and the West in the future. Both India and Iran are cooperating in Afghanistan despite hostility from the US.

There are two sets of papers that reflect on US-Iran-India relations as outlined above. This includes Mahtab Rizvi's '*US-Iran Rivalries in the Region and its Implications for India*' and Pankaj Kumar's '*Containment and Competition between US and Iran in the Caspian Sea Region: Implications for India*'. Both papers recognize the centrality of Iran in the region and for India. Mahtab explores conflicting perspectives of US and Iran by dissecting their policy orientations on the major issues that are involved between Iran and the United States. This includes Iran's nuclear issue, IPI gas pipe line, stability in Iraq and Afghanistan and the security of Persian Gulf. He then examines the impact of US-Iran rivalry in the region on India's policy options. In his analysis, he exposes the Western design to isolate and weaken Iran and cautions the Indian government from getting trapped in the Western perspective on Iran, stressing the necessity on the part of Indian government to maintain a balanced outlook between Iran and the US. Pankaj highlights the significance of Iran for India mostly from the point of view of energy security. He provides a detailed analysis of US and its Multinational companies' role to gain access to oil and gas resources of Caspian region in order to circumvent Iran's influence in that region. However the author contends that such attempts by the United States have strongly been resisted by both Iran and Russia. The author concludes that such monopolistic control over the energy resources by the United States is not in the interest of India and therefore India needs to evolve a balanced policy between Iran and US. Taken together these two papers provide a holistic picture of opportunities and challenges before the Indian foreign policy in the region of West Asia and Central Asia.

The relative decline of American prestige and influence in the Persian Gulf countries in the post 9/11 period on the one hand, and stability and growth of Asian economy on the other, has brought a discernable shift in the perception of Persian Gulf regimes towards Asian powers, particularly India and China. These two nations are fast emerging as 'safe destinations' for Arab Capital Investments and are also being increasingly viewed by Gulf Sheikhdoms as an alternative to US led security arrangement in the region. The same process has also opened the opportunities for other countries like Russia and Western European countries to gain access to market and hydrocarbon resources of the region. While the evolving relationship between India, China and the Gulf has been widely discussed and debated in the Indian media and academia, a theme that I will return to at a later stage, what is less known is Russia's growing engagement with the Persian Gulf countries. Prasanta Kumar Pradhan's '*Resurgent Russia and the Gulf*' examines the factors that led to Russia's new foray in the Gulf and discusses its possible implications for Indian policies in the Gulf.

The economic recovery of Russia during Putin's Presidency provided a context to assert its role in international affairs, including in the Persian Gulf. According to Pradhan, forging closer economic ties with Gulf, a good opportunity for the sale for Russian arms in the conflict ridden Gulf, seeking cooperation of the Arab world to manage Chechen rebels at home and to create countervailing political presence in the Gulf to offset the US political-military intervention in Eastern Europe and Central Europe that Russia considers directed against herself are some of the important factors that drives Russia's new engagement in the Persian Gulf countries. The concrete policy initiatives from Russia in this direction range from series of exchange of commercial and political visits of high ranking officials to organizing Gulf Exhibition in Moscow, to seeking observer status in Organisation of Islamic Conference (OIC), to supporting Iran on many issues including helping to construct and commissioning the Busher Nuclear Plant. The author strongly feels that this new Russian offensive has the potential to challenge the American hegemony in the region and visualizes a number of common areas of cooperation between India and Russia in the Gulf region.

Due to US' physical-militarily presence in the region and the nature of globalized capitalist economy, the contemporary strategic environment in the Persian Gulf region is increasingly becoming unpredictable, having local, regional and global implications. With windfall capital and vibrant economic growth, the region is witnessing unprecedented transformation in the social, political, economic, cultural and strategic realms. This in conjunction with growing consumption of oil and gas in Indian market has made this sub-region an arena of strategic importance for India. The region is the principal source of energy requirement of India. Hydrocarbon Vision – 2025 of government of India projects a natural gas demand of 313 million metric standard cubic meters per day (mmscmd) and 391 mmscmd by the years 2011-12 and 2024-25 from the existing demand and supply of 115 mmscmd and 65 mmscmd respectively. Peace and stability in the region is very vital for India's future growth. Gulf Cooperation Council (GCC), a six-member Arab Council namely, the Kingdom of Saudi Arabia, Kuwait, Oman, Bahrain, Qatar, and UAE, are the most important trading partners of India in the region and account for almost 70 per cent of its oil and gas requirements. As the GCC loses considerable leverage in Western export markets for its oil, India is becoming a crucial export destination for the GCC, and likewise, the GCC markets are becoming key to

India's exports of oil products. Besides, the region is home to 6 million Indian expatriates and accounts for largest remittances from Indian diaspora abroad.

Pranav Kumar's article, *'India's Energy Requirements, Natural Gas and the Persian Gulf'* highlights the importance of Persian Gulf region for India's burgeoning oil and gas needs, while Faisal Ahmed in his paper, *'India and the GCC-Trade and Geopolitical Engagements'* provides a comprehensive understanding and analysis of trade and commercial relations between India and Gulf Cooperation Council (GCC), considering both GCC as a unit as well as its ties with individual countries. The author also outlines and discusses some crucial areas of cooperation which have the potential to strengthen India-GCC ties in the emerging multi-polar world order.

The emergence of India and China as economic and regional superpowers with an increasingly global outreach and the simultaneous witnessing of economic growth in the Gulf region provide a context of mutual interdependence and convergence between the two as already indicated above. Though India's relations with China have improved considerably in the last few years, this relationship remains by and large competitive. This is particularly true with regard to the two giants trying to compete for global energy resources. China's ties with major Gulf States are on an upswing and this would be a major factor in how India shapes its regional policies in the long term. Both India and China are today engaged with similar issues in the Gulf: energy security, the security of the Arab Gulf, the security of Sea Lanes of Communication (SLOC), military cooperation, arms sales, oil and gas pipelines and flow of Arab investments in their respective domestic markets. There is no doubt that India enjoys relatively better goodwill in the Gulf on account of its historical and civilizational affinities. It is also increasingly being looked upon by the Gulf countries as a partner in their quest for managing the evolving security equations in the region. Whether India is capable of providing security cover to the Gulf Sheikhdoms or not—it has a definite desire to play that role. Its re-conceptualization of national security doctrine that now involves the security of Gulf and the Indian Ocean littoral, the series of joint naval exercises that it conducted in recent years with a number of Gulf States including Iran as well as with US, UK, and France, conclusion of military and strategic agreements with Kuwait, Oman, Bahrain, Saudi Arabia, Qatar and United Arab Emirates and its display of anti-piracy operation in the Gulf of Aden—are all indicative of its national desire to project its power in the region. Moreover, India's aspirations to emerge as a major global power may also lead it to counter China's growing influence around the globe, including Gulf.

By all accounts the current policy of US government in South Asia also aims to augment Indian powers to contain the increasing influence of China at global level. Whether India will be willing to play a junior role in the power-politics game of the United States against China only time will testify. However in hindsight it appears that while India strongly identifies with US for joint cooperation on energy security, protection of the sea-lanes, maritime policing, and counter-terrorism—and given its present capability it will prefer to benefit from, to use C. Raja Mohan words, a 'free ride' on the US role as the principal security provider in the Gulf—it will be reluctant to enter into 'strategic alliance partner' (along the pattern of UK and Israel) with the United States to achieve the desired goal. But can India contain the rising influence of China in the Gulf? Are India and China rivals in the region? Or can they cooperate together to provide a credible alternative to US-led security arrangement in the region?

The above themes and questions have been dealt in two related set of papers. Javed Ahmad Khan's paper, *'China as an Economic Rival of India in the Gulf'* examines the rise of China in Gulf region and points out how despite its late entry in the Gulf and low goodwill as compared to India, it has surged ahead in capturing the Gulf market. According to him, Gulf investments have been flowing into China on three levels: industrial ventures, refinery joint ventures and investment in the capital market. The author concludes that if India has to catch up with China and attract Arab investments to its markets, it needs to liberalize its economy at rapid pace. N. Janardhan in his paper, '*Incongruent Triangle: China Factor in India-GCC Ties*' goes beyond the evolving economic dimensions and commercial relations between India, China and GCC countries in order to examine the factors that have the potential to mutually bind China, India and GCC in the future. This will depend on whether GCC's 'Look East Policy' moves beyond the preferential trading arrangements and new-found political warmth arising out of the post-9/11 international context to address security issues as well, and whether India and China are willing to dabble beyond trade into the realm of security concerns of GCC countries. The paper also explores how US-Iran ties, GCC-Iran ties, US' approach towards China and India, Iran's relations with China and India, US-India versus China, as well as relations between India and China conditions and influences the Indo-Chinese role in the Gulf region. Contrary to Khan, Janardhan visualizes a strong possibility of cooperation between India and China in the region in many areas, including trade and commerce, security of region, counter- terrorism etcetera.

Returning to Indo-Israel relations, two interesting papers reflect two broad positions/perspectives prevalent among Indian policy makers, academia and media. This includes P. R. Kumaraswamy's '*Relations with Israel and India's Great Power Aspirations*' and K.M. Sajad Ibrahim's '*Impact of India's Partnership with Israel: Major Trends in the Post-Cold War Period*'. Both papers focus on the origin of India's Israel policy in India's pre-independence period but differ significantly in choosing the context and site for tracing its trajectory. Kumaraswamy locates the origin in India's Khilafat movement and in the 'Islamic articulation' of Mahatma

Gandhi that shaped, what he calls, India's 'recognition without relations' attitude towards Israel till 1992. In other words, he highlights the 'Muslim component' of Indian Republic and the factor of Pakistan that largely influenced India's pro-Arab Policy—and by implication non-existent relations towards Israel till 1992 when late Prime Minister, Mr. Narasimha Rao, decided to restore the full diplomatic and normal relations with Israel. Since then the relations between the two have grown rapidly despite many changes in the nature of India's ruling coalition. India's policy now is similar to those of the other major powers, all of whom maintain reasonable relations with both Arabs and Israel. Kumaraswamy sees in the post-1992 shift in India's position towards Israel as *beginning* of India's 'independent policy' dictated by the crude logic of national interest and advocates that a close relationship with Israel is essential to realize India's aspiration of becoming a global power.

In contrast to Kumaraswamy, Ibrahim interprets the same set of historical events differently: he lauds the anti-colonial and anti-imperial legacy of India's nationalist movement and thought of Jawaharlal Nehru and Mahatma Gandhi that shaped India's 'pro-Arab' and 'no-Israel' relations till 1992. He considers India's pro-active relations with Israel in post 1992 period as dictated by India's desire to become a part of US-led global power structure that emerged in the wake of disintegration of former Soviet Union in 1989 in order to realize its strategic, economic and developmental goals. Ibrahim considers this shift in India's foreign policy with special reference to Israel as 'loss of direction' and 'deviation' from the core principles of India's foreign policy, namely, its traditional anti colonial and anti-imperial thrust that will have serious implications in terms of Indo-Arab relations and its nature of support to liberation movements including the Palestine.

The book would have remained incomplete without a paper on Indo-Turkey relations. Despite deep civilizational ties and pervasive Turkish influence on Indian culture and society, the relations between the two were almost frozen until the early 1990s. The context of Cold War, divergent ideological world views and different priorities of India and Turkey kept them apart and hardly provided any opportunities to improve their relations beyond political recognition of each other. However the end of Cold War, changes in the global power structure and shift in India and Turkish approach towards international relations facilitated in improving the relations between the two. Berdal Aral's '*Turkish-Indian Relations after the Cold War: Perspectives and Policies*' provides a comprehensive historical and analytical account of changing dimensions of Indo-Turkish relations. The author explores the points of convergence as well as mutual expectations that attracted the two to one another in mid 1990s. India's economic success, its rising status both at regional and global level, its huge market potential and its expertise in the area of information technology became point of attraction for political and business class in Turkey, while India's political and economic elite recognize Turkey's growing influence in West Asia, its strategic location, its shift in position towards Kashmir and its close relationship with Europe and America that would have helped strengthening its economy. The growing convergence in terms of sharing of vision of multipolar world and multi-approach foreign policy and closer ties with the West further played an important role in bringing them closer. However, according to the author, though India and Turkey shared the perception of collectively fighting the menace of Islamic terrorism, the Western projection of Turkey-India-Israel as 'triple entente' to fight the same in the aftermath of post 9/11 year period failed to materialize.

Taken together, this collection of articles attempt to provide fresh perspectives and understanding of the evolving political and economic relationships and interactions of India with global and regional powers in the region of West Asia, with particular focus on Persian Gulf in the post-Cold War period.

In the end I would like to thank all the contributors for their valuable papers for making this book a reality. I also take this opportunity to thank the staff of New Century Publications for undertaking the strenuous task of publishing this book and bringing it in the public domain for wider debates and discussions.

August 2010 New Delhi

Notes

1. Fareed Zakaria, 'The Future of American Power', *Foreign Affairs*, Vol. 87, No. 3, May-June 2008.
2. Remarks by Tony Blair in speech at Yale University, May 25, 2008 at http://www.rediff.com/news/2008/may/26blair.htm, retrieved on 10.08. 2010.
3. http://www.indianexpress.com/news/to-engage-iran-india-looks-to-beat-us-un-sanctions-by-being-creative/655365/2 accessed on August 17 2010.

1

Relations with Israel and India's Great Power Aspirations

P.R. Kumaraswamy [1]

The decision of late Indian Prime Minister P. V. Narasimha Rao to establish full diplomatic relations with Israel in January 1992 marked a new phase in India's foreign policy in general and towards the Middle East in particular. [2] This move reversed the policy pursued by New Delhi for over four decades and signaled a new approach towards the region. Taking cue from the new international climate presented by the end of the Cold War and the disintegration of the Soviet Union, Rao brought about this course correction. In so doing he freed India's Middle East policy from prolonged pre-occupation with Pakistan and its diplomatic maneuvers in the wider Arab and Islamic world.

The absence of diplomatic relations with Israel for over four decades has to be viewed within the context of India's initial desire for such a move and its subsequent inability. For a host of domestic as well international compulsions, during the Cold War years India was unable to pursue an autonomous and independent policy towards Israel. By reversing this policy, Rao has created a new dynamism. Contrary to the conventional wisdom, India was not indifferent towards Israel and Prime Minister Jawaharlal Nehru was keen to establish a residential mission in Tel Aviv. However, he was unable to do so and non-relations remained the corner stone of India's Israel policy.

This paper argues that an independent and assertive policy towards the Middle East is a *sine qua non* for the fulfillment of India's great power aspirations. The first section gives a brief summary of the historic Indian position regarding Israel and its reluctance to maintain normal diplomatic ties with the Jewish State. The second section discusses various developments since full relations were established in January 1992. The final section discusses Israel within the context of the great power debate and argues that besides brining in bilateral benefits, relations with Israel add to India's great power aspirations.

Prelude to Normalization

The roots of India's policy regarding Israel can be traced to the early 1920s when the Indian nationalists adopted a pronouncedly pro-Arab position regarding Palestine. Coming in the midst of the Khilafat struggle, they perceived the Jewish political aspirations through an Islamic prism. Mahatma Gandhi aptly reflected this position. Even though his subsequent statement about "Palestine belongs to the Arabs" [3] acquired widespread publicity, Mahatma Gandhi was the only Indian leader to recognize the central Islamic argument against the Jewish aspirations for a homeland in Palestine. [4]

Mahatma captured the core Islamic opposition against erstwhile *Dhimmi* (non-Muslim within monotheish) acquiring sovereign rights over a *waqf* property. Under the Islamic tradition, the Jews were treated as the People of the Book (*ahl al-kitab*). In return for their acceptance of the Islamic rule, the Jewish lives and properties were protected under the Islamic rule. Hence the kind of violence, pogrom and eventually the Holocaust that plagued the Jews in the Christian Europe were alien to the Islamic Middle East. Even the most unfriendly and violent Islamic rulers could not be accused of being anti-Jewish. The current trend of anti-Semitism as manifested by the widespread distribution of *Protocols of the Elders of Zion* was primarily the contribution of the Christian missionaries. Anti-Semitism indeed had not historic basis in the Islamic Middle East.

At the same time, it is essential to recognize that protection did not imply equality between the believer and non-believer.

While the Jews were protected, Islamic rulers tolerated their presence but could not and did not recognize the People of the Book as equals. By demanding a Jewish national home in the Islamic Palestine, the Zionist sought to undo and reverse the Islamic order.

Mahatma Gandhi captured this core argument. According to him the *jazirat ul-Arab*, including Palestine enjoyed the injunctions of Prophet Mohammed and hence could not be handed over to any non-Muslim control or sovereignty. Subtly repudiating the Balfour Declaration, in April 1921 Mahatma observed:

The Muslims claim Palestine as an integral part of *Jazirat al-Arab*. They are bound to retain its custody, *as an injunction of the Prophet*. But that does not mean that the Jews and Christians cannot freely go to Palestine, or even reside their and own property. *What non-Muslims cannot do is to acquire sovereign jurisdiction.* The Jews cannot receive sovereign rights in a place, which has been held for centuries by Muslim powers by right of religious conquest.

He went on to argue that the Muslims soldiers serving in the British Indian army did not fight and shed blood in the World War I "for the purpose of surrendering Palestine out of Muslim control." [5] In short, Palestine was an Islamic property and shall remain so. Other leaders of the Congress party were less candid and wrapped themselves in the logic of nationalism.

In the post-Khilafat phase anti-imperialism and decolonization dominated the thinking of the Indian nationalists. This was compounded by the growing political rivalry between the Congress party and the Muslim League over the support of the Muslim population. This forced the former to identify itself with the Arabs of Palestine. The Zionist dependence upon the Mandate power to realize their political goals in Palestine complicated the matters. Increasingly India and its nationalist leaders adopted an unsympathetic view regarding Zionism. They did not see it as a movement for the liberation of the Jewish people but as a collaborator of the British imperialism.

The pro-Arab predisposition of the Congress party became the official Indian stand when it was elected to the 11-member United Nations Special Committee on Palestine (UNSCOP). A seven-member majority proposed partition of Palestine whereas aided by Iran and the then Yugoslavia, India put forth a Federal Plan as the solution for Palestine. Unfortunately for Israel, Nehru was advocating a federal Palestine while rejecting the same idea of a federal and unified sub-continent.

The Federal Plan disappointed both the contending parties; for the Zionist it gave them autonomy and civic rights when they were aspiring for political rights and sovereignty. The Arabs were equally disappointed as the Indian plan gave more rights to the immigrant Jews. If the Jews opposed the Indian plan because it gave them too little, the Arabs opposed it because it gave too much the Jews. Thus, both the warring sides unanimously rejected the Indian idea. Undaunted by this, on 29 November 1947 India joined the Arab and Islamic countries and voted against partitioning of Palestine.

The establishment of Israel on 14 May 1948 radically changed the Middle Eastern realities. Not only the newly formed state survived the initial onslaught by the neighboring Arab states but managed to secure the recognition of all the major powers. Despite opposition from countries such as India, in May 1949 Israel was admitted into the United Nations. Furthermore, some Arab countries such as Egypt adopted an explicitly pro-Pakistani position at the UN over the Kashmir dispute. Nehru was forced to re-examine his policy on Israel. After protracted internal debates and delays in September 1950 India recognized the Jewish state. [6]

In the initial years the Indian government gave sufficient indications that recognition would be followed by the exchange of diplomatic relations. An assurance to this effect was given to Walter Eytan when the Director General of Israel's Ministry of Foreign Affairs visited New Delhi and met

Prime Minister Nehru in March 1952. [7] This however, did not materialize. Nehru's biographer S Gopal partly holds Education Minister and senior Congress leader Maulana Abul Kalam Azad responsible for Nehru failing on his commitments. [8] Pakistan and the Kashmir issue were supposed to be Azad's principal reasoning.

Following the Suez war and the tripartite aggression against Egypt, Nehru formally ruled out diplomatic ties with Israel stating time was not ripe for such a move. This subsequently became the standard Indian position regarding Israel and non-relations emerged as the core issue of India's Middle East policy. Over the years a number of reasons and rationales were added to the absence for formal ties between the two countries.

The anomalous situation of recognition-without-relations continued until January 1992 when Prime Minister Rao normalized relations with Israel. He was helped by a number of regional and international developments including, the end of the Cold War, disintegration of the Soviet Union and the Middle East peace process inaugurated at Madrid in October 1991. These far reaching developments significantly enhanced his ability to make a break with the past. It is tempting to attribute Rao's shift to 'systemic changes.' It is essential to recognize while the Cold War accentuated the situation, the Euro-centric bloc politics was not the reason for Nehru's inability to normalize relations with Israel in 1952.

A more possible explanation has to be found in the negative repercussions of the post-Cold War situation for the Palestinians and the weakening influence of the Palestinian factor in inter-Arab politics. Their endorsement of the Iraqi invasion, occupation and annexation of Kuwait in August 1990 eventually boomeranged. The liberation of Kuwait in following February was marked by a considerable Arab alienation of the Palestinian leadership. It also resulted in the large scale expulsion of Palestinians workers from the oil-rich Gulf countries. [9] This was followed by the Madrid conference where the Palestine Liberation Organization (PLO) accepted its formal exclusion and the Israeli conditions over the format, participants and terms of reference.

This willingness of the Arabs and Palestinians to abandon past rhetoric and seek a negotiated political settlement considerably weakened the erstwhile Indian stand regarding normalization. Being more Palestinian than Yasser Arafat no longer paid political dividends. Any Indian contribution to the peace process meant abandoning the past and establishing normal ties with all the parties to the conflict, including Israel.

Though never admitted explicitly, the normalization was also fuelled by India's aspirations for great power status. Its ability to play any meaningful role internationally rested on India following a more balanced foreign policy, especially towards the Arab-Israeli conflict. Its refusal to have even minimum political relations with Israel undermined its chances of being taken seriously on the world scene. This was clearly highlighted by the consequences of the Soviet policy following the June 1967 war. Even if its political powers were limited, by breaking off ties with Israel Moscow has surrendered the Middle East to the US. If India were to avoid similar fate, it would have to have a modicum of interactions with all the principal players in the region, including Israel. With this in mind Prime Minister Narasimha Rao normalized relations literally days before the convening of the multilateral talks in Moscow in January 1992. In examining the post-1992 developments, two things have to be kept in mind; namely, the pace of relations and the reactions of the regional players.

Progress Since 1992

Until the normalization of relations in 1992, India's policy has been one of recognition-without-relations. It felt that its interests in the region, especially vis-à-vis Pakistan, could be strengthened by adopting an overtly unfriendly position towards Israel. Support for the Arabs, its leaders felt, has to be manifested by the absence of formal ties with Israel. This zero-sum, approach towards the Middle East resulted in the absence of minimal ties with the Jewish State. Even the pro-Pakistani position adopted by principal players during 1965 and 1971 wars did not result in any meaningful shift in India's Middle East policy. Unqualified and some might say unrequited friendship with the Arab and Islamic countries was seen pivotal to India's interest in this region. Thus, support for Palestinians was to be accompanied by a marked and gradual hostility towards Israel.

Normalization marked a radical shift. Under the new post-Cold War climate and growing pre-eminence of the US, India and its leaders abandoned their blinkers and discarded the zero-sum approach towards Israel. Normalization of relations was no longer seen as an anti-Arab or anti-Palestinian measure but a sign of Indian support for the Middle East peace process. In the post-Madrid situation, support for the Palestinian would demand support for the peace process and normal ties with the principal player, Israel.

Thus establishment of diplomatic relations with Israel was not accompanied by any shift in its overall attitude towards the rights of the Palestinians. India continued to argue that the right of self-determination of the Palestinians would mean the establishment of a sovereign independent Palestinian state living in peace with Israel. It reiterated its support for the PLO and treated Arafat and later on his successor Mahmud Abbas, as a head of state. Indeed on a host of issues pertaining to the Arab-Israeli conflict such as Jewish settlements in the occupied territories, borders, refugees and the Jerusalem issue there was no difference in India's pre-1992 and post-1992 positions. Unlike the past however, it has been less sermonizing.

This basic difference was reinforced in its approach to normalization. Unlike the past, India began to distinguish bilateral relations with Israel from the vagaries of the peace process. In its view it was possible and necessary to have normal relations both with Israel and the Palestinians. Such an approach was not only seen essential for Israel making that quantum leap towards the recognizing the Palestinian rights but also would be beneficial to India.

As a result, since 1992 the bilateral relations have expanded and covered a host of political, diplomatic, economic and security issues. In the initial years, it has been cautious in its approach but towards the end of 1990s relations took a significant upward turn. The formation of the National Democratic Alliance (NDA) government headed by Bharatiya Janata Party (BJP), known for its traditional support for Israel, in 1998 significantly enhanced the bilateral relations. Gradually even those parties which in the past had reservations over normalization began to review their stands.

The summer of 2000 was a defining moment in the bilateral relations. Israel not only hosted Home Minister L K Advani and Foreign Minister Jaswant Singh but also received Deputy Chairperson of the *Rajya Sabha* Najma Heptulla and veteran communist leader Jyoti Basu. The inclusion of Israel in the last foreign visit undertaken by West Bengal Chief Minister Basu did not go unnoticed. In the past, the communist parties remained were the most vocal critics of Israel and felt let down by normalization.

The initial hesitation of central leaders to visit Israel was compensated by state governments. Discarding political differences various state governments ruled by Congress, BJP and Janata Dal began interacting with Israel and signed a host of economic agreements. For its part, India became a favorite destination for various Israeli leaders, businesspersons and others. The visit of President Ezer Weizman in December 2006 and Prime Minister Ariel Sharon in September 2003 remain the high points of political contacts between the two. The leaders of the two countries have been meeting in third countries as well as during the UN General Assembly sessions in New York.

Bilateral economic relations have been increasing since 1992. From less than USUS$ 100 million in the late 1980s, the two-way trade has crossed the three billion mark and is closely inching towards billion. Israel has become one of India's major trading partners in the Middle East. This growth was in contrast to India economic ties with countries such as Egypt which had closer political ties especially during the Nehru-Nasser era. In recent years, Israeli companies have been investing in various infrastructure programs in India as well as. There has been widespread cooperation in other traditional areas such as agriculture, water management and horticulture.

The most significant growth in the bilateral ties can be noticed in the area that both countries are extremely reluctant to discuss, namely, military-security ties. Israel has been identified as India's second largest arms supplier after Russia and New Delhi has emerged as the principal export destination for Israeli weapons. Upgrading of aging Soviet inventories, border management, small arms, avionics and missile are some of the major areas of cooperation. Israel has also agreed to supply India with Phalcon advanced airborne early warning systems. The US which blocked a similar deal with China was more than happy to endorse the same spy planes being supplied to India. In July 2007 both countries have entered into a USUS$ 2.5 billion program to jointly develop missile defense. This marked a new phase in the security relations between the two. Moreover, in a major shift in January 2008 India launched Israeli spy satellite, believed to be aimed at monitoring Iran and its suspected nuclear programs. This came against the background of periodic statements of 'civilizational links' with Tehran.

What were the external reactions? With the sole exception of Egypt, none of the countries of the Middle East had adversely reacted to growing Indo-Israeli relations. Even Pakistan was less hostile on the Israeli front. Before long it recognized that its anti-Israeli clarion does not carry much weight in the region and its leaders have been suggesting a re-appraisal of the traditional anti-Israel policy. [10] Even the Islamic republic of Iran, known for its anti-Israeli rhetoric, has been more than happy to strengthen ties with New Delhi, despite growing Indo-Israeli ties. Iran has been extremely understanding of India's newly found friendship with Israel. [11] The recent unfriendly noises from Tehran have to be located within the context of India's unusual behavior over the nuclear issue at the International Atomic Energy Agency (IAEA and its growing proximity with the US. India hosting President Mohammed Khatami in January 2003 and Prime Minister Ariel Sharon a few months later highlighted that Israel has not been a major pre-occupation of the Middle East when dealing with India. Indeed significant improvements in India's relations with the Arab and Islamic countries such as Saudi Arabia and Iran happened *after* and *not before* Indo-Israeli normalization.

How does normalization with Israel serve India's great power aspirations?

Great Power Debate

In the conventional sense Israel cannot be described as a great power. Though an important player in the Middle East, it does not have some of the most important attributes of a Great Power. It lacks two of the most important ingredients, namely, territorial depth and resource basis. Its territorial vulnerability was exposed during the run up to the June 1967 and conscious of its size its military doctrine emphasized on the need to carry forward any military conflict into the enemy territory. Likewise, Israel lacks resource base and depends upon imports for all its resource requirements, including hydrocarbon needs. Even a basic resource like water is scarce forcing Israel to explore technological solutions (desalination) or commercial options ((possible imports from Turkey).

At a much wider level Israel's ability to pursue an independent foreign policy is circumscribed by its excessive reliance upon the US. Its dependence upon Washington for political support, economic largess and military supplies are too wide known to be recounted here. On occasions such a dependency has prevented Israel from seeking normal diplomatic ties with countries considered to be hostile powers by the US. For example, its hesitation to normalize relations with the People's Republic of China in the early 1950s proved costly as it had to wait until 1992 to establish ties with Beijing. At times the American disapproval has prevented Israel from pursuing lucrative military contracts in the final stages of the Apartheid regime in South Africa.

At the same time, it is undeniable that Israel has emerged as a major player in the region. A vast majority of countries perceive Israel as a major power and this perception is more acute among Israel's adversaries. Without exception no country or non-state actors in the Middle East perceive or treat Israel as another country. Even if their motives are questionable, Israel enjoys as a much wider influence than its size or resource base. This perception could be traced directly to the June war of 1967. The swift victory over larger and more powerful Arab armies during the war established not only its military supremacy but also its regional position. Since then Israel has emerged as the most important player in the Middle East.

Despite lacking a larger territorial base and natural resources, Israel has acted as a great power. A number of its political actions have the hallmark of a great power. Since the dying days of the British Mandate, it has a propensity for active intervention in defense of its interests. Since the declaration of the state hours before the departure of the British troops from Palestine on 14 May 1948, Israel has not hesitated to act in furtherance of its interests. Even if the outcomes were not always positive, its leaders were not pusillanimous. Internal differences and warnings for example, did not prevent Prime Minister David Ben-Gurion from joining hands with Britain and France and lunching the Suez war against President Gamal Abdul Nasser in October 1956.

Israel's propensity for intervention surpasses many other regional powers in the world. They often border on utter contempt for public opinion. International anger and displeasures have rarely impeded Israel from acting decisively. That it remains the only state to be formed on the basis of the UN resolution has not prevented Israel from taking unpopular decisions. On innumerable occasions it could count only the support of the US in the General Assembly. Even its traditional European friends at times opted to abstain rather than vote with it. Such glaring international isolation and condemnation have not prevented Israel from pursing its policy. In its assessment a responsible power is about leading a popular trend but about taking most unpopular decision in defense of its interests. International disapproval, for example, did not prevent Israel from killing key military and political figures belonging to the Hamas. As highlighted by its military actions against Iraqi nuclear reactor in Osiraq (June 1981) and the PLO headquarters in Tunis (April 1988) it has pursued daring military operations against its adversaries. Since the late 1970s it had actively intervened in Lebanon to minimize threats emanating from southern Lebanon (first form the PLO and later Hezbollah). The argument here is not success or failure of such military interventions but to highlight Israel's ability and willingness to pursue an assertive foreign policy.

At the same time, Israel has also perused politico-diplomatic means to neutralize its adversaries. Since mid-1950s it sought to befriend non-Arab and non-Islamic countries and groups in the region to overcome its immediate hostilities. Through this 'peripheral diplomacy' it sought to leapfrog the immediate neighborhood and befriend the non-Arab countries (Iran and Turkey) and minority groups (Kurds in Iraq and Maronites in Lebanon). During much of the Cold War Israel successfully played on the bitter memories and fears of Iran and Turkey over the Arabs. Even if the overall outcome remained mixed and questionable, this policy highlighted Israel's long-term strategic calculations. In similar vein it sought to neutralize Egypt through the Camp David accords. By agreeing to completely withdraw from the Sinai

Peninsula, it had removed the most powerful Arab nation from the anti-Israeli war coalition.

Harping on their shared opposition to an independent Palestinian state West of the Jordan River, Israel has established close politico-military ties with the Hashemite Kingdom of Jordan. Despite occasional problems (such as the June war), the close ties that the *yishuv* (Jewish community in mandate Palestine) forged with Emir Abdullah in late 1940s still continues. Of late, it is courting the Gulf state of Qatar with similar results. Doha hosting Hamas deportees from Jordan as well an Israeli mission despite regional opposition is a hallmark of its diplomatic skills in breaking political isolation. [12]

Above all, it has fully exploited the perceived influence in Washington to further its foreign policy interests. Despite the obvious failures (AWACS sale to Saudi Arabia in the 1980s and problems over loan guarantees when Yitzhak Shamir was in power in the early 1990s), many countries in the Middle East and elsewhere feel that the friends of Israel could further their interest. Accordingly they make friendly gestures or statements towards Israel before embarking upon a visit to Washington. The visits of Egyptian President Hosni Mubarak to the US, for example, have been preceded by high-level contacts with Israel, often undertaken by senior advisers of the President. Likewise while in office President Parveez Musharraf was making pro-Israeli notices on the eve of his visit to Washington and other western capitals. Real or imaginary, many countries act as if road to Washington passes through Israel.

Thus, even if it lacks the conventional attributes of a great power, Israel has been behaving, and acting as a great power. And above all it was perceived as a major player by many countries in the Middle East and beyond. India is no exception. Normalization also had an additional benefit. Israel has emerged a major convergence point for bourgeoning Indo-US relations. While alliance would be a misnomer and misleading, it is undeniable that Indo-Israeli ties have a positive vibe upon the Indo-US relations.

Though never articulated adequately, normalization of relations was part of India's new found aspiration for great power status. Ability to pursue a foreign policy independent of the diktats of others is a prime criterion for a major power. The issue is not about a great power doing the right thing but doing what that country considers right for its interest. In this sense, normalization gave an unmistakable signal to the outside world that India was prepared to pursue a policy that would serve its interests. While still seeing Arab and Islamic countries in friendlier terms, India was not prepared to accept their diktats over Israel. This approach is more visible in the manner in which India has been handling its relations with Iran and Israel. Both these countries have unique advantages that are vital for India. Military support from Israel and energy supplies from Iran are critical for India's economic growth and aspirations for greater influence beyond South Asia. In short, Iran could not offer the kind of military-technological expertise it needs and Israel could not help in its search for energy security. Hence, India has been trying to de-link Iran in its Israel policy and Israel in its Iran policy.

Notes

1. Professor, School of International Studies, Jawaharlal Nehru University, New Delhi.
2. Though West Asia is the popular nomenclature in India, the countries of the region use 'Middle East' to describe themselves and for some the 'West Asia' is seen as offensive. Hence without disputing its origin, historic circumstances and implications, this paper uses Middle East to describe the region.
3. In his article in *Harijan* published on 26 November 1938, Mahatma observed: "Palestine belongs to the Arabs in the same sense that England belongs to the English and France to the French." This is his most widely quoted statement on the Middle East. It is nearly impossible to find any discussion on India's policy towards Israel and the Middle East without this quotation.

4. For a discussion on Mahatma's attitude see, P R Kumaraswamy, "Mahatma Gandhi and the Jewish National Home: An assessment", *Asian and African Studies*, (Haifa), vol.26, no.1, March 1992, pp. 1-13.
5. Young India, 6 April 1921, *Collected Works of Mahatma Gandhi*, vol.19, p. 530. Emphasis added.
6. P R Kumaraswamy, "India's recognition of Israel, September 1950", *Middle Eastern Studies*, vol.31, no.1, January 1995, pp. 124-38.
7. Walter Eytan, *The First Ten Years: A Diplomatic History of Israel*, (London, 1958), p. 130. Citing notes of Nehru's conversation with Eytan, Gopal concurs with this assessment. Gopal, *Jawaharlal Nehru*, vol.2, p. 70.
8. S Gopal, *Jawaharlal Nehru: A Biography*, vol. 2, (New Delhi, 1979), p. 170.
9. Indeed until his very death in November 2004, Palestinian leader Yasser Arafat could not visit Kuwait and the first public state of his successor Mahmoud Abbas carried an explicit apology to Kuwait and its people for the stand taken by the PLO during the Iraqi invasion.
10. For a background discussion see, P R Kumaraswamy, "Israel and Pakistan: Public rhetoric vs. political pragmatism", in Efraim Karsh and P R Kumaraswamy (ed.), *Islamic Attitudes to Israel*, (London: Routledge, 2008), pp. 123-35.
11. This however, was not true for Israel which periodically expressed its concerns over growing Indo-Iranian ties.
12. In January 2009, following the Israeli military offensive against the Hamas-rule Gaza Strip, Qatar has ordered the closure of the Israeli mission in Doha.

2

Impact of India's Partnership with Israel: Major Trends in the Post-Cold War Period

K.M. Sajad Ibrahim

India's relation with Israel since 1992 has been viewed as an outcome of the post-cold war scenario. With the demise of the Soviet Union, India lost its long time military supplier and principal diplomatic crutch. It has also grown increasingly disenchanted with Arab sympathy for Pakistan on the Kashmir issue. As a result of the diplomatic relations, India showed keen interest in developing high level military and commercial links with Israel, especially during the period of BJP led NDA (National Democratic Alliance) government of 1998-2004. Israel is now the second largest supplier of arms to India (after Russia). It provides India with missile radar, border monitoring equipment and other similar high-tech military hardwires. In addition, several thousand Indian soldiers have been provided with "anti-insurgency training in Israel". The latest in the series was the launching of Israel's spy satellite by India in January 2008 to enhance Israel's intelligence-gathering capability. The geopolitical implications of the collaboration between India and Israel are grave and manifold. India's close collaboration with Israel is fundamentally to woo the United States as well as to build a new strategic relation vis-à-vis Pakistan and China.

India and the Palestine Question

India's relation with the West Asia was formulated by Jawaharlal Nehru in 1930s. Although Nehru took an impartial view regarding the Arab-Israeli differences in the initial period, he later took the stand of supporting the Arabs by taking into account of the denial of justice to the Palestinians. In the 1939 Resolution adopted by the Indian National Congress, it stated that "in Palestine the Jews have relied on British armed forces to advance their special privileges". [1] Even Gandhiji was not ready to recognize the Jewish nationalism, which was artificially created in Palestine at the cost of indigenous Arab population. [2] Nehru indicted Zionism for fostering Jewish settlement in Palestine at the expense of the Arab population. Jayapraksh Narayan stated:

"No doubt the Jews were entitled as a persecuted people to compassion and some compensation for the wrongs heaped upon their innocent heads through the centuries. But it was certainly not the Arabs, least of all the Palestinians, who were the persecutors. If the Christian peoples and powers of the West, some of whom had tried mercilessly to exterminate the Jews, were anxious at least to salve their conscience and do a good turn to their victims, they had no right to do it at the cost of the Arabs" [3]

Nehru in his letters to his daughter, Indira, during his prison days commented the British tactics in Palestine in favour of the Jewish immigrants violating the rights of the Palestine as another face of a colonial power. He saw the English in Palestine pitting "Jewish religious nationalism against Arab nationalism, and (making) it appear that (their) presence is necessary to act as an arbiter and to keep the peace between the two". [4] All these were some of the basic perspectives of Indian leaders regarding the Jewish colonialism in the pre-independence period.

The first task before India in its post independence period was to examine an appropriate solution to the Palestine question by becoming a member in the Special UN Committee. India supported the minority plan which recommended a federation of two Arab and Jewish states by opposing the partition plan of Palestine. (During this period the third world countries were not emerged as members of the UN General Assembly). [5] The decision of India was influenced by the perception of Indian leaders on the Palestine question as well as the partition of India.

When Israel became a reality in 1948, India had several reservations in granting recognition to it. Nehru openly stated the reason as a gesture of supporting the stand of Arab countries. [6] Moreover, India opposed U.N. membership for Israel in 1949. By 1950 a series of efforts had been made to influence the Indian government to recognize the state of Israel by the Jewish lobby as well as its counterpart in India. Finally, India accorded its recognition to the State of Israel in late 1950 without establishing any formal ties until 1992. [7]

India's Support to Palestinian Struggle

When Israel invaded Sinai on October 29, 1956 as a reaction to Egypt's decision to nationalize Suez Canal, India condemned it as a re-imposition of European colonialism in the Afro Asian world. The attack of Egypt by Israel along with British and French forces was viewed as a flagrant violation of the UN Charter and all Indian political parties, from right to left, condemned it. India cosponsored resolutions in the General Assembly urging the withdrawal of French, British and Israeli forces from Egypt. In fact, the Suez crisis drew Egypt and India closer together and its relation with Israel to low point and ended all possibility for a bilateral tie. [8]

The reemphasis given by India to the Arab cause out of Suez crisis of 1956 is reflected in the unstinting support of India to the case of Palestinian refugees. According to C.S. Jha, India's permanent representative in the UN, stated in November 1959 that "the problem of Palestinian refugees is not merely an intensely human problem; it is one of great political importance and indeed affects the entire complex of political relations in the Middle East." [9] India's hostility towards Israel increased even more after the death of Nehru in 1964. It was evident from India's refusal to accept Israeli assistance in redeveloping the barren wastes of Rajasthan. Similarly, Israeli offer of famine relief given in response to a plea by the UN Secretary General, U Thant was declined by India for political reasons. [10] India condemned the Israeli invasion of Arab lands of Palestine in the 1967 Arab-Israeli war. In December 1967, D.P. Dhar, a member of Indian delegation to the UN Special Committee, reiterated Indian position, which recognized the Palestinian as a people and not merely as refugees. It also emphasized the need for a lasting solution to ensure the just rights of the Arab people of Palestine on the basis of UN resolution 194 (III). [11]

In the meantime, the Indian political atmosphere was not fully supporting the views of the government stand. The opposition parties in India, except the Communist parties, demanded a cautious approach in the 1967 war, promoting a neutral stand. The parties like *Swathanthra Party* and *Jana Sangh* openly supported Israel. It happened on account of the neutral policy of Egypt during the Sino-Indian war of 1962 and Indo-Pak war of 1965. [12] Similarly, the Indian press also took a negative approach to official Indian position in the 1967 war. The news papers like Times of India, Indian Express, Statesman and Hindustan Times made critical remarks on Indian policy of supporting the Arabs. [13]

The first setback to India's relation with West Asia came in 1969 when India was denied participation on the Rabat conference of Islamic leaders due to the opposition of Pakistan. The meeting was convened to condemn the burning of Al-Aqsa Mosque in Jerusalem. Moreover, under the initiative of Pakistan the meeting also condemned the communal riots in Ahmedabad. As a reaction to these developments, India recalled its Senior Envoys from Morocco and Jordan. Further, Indian Foreign Affairs Minister, Dinesh Singh held a meeting with his Israeli counterpart, Abba Eban in New York, as a first sign of improving relations with Israel. [14] During the Indo-Pak war in November 1971, countries like Egypt and Syria took a neutral stand while countries like Kuwait, Jordan and Saudi Arabia condemned India. However,

Israel took a pro-India stand by criticizing Pakistan actions in East Bengal. [15]

However, India continued pro-Arab stand even in the 1973 Arab-Israeli war. At the same time India gradually moved away from the policy of supporting individual Arab countries by focusing exclusively on Palestine question. [16] Hence in the post-1973 war period India gave more importance to support the struggles of the Palestine Liberation Organization (PLO) led by Yasser Arafat. In this respect, India played considerable role in the UN to support the PLO's bid for observer status in 1974. India became the first non-Arab government to extend formal diplomatic accreditation to the representatives of the PLO in January 1975. Moreover, India was a cosponsor of General Assembly Resolution 3379, which equated Zionism with racism in November 1975. [17]

When Janata party came to power in 1977, there were speculations about the shift of India's policy towards Palestine. It was during this period Moshe Dayan, Israeli Foreign Minister made an unofficial visit to India. [18] However, there was no official action in supporting the relationship with Israel. When Camp David Accord was signed in September 1978 between Israel and Egypt, India opposed it along with the Arab world. In 1980 Indira Gandhi returned to power with the continued support of Palestinian struggle. It was during this period India accorded full diplomatic recognition to the Office of PLO in New Delhi. Moreover, Yasser Arafat paid state visits to India in 1980 and 1982. [19] This line of Indian policy continued until early 1990s. The situation in West Asian witnessed a sea change when Iraq invaded Kuwait in August 1990. It was during this period the Soviet Union was disappearing from the world map marking the era of unipolar world. In the meantime, the P.L.O. lost its prestige in West Asia on account of its support to Saddam Hussain. The United States took the initiative of holding international Middle East Peace Conference immediately after expelling Iraq out of Kuwait in 1991. This marked new era in West Asia due to different varieties of diplomatic manoeuvring. As a consequence to these developments, India also made drastic changes in its policy towards West Asia.

Ties with Israel and Shift in India's Foreign Policy

The decision of establishing formal ties with Israel was taken by P.V. Narasimha Rao, the Prime Minister of India belonging to Congress government in January 1992. The decision was a surprising one, although it looked like a long awaited decision, as remarked by Indian media. In fact, the decision of India to start formal relation with Israel was based on changes in the international scenario. It was the beginning of post-cold war period war era with the disintegration of the Soviet Union, India's strong ally for a long period. In the new situation India desired the support and collaboration with major international powers like the United States, especially in the wake of the political turmoil in Kashmir. In this respect India had two objectives in promoting its relation with the US. Firstly, to overcome the propaganda unleashed by Pakistan on Kashmir situation. Secondly, India required strategic cooperation with the US due to the demise of the Soviet Union, the leading exporter of arms to India. It was imperative for India to modernise Indian weaponry. At the same time India was fully aware of the complexities in establishing strong ties with the US. In this context India found Israel as a best option of appeasing the US line of policy. It is to be noted that India announced its decision to formally establish relations with Israel on the eve of Prime Minister Narasimha Rao's visit to the US. [20]

Moreover, the P.L.O. had already recognised the state of Israel to join as a party of the peace process in the Middle East. So India found a favourable occasion in justifying its ties with Israel. It was also remarked that India's normal relation with Israel was helpful to get the status of a mediator in the on going peace negotiations. India's relationship with Israel also marked the shift of India's foreign policy from the traditional line of anti-colonial and anti-imperialist to economic and strategic developments. In the decade following this normalisation of ties, successive governments of both the centrist Congress and the rightist BJP, irrespective of party ideology, have rapidly forged extensive military, economic and political relationship. In fact, the shift within the Indian ruling classes from the official position of non-alignment and state-centred economic development towards a pro-United States policy facilitated and encouraged this change attitude towards Israel.

Milestones in the India-Israel Relations

The most important outcome in the Indo-Israel relationship was that India emerged as Israel's second largest trading partner in Asia after Hon Kong and Israel became India's largest supplier of military equipment after Russia. [21] Although India's relation with Israel started at a low profile, a sea change took place after the NDA came to power in 1998. India soon became Israel's closest ally in Asia with strategic, defence and intelligence cooperation growing rapidly. India became the biggest market for Israeli arms. Israel supplied not only military hard wares but also several high-techs, critical weaponry such as wide array of surveillance items, electronic warfare systems, a ground based Green Pine ABM radar, and phalcon airborne warning and control systems. These arms sales were part of a declared NDA policy to forge an alliance among India, United States and Israel. [22]

The United States has given clearance to Israel's delivery of phalcon reconnaissance aircraft to India, in marked contrast to Washington's vigorous opposition to supplying them to China in 1998. The US forced Israel to cancel the deal to sell the phalcons to China out of concern altering the balance of power between China and Taiwan. In February 2003 an agreement was made to supply advanced Israeli avionic systems for the Indian Air Force's new MIG-27 combat aircraft. There were reports about the collaboration between

India and Israel on a missile defence system based on the Israel Arrow technology. [23]

India-Israeli partnership has intensified since 1998 and later led to the visiting of India's Home Minister, L.K. Advani and India's External Affairs Minister, Jaswant Singh to Israel in quick succession in mid 2000. The delegates of the Indian team with L.K. Advani consisted of Heads of India's intelligence agencies, RAW, IB, and Central Police Organisations fighting terrorism. In addition to this, India's National Security Advisor, Brijesh Mishra and Services Chiefs have paid their visit to Israel since 1998, underlining the growing strategic cooperation between India and Israel. The top officials of Indian Navy also conducted goodwill visits to Israel. [24]

The Israeli aid during the Kargil war in 1999 was considered by India as a cementing factor in the Indo-Israeli relationship. It was during the visit of Shimon Pares to India in January 2002 India and Israel made major agreements to fight 'terrorism'. Ironically, the word 'terrorism' used by Israel was about the national liberation struggle of the Palestinians, which had been strongly supported by India until late 1980s. An Indian Foreign Ministry Spokesman said during the visit of Pares: "India finds it increasingly beneficial to learn from Israel's experience in dealing with terrorism". [25] This line of Indian policy was in contradiction with the fundamental principle of Indian foreign policy, supporting all national liberation movements.

The most significant event in the Indo-Israeli relationship was the visit of Israeli Prime Minster, Ariel Sharon to India in September 2003. In fact, the visit engineered much controversy in the wake of the assassination of Palestinian leaders by Israeli military forces during the period. There were series of protests in different parts of India against the Israeli Prime Minister. However, the Indian government adopted a cautious step of either displeasing Sharon or giving much honour against the public sentiments. [26] At the same time, there were many agreements during his visit as Sharon was accompanied by a large delegation of about 30 influential businessmen, eager to forge new contracts and open new markets in India. [27]

When the UPA government under the Congress leadership came to power in mid-2004, it decided to follow the same line of the policy adopted by the earlier NDA regime. During the NDA rule the Congress party had criticised some of the close cooperation between India and Israel. But UPA government followed its relations with Israel without changing any policies. India's Navel Chief Admiral Suresh Mehta visited Israel in January 2008 to finalise several key defence projects. It was reported that Mehta had reviewed efforts to enhance the Israeli-origin barak missiles defence system. [28]

Major Implications in the Indo-Israeli Relationship

The most important outcome in the Indo-Israeli relation is the aberration in the fundamental principle of Indian foreign policy. In the first four decades after independence, successive governments sought to project India as country dedicated to decolonisation. This posture offered the basis for the principled foreign policy of Nehruvian state which drew its own legitimacy from the tumultuous anti-colonial struggle that brought about independence for the subcontinent in the late 1940s. But when India decided to establish its ties with Israel, it had far reaching implications including military and intelligence cooperation against Pakistan and Islamic terrorism. In fact, India's relation with Israel was not a normal one as it expanded into different vital fields, even foiled India's traditional relations with Arab countries and Iran. It was viewed as a tactic used by the US to bring India into its strategic orbit. As a result, it lost its independent foreign policy initiatives in the post-cold war period.

The traders and business lobby in India and Israel played a crucial role in fostering the ties between the two countries for promoting their interests. The Indian business lobby was not interested in any matters regarding the case of Palestinians. Since Palestine has little to offer financially or technologically, while Israel can sell to India what the US refuses to India, these pragmatists insisted that New Delhi had no option but to court the more "valuable" Israel. [29] The official Israeli figures show that Israel exports to India valued US$ 1.270 billion in 2006 and imports US$ 1.433 billion to Israel. Agricultural, water and IT technologies in addition to fertilisers and diamonds are major mutual trade concerns. The State Bank of India became the first foreign bank to open a branch in Israel's diamond exchange. [30]

The India-Israeli alliance strengthens the US strategic designs for India and the region. India holds significant place in the September 20, 2002 National Security Strategy of the US, a policy document to support the actions of the current US President, George Bush. [31] Like Israel in West Asia, the US needed a close ally in South Asia to confront terrorists in Afghanistan and Pakistan as well as to overcome the challenges posed by China. The Indo-US nuclear deal is the most significant outcome of this kind of policy initiatives of the United States.

"Pakistan factor" was another aspect which cemented the relation between India and Israel. For India, the growing nuclear arsenal of Pakistan and its support to terrorism in Kashmir and different parts of India were most important challenges. In the case of Israel, the nuclear capability of Pakistan and its support to Palestinian extremists posed a threat to its security. In this context Pakistan was a common threat to India and Israel and any alliance in this direction was considered as most valuable. There were reports about the Israeli clandestine support to Indian nuclear explosion, Pokhran II in May 1998. [32] Even the *Sangh Parivar* was demanding for an alliance with Israel way back in 1960s and 1970s to face the "Islamic threat" from Pakistan and Kashmir.

India's relationship with the West Asian countries, most specifically Iran, has been a point of contention in the Indo-

Israeli partnership. Israel's relationship with Iran is extremely antagonistic and unstable. Israel viewed Iran as the most important threat to its security in the region due to the kind of support it extended to Hezbollah and Palestinian extremists. In the case of India, Iran is considered as the most important ally in the region. India paid a lot of respect to Iran on account of its support to Kashmir issue against Pakistan. So India treated Iran as an ideal power in the region to counter Pakistan influence in West Asia. But with the inception of Indo-Israeli ties India's traditional relationship with Iran badly damaged. [33] Israel's spy satellite, Tecsar (Polaris), was launched by India in January 2008 to enhance Israel's intelligence gathering capability. In fact, the real objective behind the launching of the satellite was to undermine the Iranian nuclear programme. Moreover, India voted twice on the IAEA governing body against Iran under the compulsion from the United States. All these created rifts between India and Iran. [34]

However, it is not possible to follow a negative policy towards the Arab countries by taking into account of many realities. It is estimated that more than five million Indian expatriate work in the Arab countries. Moreover, nearly US$ 25 billion worth of Indo-Arab trade, including 60 percent of Indian oil and gas imports worth US$ 20 billion, is the basic support of Indian economy. [35] In this respect, India had to follow a soft policy towards the question of Palestine. In order to overcome this dilemma an attempt had been made by Indian foreign policy makers to separate its Israeli policy from the Arab-Israeli conflict. To realise this objective, India has taken a more tactical neutral position on the Palestine question, publicly stating its continued support for the Palestinian case and making deliberative effort to further strengthen ties with ties Arab neighbours. [36] This is more evident from India's attitude during the Israeli invasion of Gaza Strip in January 2009 in which more than 1000 Palestinians were killed. India was ready to condemn the attack only in a mild manner without affecting the normal relations. This was questioned by some Indian political parties, especially the left wing groups. [37]

Conclusion

As a result of India's new foreign policy decisions, its traditional line of supporting national liberation movements and ant-colonial and anti-imperial stands has been fizzled out. The Palestinians have been waging a struggle for their nationhood for the last six decades against Israeli illegal occupation of lands. India was one of the leading countries which extended all support to the Palestinian cause. India has always opposed the continued illegal occupation of West Bank and Gaza. However, India's changed policy since 1992 is a blatant contradiction to its avowed policy of supporting the Palestinian cause due to the transformation in the international politics resulted in the disintegration of the Soviet Union. Moreover, India had enough justifications in establishing ties with Israel by taking into account of the factors like the recognition of Israel by the P.L.O. and some Arab countries. However, the current phase of India's relation with Israel goes beyond the level of normalcy and reached a stage of much clandestine cooperation for defence and strategic purposes. Ironically, India wants to borrow the ideas of Israeli tactics of eliminating the Palestinian leaders in its efforts to combat terrorism in Jammu and Kashmir. For a long period India had been condemning these Israeli policies against the Palestinians. Now the cooperation in the same field with Israel is against its foreign policy principle and the support to the Palestinian struggle.

Moreover, India never used its relation with Israel to resolve the issue of Palestinians. At present India is in a commanding position of using its good offices to influence Israel. However, no attempt was made to pressurise Israel to withdraw its forces from the occupied territories. Since 1992 India was not ready to condemn Israeli atrocities against the

Palestinians by sticking to a passive stand of supporting a 'peaceful solution' to the crisis. The new diplomatic initiatives of India target only its vested interest against the traditional principle of solidarity with the third world countries. The current trends indicate India's keen interest to develop close ties with imperialist global powers like the United States for economic and defence benefits undermining its values and principles. In other words, Indian foreign policy lost its direction as it is dictated by the external powers to realise their objectives.

Notes

1. N.V. Raj Kumar (Ed.), *The Background of India's Foreign Policy* (New Delhi: Indian National Congress, 1952), p. 57.
2. Leonard A. Gordon, "Indian Nationalist Ideas about Palestine and Israel", *Jewish Social Studies*, 37, Summer-Fall, 1975, p. 223.
3. Jayaprakash Narayan, "The Arab-Israeli Question", *Indian and Foreign Review*, Vol. 6, July 15, 1969, pp. 1-2.
4. Jawaharlal Nehru, *Glimpses of World History* (Bombay: Asia Publishing House, 1962), p. 789.
5. For details see United Nations, *Official Records of the General Assembly*, Second Session, Supplement No.11, Document A/364 (UNSCOP Report).
6. G. Parthasarathi (ed.), Jawaharlal Nehru, *Letters to Chief Ministers 1947-1964*, Vol. 2, 1950-52, "1 October 1950", (Delhi: Oxford University Press for the Jawaharlal Nehru Trust, 1986), p. 217.
7. Subhash Kapila, *India-Israel Relations: The Imperatives for Enhanced Strategic Cooperation*, South Asia Analysis Group : Papers, cited at http://www.southasiaanalysis.org/papers2/paper131.html retrieved on 12-09-2008.
8. Sudha Rao, *The Arab-Israeli Conflict: The Indian View* (Delhi: Orient Longman, 19720, p. 60.
9. Krishna Gopal and Kokila Krishna Gopal, *West Asia and North Africa* (New Delhi: V.I. Publications, 1981), pp. 274-277.
10. Arthur G. Rubinoff, "Normalisation of India-Israel Relations: Stillborn for Forty Years", *Asian Survey*, Vol. 35, No. 5, May 1995, p. 493.

11. Krishna Gopal Swamy, n.9, pp. 278-279.
12. Farah Naaz, *West Asia: Changing Perspectives* (Delhi: Shipra Publications, 2005), p. 95.
13. See *Indian Opinion on the West Asian Crisis* (Bombay: Indo-Israeli Friendship League, 1967).
14. Arthur G. Rubinoff, n.10, p. 498.
15. Ibid.
16. K.R. Singh, "India and West Asia: Retrospects and Prospects" in Nancy Jetly (ed.), *India's Foreign Policy: Challenges and Prospects* (New Delhi: Vikas Publishing House, 1999). p. 227.
17. Raja Swamy, "The Case against Collaboration between Indian and Israel", *MR Zine*, 30-08-06 cited in http://mrzine.monthlyreview.org/swamy300806.html, retrieved on 11-09-08.
18. Moshe Dayan, *Breakthrough: A Personal Account of the Egypt-Israeli Peace Negotiations* (New Delhi: Vikas, 1978), p. 28.
19. *Hindustan Times* (New Delhi), March 27, 1980.
20. *New York Times*, January 30, 1992.
21. Nicola Nasser, "Indian - Israeli Ties Could Neutralize Delhi's Palestinian Policy", 12 July 2007, *Arabic Media Internet Network*, cited at http://www.amin.org/look/amin/en.tpl?IdLanguage=1&IdPublication=7&NrArticle=41334&NrIssue=1&NrSection=3 , retrieved on 09-09-2008.
22. Ninan Koshy, "India and Israel Eye Iran", FPIF foreign Policy in Focus, February 13, 2008, cited at http://www.fpif.org/fpiftxt/4959 retrieved on 10-09-2008.
23. Ninan Koshy, US plays matchmaker to India, Israel, Asia Times on line, June 10, 2003, cited http://www.atimes.com/atimes/South_Asia/EF10Df03.html retrieved on 21-09-2008.
24. Subhash Kapila, n.7.
25. Ninan Koshy, n.23.
26. Bansidhar Pradhan, "Globalisation and the Shift in India's Palestine Policy", in Anwar Alam (Ed.), *India and West Asia in the Era of Globalisation* (New Delhi: New Century Publications, 2008), pp. 296-297.
27. Harsh V. Pant, "India-Israel Partnership: Convergence and Constraints", *The Middle East Review of International Affairs*, Vol8, No.4, December 2004, cited at

http://meria.idc.ac.il/journal/2004/issue4/jv8no4a6.html.

28. Ninan Koshy, n. 22.
29. Ramtanu Maitra, "Palestinians Pay for Indian Ambitions", *Asian Times on line*, September 10, 2003, cited at http://www.atimes.com/atimes/South_Asia/EI10Df03.html, retrieved on 25-09-2008.
30. Nicola Nasser, n. 21.
31. Ninan Koshy, n. 23.
32. S.R. Chaudhari, "Indo-Israeli N-Nexus", *The Hindu* (Delhi), February 10, 1999.
33. Adam C Castillo, "India and Israel: A Balancing Alliance, International Relations and Security Network", cited at: http://www.isn.ethz.ch/news/sw/details.cfm?ID=19199 retrieved on 23-09-2008.
34. Ninan Koshy, n. 22.
35. Nicola Nasser, n. 21.
36. Frederick Stakelbeck, Jr., "India and Israel Shape a New Strategic Relationship", *Global Politician* , cited at http://www.globalpolitician.com/2345-Israel.
37. *The Hindu* (Thiruvananthapuram), January 9, 2009.

3

Turkish-Indian Relations after the Cold War: Perspectives and Policies

Berdal Aral

Introduction

While Turkey was a staunch ally of the United States (US) during the Cold War, Turkey's favourite partner in South Asia was Pakistan: it was after all a Muslim state and an ally of the United States. Not unexpectedly, at that time, Turkey supported the right of self-determination for the people of Kashmir based on United Nations resolutions. Economic and political prowess of India during the Cold War was not sufficiently appealing to convince Turkey to act otherwise. India was a founding and prominent member of the Non-Aligned Group of States, while Turkey considered itself as a loyal ally of the "Western camp" also played its part for distant relations. From the early 1950s, India acted as an ardent supporter of the search for a new international economic, political and cultural order. The key words of this endeavour were disarmament, decolonisation, and the right to development. Although, Turkey manifested characteristics which resembled to those of Third World countries, as it was economically a developing nation with shortage of capital and technology, it generally remained quite aloof to demands for a radical restructuring of the international system and calls for the elimination of antagonistic alliances. [1]

The lack of rapport between Turkey and India during the Cold War was also manifest in the slightness of their economic relations. While the bilateral trade between the parties was negligible before the 1980s, recorded improvements in the 1990s were still discouraging. Even at a time when the Cold

War was nearing its end, the overall trade which the parties recorded in 1987 was less than 110 million US dollars. [2]

The end of the Cold War has been the key event which laid the international systemic foundations for Turkish-Indian rapprochement. Indeed the polarity and rigid partisanship generated by the East-West conflict disappeared in the early 1990s, thus providing Turkey with greater leeway in its quest for new diplomatic openings. Turkey sought to expand its influence in Central Asia, Caucasia and West Asia where ethnic (Turkic), linguistic (languages akin to Turkish) and/or religious (Islam) affinities played a major part, although main emphasis was laid on economic cooperation. In the meantime, Russia became one of Turkey's major trading partners in the 1990s, with the Blue Stream pipeline delivering Russian natural gas into Turkish territory by traversing the Black Sea.

A similar shift has been observed vis-à-vis the Indian foreign policy in this period. Indeed India made significant modifications to its foreign policy course in the aftermath of the Cold War by making overtures with unlikely states such as China, a historic rival with acute border problems, and Pakistan, arch-enemy with which it went to a number of wars during the Cold War. India has also made a series of strategic openings towards the US with crucial economic, political, military and geostrategic consequences.

Turkish-Indian rapprochement is, not surprisingly, supported and even encouraged by the US. This is presumably predictable when considering that Turkey has been a member of NATO (North Atlantic Treaty Organization), a Western military alliance, and a loyal partner of the US since the early 1950s. This substantive change of policy is well put by an Indian scholar, Subhash Kapila:

"The foreign policies of both Turkey and India adopted newer hues to grapple with the new emerging strategic realities. Turkish and Indian foreign policies started breaking out of their traditional moulds. Turkey while still remaining a staunch United States and Western ally started adopting more independent stances including initiatives for more cooperative relations with Russia. India on the other hand shifted away from its idealistic and delusional fixations with non-alignment. India today while maintaining its traditional strategic partnership with Russia is in the process of evolving a significant and wide ranging US-India Strategic Partnership". [3]

As said above, the passing of the Cold War and the dissolution of the polarization between eastern and western blocs opened up a large breathing space for India as well as Turkey. This is the *international* determinant of the bourgeoning ties between Turkey and India. The external dimension has had a decisive impact on the way the parties began to perceive one another. Indian-Turkish relations have, not unexpectedly, been influenced by the specific policy-choices of governments in both countries. In the Turkish case, the international and *domestic* contexts have never overlapped as neatly as it is during the tenure of the currently ruling Justice and Development Party (AK Party) government which took office in November 2002. This government has been an advocate of a multi-dimensional foreign policy perspective and behaviour that are reflective of Turkey's potential as a regional power with long and colourful history. Turkey has, in the last six years, manifested powerful impulses towards transforming itself into an "axis" state with its own diplomatic agenda. The new agenda, *inter alia,* requires that Turkey project its influence into distant geographies and civilizational spheres. This imaginative outlook, it is argued, much resembles the multipolarity of Indian diplomacy based on a broad vision whose imprint has been put by the Congress Party of India.

The first part of this paper will look at the points of convergence as well as mutual expectations which attracted Turkey and India towards one another. The fruits of this relationship in the 1990s will then be explored. Then, the question will be raised as to whether a "triple entente" was being formed between Turkey-India-Israel after September 11

(2001). The second part of this paper will take a look at the diplomatic relations between Turkey and India during the term of office of the AK Party government (2002-) and the premiership of Tayyip Erdoğan. It is argued that, even if there ever was a triple entente between Turkey-India-Israel, it has failed to deliver the kind of promises which the US and Israel had initially hoped.

Points of Convergence and Mutual Expectations

A cursory glance at the peculiarities of Turkey and India cannot possibly yield itself to discovering too many similarities between them: Turkey is a West Asian, whereas India is a South Asian state; people in Turkey are overwhelmingly Muslim, whereas Indians are overwhelmingly Hindu; Turkish foreign policy is oriented towards the West, e.g. Turkey is part of NATO and is currently negotiating for membership of the European Union (EU), whereas India is a founding member of the Non-Aligned Movement which has had a critical view of the West and its imperial role in world politics. However, a deeper look at the issue may indicate some very interesting similarities between the two states which have played some part in the bourgeoning relations between Turkey and India after the Cold War. The first set of similarities which visiting Turkish and Indian statesmen have been fond of emphasizing is their potential role in *contributing to regional and international peace* and their commitment to *secularism* [4] *and democracy.* Here is an excerpt from a speech by Turkish Foreign Minister Ali Babacan during his India visit in February 2008:

"Rich historical legacy, today, the modern principles of democracy combined with secularism, the rule of law, tolerance and pluralism are the common constitutional pillars of our states. As we consider Turkey's future role in regional and global politics, we draw some parallels with the rise of a democratic and increasingly powerful India in her region and the world". [5]

Similar remarks have also been made by Indian statesmen. On the occasion of his meeting with his Turkish counterpart, Tayyip Erdoğan, in September 2003, Indian Prime Minister Shri A. B. Vajpayee had this to say:

"We have some obvious shared strengths and commonalities, which are valuable in today's world: Both our countries are secular in our philosophy and democratic in our institutions. The will of our peoples is embodied in the supremacy of our parliaments.... There is an important role, which India and Turkey can play in maintaining regional peace and stability". [6]

Their joint emphasis on secularism and democracy, combined with strategic partnership with the US, meant that, Turkey and India have had little inhibitions about providing active support for the US-led "war on terror" after September 11. Both states had already become part of the Western-led struggle to stem the tide of "Islamic fundamentalism" from the early stages of the post-Cold War period. (This issue will be taken up later) Observers generally draw on the fact that India and Turkey are *regional powers*, although some would say that India is fast becoming a *global power*, which is presumably implicated when statesmen from both countries talk about contributing to regional and international peace. Kapila makes a strong point about another similarity between the parties linked to their strategic choice: "Despite any differences with the United States at the regional level, both Turkey and India can be said to realistically be considered *in the United States strategic orbit*." [7] On the strategic front, Kapila also notes that "there are *no strategic issues which divide Turkey and India* and nor are there any competing strategic interests between the two even in the areas tentatively defined as 'India's strategic frontiers'". [8] (*Emphasis mine*) The same point was also made by Prime Minister Vajpayee of India during his visit to Turkey in 2003: "We do not share physical borders, but we do have a vast common extended neighbourhood -- in Central Asia, western Asia and the Gulf. It is of even greater significance that, while our interests overlap in this area, nowhere do they clash." [9]

Indian-Turkish rapprochement, of course, is not simply the product of mutual similarities, although these similarities provide a suitable political and psychological context within which to cultivate relations. Their resemblance has also propelled India and Turkey to search ways to diversify existing ties so as to make fuller use of similarities. Turkey has a number of assets which India finds appealing. They include the following: a) with its strategic location at the crossroads of three continents, with its long and colourful experience in statehood, and military prowess, Turkey has the making of a prominent regional power. Keenly aware of these qualities, India conceives Turkey as a "prime strategic partner" [10] in West Asia; b) With a population of well above 70 million and rising consumption patterns, Turkey offers a lucrative outlet for Indian exports; c) As a candidate for membership of the European Union, Turkey could prove instrumental in creating better terms of dialogue, trade and economic cooperation between India and Europe; d) Indian investors may find in Turkey a profitable base for production, granting that the Turkish-EU customs union arrangement has eliminated all customs taxes and quantitative restrictions in the respective trade of the parties.

India too has a number of attractions for Turkey: a) India's great economic leap forward since the early 1990s and its increasing political clout, both at regional and global level, which has elevated it to a great power status, makes it an appealing partner for Turkey; b) With its huge population (1,2 billion) and rising trends of consumption, India is a very attractive market for Turkish exports; c) India has steadily turned its face to the West in the aftermath of the Cold War which Western-oriented Turkish diplomacy finds comforting; d) Turkey wants to attract Indian investors to increase its capital stock and to improve the quality of its technology, first and foremost, in the area of information technology and computer programming.

From the Early 1990s up until September 11, 2001

Soon after the Cold War was over, India began to show signs of a redefinition of its strategic position in the international system. A major outcome of this rethinking process was the bending of Indian diplomacy towards the US. During the course of the Cold War, India's relations with the US had remained cool for a number of reasons: US was the vanguard of the Western bloc, while India was a founding member of the Non-Aligned Movement; India was a close associate of the Soviet Union; Pakistan was an ally of the US in its struggle against communism. However Pakistan began to fall from Washington's favour when the Soviet armies pulled out from Afghanistan by the end of the 1980s. Besides, US President George Bush refused to certify that Pakistan was not in possession of nuclear weapons in 1990. [11] Combined with the end of the Cold War and the disintegration of the Soviet Union, Pakistan's fall from grace created a more positive climate for Indian-US rapprochement. The collapse of the Soviet Union was in some ways disastrous for India, because that state was India's principal arms supplier and major supporter in international diplomatic forums. [12] India wanted afterwards to turn to the US for arms supplies. India was also keen to get the US support on the Kashmir problem.

Such mutual considerations explain why, although in disagreement on a host of issues, the parties nevertheless began to enter into military and security cooperation in the 1990s. India decided to pursue a more liberal economic policy in the early 1990s which was viewed favourably by the US. [13] The US began to see in India an attractive market and a promising investment outlet. US-Indian relations, however, suffered a temporary stroke when the US reacted heavily to India's nuclear tests in May 1998. However, this disenchantment proved short-lived. The relations gained a new lease of life when US President Bill Clinton and India's Prime Minister Atal Bihari Vajpayee met on 21 March 2000, to "create a closer and qualitatively new relationship between the United States and India". [14] US-Indian relations have indeed grown beyond expectations since then, and particularly in the aftermath of September 11 (2001) terror attacks which paved the way for a "strategic partnership" between the US and India. A speech made by the then Foreign Secretary of India, Kanwal Sibal, in the Geneva Forum in 2003 provides us with a number of clues for this rapidly expanding and deepening relationship, in addition to the ones mentioned above: "The combat against international terrorism presents an immense challenge."; "The menace of Islamic fundamentalism...is internationally recognized as a problem that needs to be collectively dealt with."; "India and the United States are, respectively, the world's most populous and the most powerful democracies"; "the US is our largest trading partner..., the predominant destination of our IT services exports...and the major source of foreign investments"; areas of dialogue, in addition to economic issues, include "combating terrorism and missile defence." [15]

Apparently, the strategic shift in Indian foreign policy towards the US and Europe in the 1990s was welcome news for Turkey, as it overlapped with Turkey's foreign policy orientation towards the West. [16] Before everything else, their economic and commercial relations have expanded in the 1990s, although their overall annual trade never exceeded 500 million dollars.

In the diplomatic front, with American encouragement, India began approaching Israel soon after the Cold War was over. While there had been no diplomatic contacts between India and Israel during the Cold War, since India had refused to recognize Israel, a rapprochement began to take shape between them soon after India established diplomatic relations with Israel in January 1992. The crux of Indian-Israeli relations, similar to that of Turkish-Israeli relations, has been security cooperation. This cooperation is outlined by Berman: Contacts between the two countries, ...quickly evolved into a robust military and defense dialogue which today includes steady military-to-military contacts (more than fifty liaisons between 1992 and 2000) and intelligence sharing, as well as counterterrorism coordination. Jerusalem has also become an important player in a number of prominent Indian defense projects, ranging from aircraft upgrades to the development of the Arjun main battle tank. [17]

As regards Turkey, we note that under the premiership of Bülent Ecevit (1999-2002), Turkey scaled down its traditional intimacy with Pakistan and came to distance itself on a host of issues dear to Pakistan. During this period, Ankara began calling for a settlement of the Kashmiri problem on the basis of bilateral negotiations between India and Pakistan, instead of drawing on the United Nations (UN) resolutions that envisage referendum in Kashmir. [18] In March 2000, Turkish Prime Minister Bülent Ecevit visited India, while bypassing Pakistan as Turkey's traditional friend. [19] When asked why he did not visit Pakistan, Ecevit said: "We are friends with Pakistan, however we cannot support a military regime." [20] During his visit, he declared that Turkey considered armed groups fighting for the independence of Kashmir as "terrorists".

Ecevit's March 2000 visit was, then, considered by some observers, such as Ilan Berman and İbrahim Karagül, as part of a bigger picture named as a "triple entente" [21] in-the-making between Turkey-India-Israel. According to Karagül, the Ecevit visit signified that Turkey was happy to forge ahead with the approaching triple entente. [22] Assuming that this was a triple entente, which of course was a US-sponsored project, the Turkish-Israeli component was beginning to shape in the middle of the 1990s. The degree of collaboration between Turkey and Israel peaked during this time to cover issues like intelligence sharing, conducting joint military exercises, joint training, allowing Israeli pilots to use Turkish air space for training purposes, growing Israeli share of Turkish imports of armaments and equipment. The extent and depth of Turkish liaison with Israel has been mostly determined by the Turkish army.

The laicist ruling and bureaucratic elites who gradually restored their authority after Özal's death in 1993, rather like the Israeli establishment, consider Turkey as the vanguard of Western values and strategies in a terrain infected by the "virus of Islamism and irrational resistance to Western civilisation".

The Turkish army, supported by the dominant laicist media and western-oriented business lobbies, thus conceives of Israel as a strategic partner and an enlightened state struggling against "the forces of darkness" in West Asia.

Needless to say, the "forces of darkness" refer to all the actors, such as Iran, Syria, Hamas, Hizbullah and the large mass of Arab peoples, who have the desire and courage to rise up against externally-imposed imperial projects whose goal, they believe, is ultimately to pave the way for "greater Israel" and for the control of all energy resources and lines of delivery. This is the backdrop of the security conception which Turkey's pro-Israeli elites [23], alongside Israel, have had in their mind.

This explains, as Berman does, the "retooling of the nation's military strategy toward a substantially broader conflict scenario in the Persian Gulf and the eastern Mediterranean. Within the Turkish military—the main driver of Ankara's strategic relationship with Jerusalem—cooperation with Israel is perceived as essential to fulfilling this demanding security agenda." [24]

Although this artificially-hyped up and dangerous flirtation with Israel was not well received by the public in Turkey, no Turkish government, out of fear of US retaliation, has ever dared to challenge it. [25]

After September 11

The momentum for the triple entente-in-the-making, according to Berman, came with the horrific attacks in September 11 (2001). He says:

"Al-Qa'ida's attacks on Washington and New York have galvanized a broad international consensus about the threat posed by terrorism. For Israel and Turkey, this new focus provides an unprecedented opportunity to expand their strategic dialogue... In the wake of the terrorist attacks on the United States,...Jerusalem and New Delhi have demonstrated a new accord regarding the terrorism threat posed by transnational Islamist extremism". [26]

September 11 terror attacks were the second in the chain of events that brought Turkey and India together. This is well put by Kapila: "The end of the Cold War and the strategic compulsions in the post 9/11 era have erased away the strategic and political inhibitions which held back Turkey and India from moving towards a strategic partnership." [27]

The international struggle against terrorism and Islamic fundamentalism, as a crusade led by the US particularly after September 11, provided India with new opportunities that it could exploit. The new jargon about the "war on terror" permitted India to portray Kashmiri armed groups fighting for independence as "Islamic fundamentalist terrorists". In the murky atmosphere of the turbulence of "global war on terror", India, like many other states under challenge by separatist movements, was able to mobilize excessive and arbitrary force against all resistance movements in Kashmir–armed or unarmed-with dramatic human consequences. Indeed India has set to gain enormously after the War on Terror and new definitions and interpretations which it engendered.

This geopolitical axis, formed under US patronage, was intended to constitute a major pillar of US imperial strategy in Eurasia. This triple entente was in fact derivative of the global axis between the US-Britain-Israel. The September 2003 visit of Israeli Prime Minister Ariel Sharon in the Turkish capital, followed by that of Indian Prime Minister Atal Bihari Vajpayee after a week, was meant to cement the foundations of a strategic axis between these three states. [28] A major goal of the triple axis between Turkey-India-Israel was to collaborate against the so-called "Islamic threat" in Central Asia, South Asia and West Asia. A second goal was to prepare the ground for an increased US political role in the region. Eurasian states that challenged the US hegemony, such as China, Russia, Pakistan, Iran, and Syria stood to suffer from this hawkish entente. Subduing West Asia to make its state system serve US and Israeli interests was known as a prominent objective of the US-Israeli strategic partnership. That Turkey and India accommodated themselves to this imperial design strengthened the applicability of this goal. A third goal was to get the lion's share of rich energy resources of Eurasia and take the upper hand over energy terminals and pipelines. Last, but not least, the parties wanted to create, under the aegis of the US, the fundamentals of a security system which was in tune with the overall objectives of this axis. This required, *inter alia,* enhanced military cooperation between Turkey, India and Israel like holding joint military exercises, cooperation in the area of nuclear technology, generous trade in military hardware, and the opening of one's territory for the military training of others. Of course, the whole project, to repeat, would proceed under US patronage. [29]

Turkish-Indian Relations during the AK Party Rule in Turkey

As said above, contrary to some expectations, the triple entente has not taken hold to the extent which the US and Israel had envisaged. This entente drew a flurry of criticisms within India and Turkey. The critics argued that the entente was damaging to their country's international image without delivering much gains in return. They argued that it was the US and Israel which stood to gain most from the entente.

Indeed, as its most enthusiastic champion, Berman himself accepts that the true beneficiary of the entente would be the US:

For the United States, this potential entente is also an opportunity. All three countries—pro-Western in orientation, stable, and democratic—are natural allies for Washington. Their interaction, spurred by a mutual focus on regional deterrence, missile defense, and counterterrorism, could create a pro-Western nexus capable of dramatically bolstering both U.S. interests and initiatives. In fact, the prime beneficiary of such an entente would be the United States, since the triad would provide a powerful counterweight to the very states and movements that wish to undermine the U.S. position between the Mediterranean and the Indian Ocean: Iran, Iraq, Syria, and the Islamist internationale. [30]

Misgivings about the triple entente then came to dominate the official posture in India and Turkey whose enthusiasm soon vanished for a number of reasons: First, neither Ankara nor Delhi acted on the threat perceptions which the US and Israel were too keen to propound. These two countries had a distinct history of their own and set of priorities which hardly coincided with those of the US or Israel. While Israel considered Iran as a major threat in West Asia, India saw in Iran more a partner than a menace. The Indian perspective was visibly evident in a speech made by Indian Foreign Minister during the Geneva Forum in 2003:

Both countries [India and Iran] are interested in forging a long term strategic relationship built around energy security and transit arrangements. Iran is ready to work with India to provide viable and rapid access to Afghanistan, Central Asia and Russia and some projects have already been agreed upon. India and Iran have shared geo-political interests in the pursuit of which this part of Asia can be knit into networks of economic cooperation with increased stability as a consequence. [31]

Secondly, governments in Turkey and India that forged this unofficial alliance were replaced by less US-centric and more independent-minded governments in the intervening years. [32] The rejection of March 1 Memorandum, drafted to allow American troops to use the Turkish territory in order to invade Iraq from the northern frontier, by the Turkish Parliament in 2003 and the multilateral and multidimensional foreign policy strategy pursued by the new AK Party government, meant that the US was no longer able to manipulate Ankara in the service of eccentric alliances and projects devised in Washington to serve US imperial goals. Not unexpectedly, present Turkish government does not have a hawkish view of Iran or the Arab West Asia.

Thirdly, Turkish-Pakistani ties proved more resilient than some had initially thought. The extent of military cooperation and strategic contacts between Ankara and Islamabad was so deeply-rooted that, this long-time friendship was only marginally harmed as a result of Turkish-Indian rapprochement. In any case, the AK Party government had no desire to tilt the balance against Pakistan for a number of reasons, in addition to the one mentioned above: first, people in Turkey consider 'Muslim' Pakistan and its people as a true friend of Turkey and Turkish people. Granting that the Muslim consciousness is a key mental element that shapes the worldview of the founders of the AK Party as well as the hard core of its supporters, the current government detests the idea of betraying a 'brother nation'. Thirdly, under the rule of the current AK Party government, Turkey has started to play a prominent role in the Islamic world. Suffice to note that the current secretary-general of the Islamic Conference Organization is from Turkey.

Finally, steering a middle course between a variety of international actors, *inter alia*, so as to play an imaginative role in the resolution of conflicts in its near abroad, as well as in the larger Muslim world, has become a marked characteristic of Turkish foreign policy in recent years. Turkey has indeed proven itself to be an able and reliable mediator or facilitator that can bring together even the most ardent of enemies, states or other actors, or that can at least act as an intermediary between them: Syria and Israel; USA and Iran; different political groups in Iraq; Russia and Georgia. Turkey assumed a similar role by acting as an intermediary between Pakistan and Afghanistan a few years ago. If Turkey sacrifices one set of relations at the expense of the other, it will not be able to play the type of active and prestigious role which it has playing in the last few years.

There is at least one striking similarity between the AK Party and the Congress Party of India. Both of them, currently in power, are keen to forge harmonious relations with all the great powers such as the USA, EU, China, Russia, Non-Aligned Group of States, and the Muslim world. Both consider the role of Turkey and India respectively, *inter alia,* as "bridge-builder" between antagonistic power blocs. They share a common vision that emphasizes the positive assets of other international actors, and then seek ways to build on them. In other words, both parties reject the exclusivist categorisation of the world as "friendly" and "unfriendly". Since neither of them is nationalist in their ideology, both ruling governments refuse the idea of dubbing some states, especially immediate neighbours, as "eternal enemies". India has come to open a new diplomatic page with China and Pakistan as its arch-rivals through a series of diplomatic initiatives, while establishing strategic partnership with the US. [33] Turkey too has taken similar historic steps under the AK Party government by supporting the UN proposed (Annan Plan) formula for uniting Cyprus, securing cordial and extensive relations with Iran and Syria, and making a monumental diplomatic gesture in the visit to Armenia of the Turkish president in September 2008. To continue, both parties are averse to pitting one set of its relations against other groups of states. Although multipolarity and multidimensionality of Turkish foreign policy is undeniable today, the main crux of Turkish diplomacy still remains embedded in the Western alliance such as NATO, the European Union, Council of Europe, and the Organization for Security and Co-operation in Europe. Turkey has managed to put into positive use its Western connections in the realm of diplomacy in the near past. A few examples may suffice: Turkey was the architect of the series of meetings which began in 2003 under the title, "Iraq's Neighbours Conference", intended to contribute to stability in Iraq. Although the US initially expressed strong misgivings about this diplomatic initiative, it has since become part of it, alongside some other international actors such as the UN. This means that, from the perspective of decision-makers in both countries, US needs Turkey as much as Turkey needs the US. Likewise, Turkey tried to defuse the crisis that erupted in the Black Sea basin and escalated into a possible head-on-collision between the US and Russia following the war between Russia and Georgia in August 2008 by proposing a *Caucasian Platform* for security and stability. Turkey's Western engagements did not prevent the Turkish government from defending the integrity of Iraq, Lebanon, or from establishing diplomatic contact with the Hamas government as an elected and legitimate representative of the Palestinian people, or from (also) voicing the concerns of Syria and Iran against the background of Western hostility and aggressive posture towards them. India has likewise continued to voice the concerns, priorities and demands of developing non-Western states in international platforms, although it has become a strategic partner of the US and the Western world.

Like Turkey, India has figured more prominently in the international system in recent years. A major concern of Indian foreign policy is to provide utmost security for the country. India has a rather broad definition of its key security concerns which include the following:

"External security; internal security; sustained economic growth; energy security; maritime security; access to technology." [34] India has been trying to "secure for itself strategic autonomy so that it can pursue its national interest" [35] As part of this strategic goal, India decided long ago that it should possess nuclear weapons in order to enjoy "strategic autonomy", which it did in 1998 allegedly for purposes of "deterrence". India has officially announced that its main strategy about nuclear weapons is "no-first-use policy". India, rather like Israel and Pakistan which are likewise members of the "nuclear club", has refused to be a party to the Non-Proliferation Treaty of 1968. The nuclear issue, combined with India's impressive economic performance in recent years and the sheer size and quality of its scientists and intellectuals, has undoubtedly elevated the international stature of India. In the words of Pant, "as India's weight has grown in the international system in recent years, there's a perception that India is on the cusp of achieving 'great power' status." [36] India has thus become a major power and a pole of attraction both for small and big states alike. Interestingly, India is fond of describing its relationship with major international actors as a "strategic partnership". [37] At least in the case of US-Indian relations, there is a degree of truth in this. Indeed, US-Indian relations have continued to expand in recent years with special focus on economic and strategic cooperation. The parties have decided to engage in nuclear cooperation following a landmark visit by US President George Bush to Delhi in March 2006. [38]

However, although it has come to play a prominent role in international politics and established strategic partnership with the US, "India would like a world that is non-polarised and non-hegemonic – an aspiration no doubt – for these would maximise Indian autonomy." [39] Indeed India has not necessarily dissociated itself from the search for a "new international order" that can better echo the needs and priorities of poorer nations of the non-Western world. The debate still rages in India about the Non-Aligned Movement and India's role in it. Some twenty years after the Cold War ended, India is still an active member of the Non-Aligned

Movement. Therefore it is deceptive to jump to the conclusion that, because India has chosen to act more in tandem with the overall geostrategic environment defined by the US and its Western allies, it has abandoned its critique of the international system.

While, as a matter of strategic choice, both Turkey and India can be placed in the Western orbit, they take caution not to antagonize the international system through unilateralist moves and aggressive gestures. Turkey has come to pay more attention to the malaise endemic in the global economic system. Furthermore, it no longer suffers from inhibitions about making diplomatic openings to distant geographies as, for instance, it has done with Africa and East Asia. What is more, through effective lobbying premised on the government's track record of multilateral diplomacy and constructive engagement with disparate international actors, Turkey began to brace itself for possible membership in the UN Security Council. This aspiration came true when, on 17 October 2008, Turkey was elected to the Council membership for a period of two years with overwhelming support from the UN General Assembly. Their common strategic outlook, imaginative, flexible and constructive, combined with liberal economic policy and achievements in the economic front have naturally brought Turkey and India together. Therefore, today, Turkey and India have stronger motives than before to forge closer political and economic ties. As far as Turkey is concerned, Pakistan no longer occupies the central place in its strategic evaluation of, and concrete diplomatic initiatives for, South Asia. Since taking office in November 2002, Turkey's AK Party government has improved its existing set of relations with India and Pakistan simultaneously. Turkish Foreign Minister Ali Babacan's five-day visit to India in February 2008 was a clear manifestation of the growing significance of India in Turkey's new strategic thinking. [40] During his visit, Babacan gave particular emphasis on economic issues, as the following passage from his speech testifies: "The legal framework for the expansion of our economic and commercial relations has almost been completed. Hence, there is a wider scope of cooperation between our private sectors in terms of more trade and mutual investments." [41] The *range of economic activities* that may bring Turkey and India together appear to include the following: Indian companies could invest in Turkey, cooperation in the area of energy (India could build nuclear power plants), iron and steel, tourism, agriculture, information technologies including computer hardware and software, electronics, pharmaceuticals, automotive, etc. Turkey has been calling for a fairer balance of trade with India on account of its huge trade deficit against India. While in India, the Turkish Foreign Minister also drew on the economic integration between Turkey and the EU as a factor that enhanced the rewards which foreign investors could reap in Turkey: "Turkey's Customs Union with the EU since 1996 provides another opportunity for furthering its economic relations with India by providing Indian companies access to European markets without being subjected to customs duties. Several Indian companies are already utilizing this advantage by investing in Turkey." [42] Encouraged by the current level of trade and economic cooperation, Turkey has now been pushing for a free trade deal with India.

Conclusion

While India and Turkey kept a respectable distance during the Cold War, the parties began making mutual overtures from the early 1990s. Growing diplomatic, economic and strategic links between Turkey and India in the aftermath of the Cold War can be understood as a mixture of their economic and political pragmatism on the one hand, and a deliberate strategic and geo-political preference for global American strategies on the other. We may also refer to the absence of geopolitical clash between the two states. When looked at from Indian perspective, Turkey "shines out significantly as a stable, democratic and moderate and more importantly a 'secular' state, despite being a predominantly Muslim state." [43] From the Turkish perspective, India is likewise a moderate and stable state that stands out as the largest democracy with enormous market opportunities.

Both Turkey and India have acted as partners of the US in its "war against terrorism", whose primary target has been "Islamic terrorists", a position greatly aided by both states' attachment to secularism and their protracted struggle against separatist insurgents, PKK in Turkey and Kashmiri jihadists in India. Even before the September 11 attacks, both of these international actors had chosen to act in tandem with the global strategies which the US and its European allies pursued. The moderate, or non-revolutionary, role which India and Turkey assumed in the aftermath of the Cold War was also manifest in the extensive relations which they established with Israel from the middle of the 1990s. One major motive commonly held by India and Turkey was to improve their missile defence system against regional adversaries through US and Israeli assistance.

The complex web of security arrangements and other diplomatic contacts between Turkey-India-Israel under US patronage, premised on a confrontational rhetoric towards some neighbours, which intensified in the immediate aftermath of September 11 attacks, has prompted some observers to call this relationship as a "triple entente". However if it ever was a "triple entente", it did not take firm roots. As significant political actors with diverse goals, neither India nor Turkey has had any desire to see its international role reduced to the confines of an axis that would gain them new enemies rather than friends. Both Turkey and India knew that such an entente would mostly serve the imperial goals of the US and Israel. This critical outlook, overwhelmingly shared by the public opinion in both countries, was facilitated by the rise to power of the Congress Party in India (2004) and the AK Party in Turkey (2002).

Although the size of their current trade is not satisfactory, there is every reason to believe that, at least in the medium term, Turkey and India are likely to become major trading partners. Turkey, as a regional power with greatly enhanced international standing, is likely to discover new channels of communication and new issues to explore so as to lay the foundations for a fruitful and sustainable relationship with India. Seen through the eyes of the current Turkish government, Indian-Turkish rapprochement is not however likely to damage its traditional friendship with Pakistan.

Notes

1. On how Turkey voted in the United Nations General Assembly on "progressive issues" of international law during the Cold War and a few years beyond, see Berdal Aral, "Fifty Years On: Turkey's Voting Orientation at the UN General Assembly, 1948-1997", *Middle Eastern Studies*, Vol. 40, No. 2, March 2004, pp. 137-160.
2. http://www.ficci.com/international/countries/Turkey/turkeycom mercialrelation.htm
3. Subhash Kapila, "Turkey – India Strategic Partnership: The Indian Imperatives", South Asia Analysis Group, Paper No. 2788, 29 July 2008, http://www.southasiaanalysis.org/percent5Cpapers28 percent5Cpaper2788.html.
4. Both states consider themselves as secular and democratic. But this claim is at least debatable in the case of Turkey. Turkey is not truly a "secular" state, because Turkish type of secularism positions itself **against** religion, seeks to control religion and confine it to the private sphere. The Turkish version may be dubbed as "authoritarian" or "rigid" secularism. Turkey is not a sufficiently "democratic" state either, as the country has witnessed a handful of military and/or political interventions and manoeuvres by the army, which have distorted civilian politics in recent past. Sadly, segments of the media and most of the political parties in Turkey have chosen to go along with the army when it attempted to topple unwanted governments either directly or through political pressure.
5. Speech Delivered by H.E. Ali Babacan, Minister of Foreign Affairs of Turkey, entitled "Turkey-India: Rich Past/Bright Future" at an Interaction Session with the Industry Heads

organized by the Turkish Embassy in New Delhi and the Confederation of Indian Industry (CII), Hyderabad, Taj Krishna Hotel, 7 February 2008, http://www.mfa.gov.tr/speech-delivered-by-h_e_-ali-babacan_-minister-of-foreign-affairs-of-turkey_-entitled-_turkey-india_-rich-past_bright-future_.en.mfa

6. Shri A. B. Vajpayee, Daily World EU News, "India-Turkey relations in the 21st century", 20 September 2003, http://www.turks.us/article.php?story=20030920002222695.
7. Kapila, op.cit.
8. Ibid.
9. Vajpayee, op.cit.
10. This description belongs to Kapila, op.cit.
11. Ravi Tomar, India–US Relations in a Changing Strategic Environment , Research Paper No. 20 2001–02, 25 June 2002, p. 22.
12. Ilan Berman, "Israel, India, and Turkey: Triple Entente?", *West Asia Quarterly*, Fall 2002.
13. Tomar, op.cit. p. 15.
14. Joint India-US Statement, March 21, 2000, http://www.indianembassy.org/indusrel/clinton_india/joint_india_us_statement_mar_21_2000.htm.
15. "Indian Foreign Policy: Challenges and Prospects", Presentation at the Geneva Forum by H.E. Mr. Kanwal Sibal, Foreign Secretary of India , January 23, 2003, http://www.geneva-forum.org/Reports/20030123.pdf.
16. Kapila, op.cit.
17. Berman, op.cit.
18. Ibid.
19. During the Cold War, aside from the fact that Turkey and India were in different strategic camps, the Pakistan factor had kept Turkey and India apart.
20. http://www.hri.org/news/turkey/anadolu/2000/00-04-02.anadolu.html.
21. The term "triple entente" was coined by a Zionist American scholar, Ilan Berman, who hailed it as a "monumental regional realignment" in an article which he wrote in the *West Asia Quarterly* back in 2002, op.cit.
22. İbrahim Karagül, "Türkiye-İsrail-Hindistan ekseni: Amerika'nın 'Avrasya harekatı", (The Axis between Turkey-Israel-India:

America's 'Eurasian Operation') *Yeni Şafak,* 16 September 2003.

23. Not all elites in Turkey are pro-Israeli, of course. Among the advocates of Turkish membership of the European Union, there are those who consider the intricacies of Turkish-Israeli connection as a "burden", not an asset. Part of the Turkish ruling elite and the intelligentsia with Muslim awareness likewise challenge the wisdom of this hugely unpopular entente which elicits the fury of the Muslim world.
24. Berman, op.cit.
25. For instance, a public opinion poll conducted by German Marshall Fund in 2008 showed that, among a group of international actors such as China, Iran, the European Union, Russia and the US, Turkish public opinion fostered the least positive feelings towards Israel with only 8 percent of the interviewees expressing warm feelings towards it. (*Taraf* , Turkish daily, September 11, 2008).
26. Berman, op.cit.
27. Kapila, op.cit.
28. Karagül, op.cit.
29. Ibid.
30. Berman, op.cit.
31. Sibal, op.cit.
32. Anne Andlauer, "Indian-Turkish relations poised on the brink of redefinition", *Sunday's Zaman*, 13 April 2008.
33. In fairness, one needs to note that the process of Indian rapprochement with archrivals did not wane during the rule of the less cosmopolitan Bharatiya Janata Party.
34. Ummu Salma Bava, "New Powers for Global Change? India's Role in the Emerging World Order", FES Briefing Paper, 4 March 2007, http://library.fes.de/pdf-files/iez/global/04372.pdf
35. Ibid.
36. Harsh V. Pant, "India's Search for a Foreign Policy", 26 June 2008, *YaleGlobal Online*, http://yaleglobal.yale.edu/display.article?id=11003.
37. Ibid.
38. This agreement has not however come to the implementation stage at the time of writing, since the coalition government in India did not bring the deal before the parliament for ratification out of fear of rejection. The Communist allies of the ruling

coalition in India have been adamantly opposed to the deal which would "give Washington too much control over India's foreign policy and nuclear programme." The Communists thus threatened to withhold their support for the government if it went ahead. Against this outstanding opposition, the government has skilfully managed to convince one of the rival parties at the end of June 2008 to vote for the nuclear agreement when it is brought to the parliament. Thus the deal was in his pocket when India's Prime Minister Manmohan Singh went to the G-8 summit in July 2008. ("India's PM, Manmohan Singh saves nuclear agreement with US", July 7, 2008, *TimesOnline*, http://www.timesonline.co.uk/tol/news/world/asia/article4282146.ece)

39. Bava, op.cit.
40. Andlauer, op.cit.
41. Babacan, op.cit.
42. Ibid.
43. Kapila, op.cit.

4

Incongruent Triangle: China Factor in India-GCC Ties [1]

N. Janardhan

Introduction

China and India are two great civilizations with different post-colonial development models, different social, as well as political setups, different oriental attributes, and most importantly, different economies that together account for more than a third of the world's population. Both are not only consolidating their place in Asia, but also making their presence felt on the global stage.

As the search intensifies for energy and raw materials to feed their rapidly growing economies -- as seen in both wooing Africa, something that could become more apparent in their relations with the energy-rich Gulf Cooperation Council (GCC) countries in the future -- and their naval presence expands to protect the supply routes in the Indian Ocean, the discourse on a potential Indo-Sino rivalry in the Gulf region in future is gaining pace.

This apprehension comes in the midst of the GCC countries recognising the significance of Asia as an economic ally at a time when, first, the GCC economies are robust following high oii prices and need new avenues to invest and diversify; and, second, when Asia's oil consumption is soaring amid an economic boom. The six-country alliance, which boasts of nearly half the world's crude proven reserves, produces around 16 million barrels of oil per day, or about 20 percent of the world's consumption. Asia imports more crude oil than any other region in the world and is the single most important market for the GCC producers.

It is also important to note the good health of the GCC wealth (*despite the global financial crisis and the recent steep fall in oil prices*), which will drive ties with India and China. After earning US$ 364 billion in 2007, the International Monetary Fund's Institute of International Finance estimates the GCC countries would have earned about US$ 2 trillion through oil sales in the last six years and that their public and private overseas wealth would top US$ 2 trillion by the end of 2008. [2] Further, a Goldman Sachs report titled "The GCC Dream" also estimates that the cumulative oil and natural gas revenues for the 2005-2030 period would amount to US$ 5.5 trillion. This would also help the region's GDP overtake the United Kingdom and Germany by 2050.

A combination of the above factors, as well as the fallout of the events of 9/11—especially Western suspicion about the region and its financial dealings—made the GCC countries approach the East as their preferred market. This, according to a study by consulting firm McKinsey in 2006, would lead Gulf investors to shift their portfolio allocation toward Asia by 10 to 30 percent, which translates into about US$ 250 billion being available for investment in Asia by 2011. The 'Look East' policy in the economic realm also comes at a time of regional introspection in the political arena, which is likely to influence the long-term political economy of the GCC countries and shape international relations in the coming decades. [3]

While being rooted in the prevalent economic dynamics, this paper explores what the future course of the relationship will be between India, China and the GCC countries beyond the economic realm. The premises are: first, the GCC's new 'Look East' policy has to go beyond preferential trading arrangements and newfound political warmth, and address security strategies as well; and second, the GCC countries would take India and China seriously only if they are willing to be involved beyond trade.

The paper also explores another equally-important dynamic -- the factors that may condition Indian and Chinese role in the Gulf region–especially US-Iran ties, GCC-Iran ties, US approach towards China and India, Iran's relations with China and India, US-India versus China, as well as relations between India and China itself. The fundamental question is: Will India and China cooperate, compete or confront on matters related to the Gulf, which is a strategic partner for both? [4]

China-GCC Economic Ties

China neither has strong historical ties nor has it developed long-term strategic interests in the Gulf till now. Any role that it did have in the Middle East was laced with Maoist ideology and influenced by Third World solidarity for leftist independence movements. Yet, its relationship with the region has assumed dynamic proportions, chiefly due to its energy requirements to feed its thriving economy.

But, unlike *China's* ties with Africa, which have been seen by some as "resource imperialism", *Beijing*'s renewed interest in the *Middle East*, particularly the GCC countries, has been termed as a "joining of equals–newly rich Chinese manufacturers cutting deals with flush petro-princes from a tradition of unfettered trade as rich and old as China's." Starting with "exchange of Arab oil for Chinese capital," it has developed during the last decade into a web of two-way deals in banking, property development, industry and tourism. [5] This expansion has been aided by the two being among the world's "most liquid economies", thus opening the doors for improving political ties as well.

The new Silk Road trade, between China and the Middle East, has doubled since 2000, to US$ 240 billion, according to the Dubai International Financial Centre. The GCC-China trade bill was about US$ 57 billion in 2007, more than doubling since 2003. According to McKinsey, trade flows between China and the Middle East is estimated to reach between US$ 350 billion and US$ 500 billion by 2020, with China-GCC trade accounting for much of that growth. [6] For example, the UAE projects that its two-way trade with China will grow seven-fold by 2015, to US$ 100 million from US$ 14.2 billion in 2006; and Saudi Arabia too has expressed a similar intent. [7]

GCC-China Trade, 2001-2007

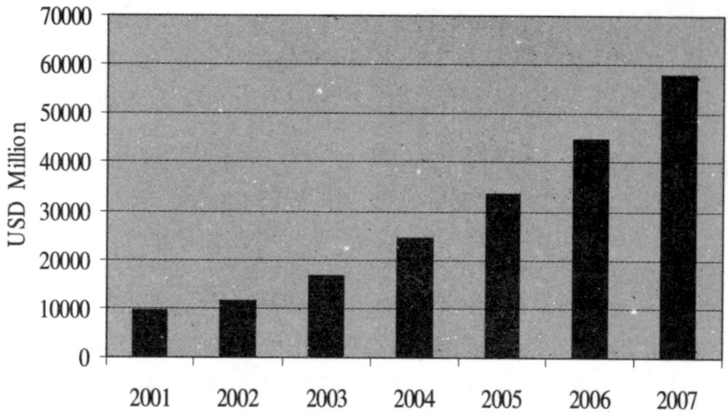

Source: Trade Map, International Trade Centre UNCTAD/WTO (ITC)

GCC-China Trade, 2007 (billion USD)

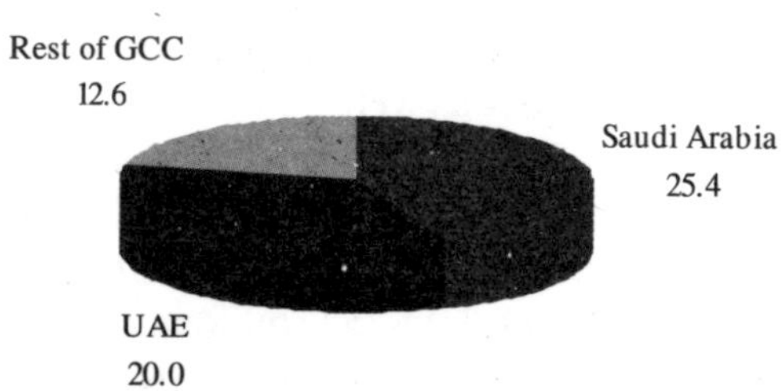

Source: Trade Map, International Trade Centre, UNCTAD/WTO.

The GCC-China trade ties are still rooted in oil — China relies on imports for more than half of the nearly eight million barrels of oil it consumes every day. China is the second largest oil importer in the world, accounting for at least 12 percent of the world's energy consumption, with a third of its supply coming from abroad. The International Energy Agency predicts that over the next 25 years, Chinese industry is expected to account for over 20 percent of growth in world energy demand. China currently imports 32 percent of its oil, a figure that is likely to double over the next five years. Its gas consumption is rising at an even faster pace, with imports projected to increase from zero in 2000 to 20-25 million cubic meters by 2010. [8]

As a result, China has forged several joint ventures to strengthen the energy ties in the region. For examples, Saudi Aramco — the Saudi state oil company, Sinopec — one of China's biggest oil firms, and the US firm Exxon Mobil signed a deal in 2007, through which Exxon and Aramco will help fund a Chinese petrochemical refinery, in exchange for export rights (for Saudi Aramco) and rights to operate 750 gas stations in China (for Exxon). In another arrangement, Chinalco, China's state-run aluminum manufacturer, is funding phosphate projects in northern Saudi Arabia, and plans to set up a production facility in the Kingdom's Jazan Economic City. Sinopec also signed in 2005 a US$ 5-billion agreement with Kuwait Petroleum Corp. to develop the southern Guangdong Province.

Further, China seeks to import energy-intensive goods like phosphate and aluminum, which the energy-rich GCC countries can produce more cheaply. Thus, "the theory of comparative advantage would lead to a situation where energy-intensive goods from Saudi Arabia are traded for labour-intensive goods from China." [9] Given this strong synergy, McKinsey predicts that GCC oil exports to China will grow by an average of 3.7 percent per annum until 2030.

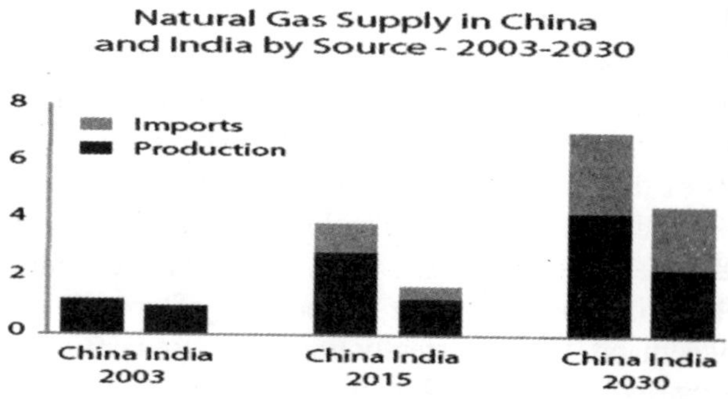

Source: US Energy Information Administration, International Energy Outlook 2006

Cross investments have successfully improved the effectiveness of preexisting trading relationships, or formulating new ones. For example, Maaden, the Saudi national mining company has acknowledged that Chinese direct investment has helped enhance the company's competitiveness in mining projects, in turn bolstering the quantities of commodities the firm is able to export to China.

Several non-oil sector partnerships in the recent past also reflect the growing synergy between the UAE and China. Dubai International Capital and Hong Kong-based First Eastern Investment Group announced in April 2008 a US$ 1-billion investment fund to prepare Chinese companies for listings on Arab stock markets; real estate giant Damac entered the Chinese market with a US$2.7 billion mix-use development in Tanggu district; Dubai Ports World, which operates container berths in six Chinese ports, and Tianjin Port Group Company Limited announced in 2006 that they will build a US$ 500-million container terminal in Tianjin; Emaar Properties has opened an office in Shanghai with a plan to roll out a number of real estate projects; and Emaar Industries and Investments intends to set up an automobile-related plant in China. On the other hand, Zhongon Construction Group is investing in Dubai's real estate projects, in partnership with

Fkamber Holdings; and Dubai's retail sector is likely to receive substantial investments from Dalian-based retail giant Dashang.

Further, since 2006, two high-profile Chinese companies, CNOOC and Huawei telecommunications, were forced to abandon plans to buy stakes in US companies amid politically charged security concerns. In April 2008, both companies signed major deals in Qatar and the UAE respectively. And, a consortium led by Gulf Finance House, the Bahraini Islamic investment bank, unveiled plans in July 2007 to build a US$ 5-billion residential and industrial city in China. [10]

In an indication of things to expect, a May 2008 report issued by JL McGregor & Co., a Beijing-based consultancy, estimates that the amount of Middle East money flowing into China could reach US$ 250 billion over the next five years. This compares with the US$ 200 billion that Gulf investors have divested in the United States since 2003.

These statistics provide a better overview of the fact that while energy might be driving the GCC-China relationship, ties have increasingly developed across the entire economic sphere as well. The GCC countries have also been motivated to expand their non-oil revenues. For this, China represents a potentially highly lucrative market. China's steel industry, for example, has been a net exporter since 2004, which – given its competitive prices – is good news for the booming construction sector in the region.

Moreover, China's shift from exporter to consumer market is being seen as an opportunity for the GCC countries to sharpen their competitive edge and increase their share in the world's largest market, as well as play a pivotal role in re-exporting Chinese goods to European countries. The region is already benefiting from access to cheaper Chinese products, with enormous demand for garments, fabrics, electronic and telecommunications products. The result is that the region's petro-diplomacy is emerging as a crucial foreign policy tool aiding China's economic modernisation.

The growing presence of Chinese companies in the GCC countries is having a social impact too — rapid increase in the number of Chinese workers. For example, the UAE is calling on the Chinese authorities to provide capable manpower in the fields of health, medicine, tourism, hospitality and construction, and is planning to increase the number of Chinese workers in the country, currently estimated at 80,000, to more than 200,000 during the next two years. [11]

India-GCC Economic Ties

Relations between India and the GCC countries have evolved greatly since Bombay's days as a premier marketing centre for pearls and dates from the region, and Indian currency and postage stamps were in circulation in the Gulf.

India's current economic relations are nearly similar to China – in terms of the trade basket, volume of trade, oil supply, as well as investments and cross investments. Two-way non-oil trade turnover with the GCC in 2007-08 was US$ 47 billion, more than doubling since 2005-06. If the oil bill and remittances were added the trade volume jumps to about US$ 110 billion. [12]

The GCC countries account for more than 12 percent of India's total global exports, supply nearly two-thirds of India's energy needs and host nearly five million Indians who contribute to the region's economic development. The region's importance lies in India's increasing dependence on Gulf crude oil, which may grow to 90 percent by 2020.

Apart from the UAE, which is India's third-largest trading partner in the world after China and the US, being a major source for investment in India, the GCC countries together are also emerging as India's premier investment partner.

India-GCC Non-oil Trade

To meet its forecasted growth rates, India has revealed plans to invest up to US$ 25 billion for acquiring oil and gas fields overseas in a dozen countries, including some from the

GCC bloc. This and other attempts to develop infrastructure facilities in India and economic diversification in the GCC countries set the stage for cross investment in both oil and non-oil sectors.

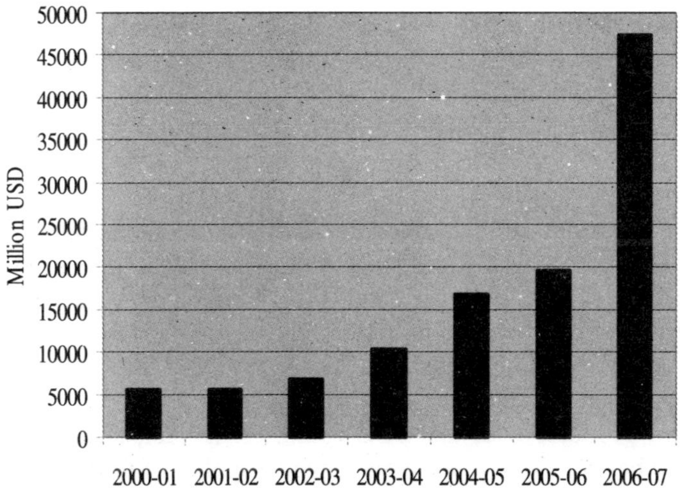

Table 4.1 India-GCC Trade (Individual Countries; US$ million)

Country	2005-06	2006-2007
Bahrain	381.8	654.0
Kuwait	975.6	6601.3
Oman	674.0	1089.8
Qatar	1161.0	2397.8
S. Arabia	3442.1	15959.6
UAE	12945.9	20673.5
Total	19580.4	47376.1

Source: Export Import Databank, Ministry of Commerce and Industry, Government of India, 2008.

Note: India's total imports since 2000-2001 do not include import of petroleum products and crude oil.

"The challenge before us is to transform the present buyer-seller relationship into something more substantial and enduring...Indian companies could participate in exploration and development projects in the Gulf, while Gulf companies could invest in India's downstream and petro-chemical sectors. Both also recognise the need for trained personnel in the hydrocarbon sector. Thus, we can collaborate in the development of educational and training institutions, not only covering the technological aspects of the industry, but also related areas such as health, safety and environment sensitivity," Indian External Affairs Minister Pranab Mukherjee said recently.

Accordingly, for example, Reliance India Limited has announced that it would reposition its global operation to Dubai before investing around US$ 24 billion over the next 10 years in petrochemical projects in the region. [13]

Beyond oil, while real estate is the 'hot' sector for investments, India has expressed interest in greater trade in agro products with the GCC countries. In fact, according to Mukherjee: "Today, we are a reliable supplier of food products to the Gulf countries and this will only expand in keeping with the expansion of Indian agriculture. I thus see India's requirement for energy security and that of the GCC countries for food security as opportunities that can be leveraged to mutual advantage."

The GCC interest in India is also gaining momentum amid a changing perception of India and Indians in the Gulf. [14]

A 2003 study by Goldman Sachs projects that over the next 50 years, India will be the fastest-growing of the world's major economies (largely because its workforce will not age as fast as the others). The report calculates that in 10 years, India's economy will be larger than Italy's and in 15 years will have overtaken Britain's. By 2040, it will boast the world's third largest economy. And, by 2050 it will be five times the size of Japan's, and its per capita income will have risen to 35 times its current level.

"In the past, India has been called a caged tiger, a lumbering elephant, and various other exotic animals in the zoo. I think it would not be boastful to say that today we have moved out of the zoo -- and on to the race course," is a sentiment that is striking a chord in the region. [15]

It is now evident to the GCC countries that the beneficiaries of India's knowledge economy include the United States and Europe, which will help India play a bigger role in the region's service industry. Further, the expanding private sector in the region has given Indians a level playing field over Western expatriates, and an opportunity to showcase their professional skills. After being the major source of unskilled and semi-skilled workforce to the Gulf for decades, India is now ready to increase its share of skilled and professional workforce in the region's quest to build a knowledge-based economy, which is bound to alter the composition of the Indian workforce in the region to some degree. [16]

Security Dynamics

Looking beyond the economic ties, there has been an increasing call, in recent years, for the GCC countries to act independently, take stock of the situation, and design future security arrangements, without leaving everything for the United States to formulate, thus opening a window for Asian countries. It is true that though the GCC's ties with both Asia and Europe are expanding, no other international actor can replace the United States in the short- or even medium-term future of the region. But that could change in the long term.

GCC Perspective

The GCC countries are increasingly finding themselves in a fix having to choose between their traditional security guarantor, the United States, and their disagreements with many aspects of recent US policy. They are increasingly convinced that events in the region, especially in Iran and Iraq, are beyond the US's scope of influence and certainly not in the best interests of the GCC countries. Given the added pressure of the region's leadership being unable to provide the necessary vision, two schools of thought prevail in the region: one urging less international involvement in the region's affairs and the other, more.

Those arguing that the way out of the dilemma is through the withdrawal of external powers from the Gulf, feel that they have precipitated the crises rather than contribute positively. Therefore, the new mantra is that "a lasting Gulf security system can only function if it is based on a regional initiative". But the situation on the ground is really not conducive to the complete removal of external forces. As a result, an indigenous alternative and viable security architecture is highly unlikely. [17]

In such a situation, the only option is further internationalisation of the region. Hence, the GCC countries are willing to consider intense political, economic and social ties with other countries to counter the prevailing notion that only American military power counts.

An example that illustrates this approach is Saudi Foreign Minister Saud Al-Faisal's statement, at the Gulf Dialogue in Bahrain in December 2004, which guarantees for Gulf security cannot be provided unilaterally "even by the only superpower in the world". The region requires guarantees "provided by the collective will of the international community."

The events leading to these and similar reactions in the region have forced the GCC countries to explore the idea of incorporating several international actors who could act as security guarantors of a regional security arrangement. While cultivating the new relationship, the region is linking its economic interests and security needs. And, apart from the importance of energy, Europe and Asia are showing signs of relating the relevance of the Gulf region to transnational security issues such as proliferation of weapons, crime, drugs and terrorism, and their impact on their domestic scenarios.

Asian Perspective

Three countries in Asia can be easily identified as having the potential and the inclination to play a security role in the region – China, India and Pakistan. All these countries are military powers in their own right and given the current level of economic engagement, they are bound to take part in any arrangement that safeguards their interests, thereby overlapping with the security of the region. Some of the developments in and statements of each of these countries suggest that the possibility of an Asian role in the security architecture in the Gulf is more than theoretical in the long run.

China

For a long time, Beijing has been, what historian John Gittings calls, a "status quo power that often punches below its weight in international politics." China's current Middle East policy is just one element of its overall goal of addressing this. While Chinese policies are clearly aimed at ensuring energy security, China is equally interested in increasing its influence in a region that is increasingly weighing the US presence, thereby challenging American control to complement its own global ambitions. [18]

Beyond this dimension, China is also beginning to look at protecting the valuable energy routes to maintain its development needs. In the past, China raised some eyebrows with its sale of ballistic missiles and related technology to Iran and Iraq during the Iran-Iraq conflict, as well as the long-range CSS-2 missiles to Saudi Arabia. [19] Such sales occurred in a different political environment. Though there is nothing to suggest that China is engaged in any form of military offensive, it is not too long before it starts engaging increasingly in the security debate in the region to have its voice heard or before its real plans for the region crystallise or receive more attention.

The fact is that by 2025, the Indian Ocean and the Straits of Malacca are likely to facilitate about 75 percent of China's energy imports, which explains its plan to provide more than a billion dollars in aid and loan guarantees for building its "String of Pearls" at the Pakistani port of Gwadar, which is on the doorsteps of the Gulf and the Strait of Hormuz. [20] Beijing is keen to use Gwadar as a transit terminal for Iranian and African crude oil imports, which leaves open the possibility of a role for the Chinese naval patrol. A road, and eventually a pipeline, from Gwadar could give China the alternative energy route that it urgently needs and spur the development of its western provinces. This and the other surveillance stations, naval facilities and airstrips that Beijing is either building or contemplating to safeguard the oil route have long-term strategic ramifications. [21]

China has also been busy strengthening its military capacity along its Middle East oil supply routes from Central Asia through to Iran. This is a direct response to the Chinese fear that the United States, as the pre-eminent power in the region, could check Chinese oil imports and, in doing so, severely damage its economy. As such, the Chinese government wishes to reduce the vulnerability of its Middle Eastern oil supply to US power.

The current Chinese views on regional security were mentioned in a government 'white paper' on national defense in December 2006. It provided a rare glimpse into the strategic assessments that underlie decisions and priorities of the Chinese military and the Communist Party's policymaking Central Military Commission. The main aim of releasing the contents of the white paper was to counter Washington's accusation that Beijing had not explained the rationale behind its long-term military modernization program, which hiked its defense budget to US$ 35.4 billion in 2006. The US estimates that counting equipment expenditures would more than double it.

The document said the military improvements are part of the country's overall modernization and economic expansion. It is meant to "lay a solid foundation" by 2010, make "major progress" by the end of the next decade and "reach the strategic goal of building informationised armed forces and being capable of winning informationised wars by the mid-21st century." It particularly aims to shift from infantry to high-tech naval and aerial warfare. It has dropped thousands of untrained foot soldiers and replaced them with trained technicians with skills to operate computerized weaponry. In fact, the People's Liberation Army "has made new progress toward the goal of being proper in size, optimal in structure, streamlined in organization, swift and flexible in command and powerful in fighting capacity." [22]

Thus, the bottom line is that security is an issue weighing heavily on the minds of the Chinese security officials and that, as a result, the strategic consequences for the wider involvement of the China in the Gulf will have to be taken more seriously.

India

While energy security is certainly a factor, India is also willing to showcase its power and influence in the region. This expanded security perspective is driven by necessity, ambition and opportunity. The desire to lead coincides with its rise as a major power with continental aspirations. Former premier Atal Behari Vajpayee and current Prime Minister Dr Manmohan Singh urged looking beyond the immediate neighbourhood. Singh said "the Gulf region is a part of our natural economic hinterland. We must pursue closer economic relations with all neighbours in our wider Asian neighbourhood." [23]

After Pakistan, China, Russia and the US, the Gulf is the focus to ensure against any maritime or landward threat to it from the region, serve as a base to pursue India's interests, confront terrorism and extremism, as well as tap the investment potential. By focusing on the Gulf and restoring traditional linkages with the immediate and extended neighbourhood, India is seeking to address its "four deficits" in the historical, security, economic and global decision-making realms. [24]

India is now talking about "soft power" and diplomacy – the security of the Gulf countries, as well as the wider Middle East, is of "paramount concern" and New Delhi is ready to contribute to the stability of the region by sharing its experience in combating terrorism, maritime security and military training.

According to India's National Security Adviser M.K. Narayanan, "The key focus in our external relations today is ensuring the stability and security of the region, comprising the arc of nations from the Gulf to East Asia…" [25]

The latest military capacity-building plan dates back to 2001. On a visit to Washington, then external affairs minister Jaswant Singh said:

"For a long time, India has not been seen in its true dimensions. How many people know that Indonesia is only 65 miles from the southernmost Indian island? Or that but for Pakistan-occupied Kashmir, Tajikistan is just 27 miles from India. That we had a border with Iran in 1947? Or that the legal tender of Kuwait was the rupee? So when we talk about Indonesia or central Asia or the Gulf, it is because of our interest and our sphere of influence."

With this in mind, the government launched "a 20-year program to become a world power whose influence is felt across the Indian Ocean, the Arabian Gulf, and all of Asia" in November 2003. [26]

A key role in this program is that of the Indian Navy. In October 2003, then navy chief Admiral Madhvendra Singh said: "Fulfilling India's dream to have a full-fledged blue-water navy would need at least three aircraft carriers, 20 more frigates, 20 more destroyers with helicopters, and large numbers of missile corvettes and anti-submarine warfare corvettes." The Navy's acquisitions program was then worth US$ 20 billion. The plan includes acquiring or constructing a submarine that could launch nuclear missiles, aircraft carriers, and long-range missiles with a reach of over 2,500 kilometers.

The Navy's aim is not just to patrol the seas, but have the capacity to create and "deploy battalion-sized forces at various strategic points... [on] short notice, and disperse them quickly from the landing or dropping zone before any adequate enemy response". The inference is that the expansion program envisions possible intervention in countries in India's "sphere of influence".

These plans were reflected in the government's Maritime Doctrine in 2004. According to a US War College study:

"Whereas (India's) earlier doctrine focused on inward-looking strategies, the new doctrine attempts to deal with conflict with (an) extra-regional power and protecting persons of Indian origin and interest abroad," (which perhaps brings the Gulf on the radar screens). [27]

Maintaining that the 'challenge' lies in India becoming a maritime power, former Indian Navy chief Admiral Arun Prakash promised in August 2006 a fully balanced, technologically fighting fit force in the next decade.

"No one can stop India from becoming a maritime power...Though our maritime interests are now all over, anything that happens between the east coast of Africa and the Malacca Straits is of immediate concern to India. We have the business to know what is happening in this part of the Indian Ocean. So, this is the immediate footprint of the Indian Navy..." [28]

It is relevant here to point out that Alfred Thayer Mahan, an American naval officer and historian from the 19th and 20th centuries, said that "whoever controls the Indian Ocean dominates Asia. This ocean is the key to the seven seas in the 21st century, the destiny of the world will be decided in these waters." Thus, India's naval plans and assertions have led some to ask, with concern, if India is turning the Indian Ocean into India's ocean. [29]

China, a Cause for Concern?

In order to limit dependency, both India and China have their fingers in the energy pies of more than 20 countries. Diversification away from the Gulf, however, has its limits -- not only are two-thirds of proven oil reserves in the Gulf region, but reserve-to-production ratios show that the reserves of non-Middle Eastern producers are depleting. In the medium-term, both countries have few alternatives to Gulf energy supplies, which could trigger competition.

But, China has not been a factor in India's relations with the GCC countries so far. India has had a more longstanding interaction with the region and its people. The socio-cultural compatibility and geographical proximity between India and the GCC countries are unparalleled. India's image as a benign and unthreatening major power is another comparative advantage that India has over China. [30]

Despite the surge in trade since 2000, there are several factors -- mutual suspicions, lack of developed business relationships, cultural and language barriers -- that could hinder China-GCC association in the long run, which indirectly benefits India. "We're talking about capital plus...That plus must include the relationship (built over a long period of time that can make or break deals)...One underestimates the importance of values and culture in both regions." [31]

Further, "businesses from either side don't always know what to expect when they venture into the other: Going into the (Saudi) economic cities, companies like Chinalco wonder who's in charge. Is it Bin Laden Group? Is it the central government? Is it the regional government? When large amounts of money are on the table, these unknowns become very real business risks. Local companies are often able to work around these market eccentricities and skirt bureaucracy through connections, but it takes time to develop these relationships and to garner the trust that makes them work effectively." [32]

But, while India and China appear to be on par, thus far, both in tapping the GCC potential as well attracting GCC interest in both countries, China appears to be pulling ahead in some respects, which must be assessed seriously to ensure that India doesn't lag behind in future.

For example, while the outlook for the UAE-China trade is very optimistic with a recent report envisaging a US$ 100 billion business by 2015, the UAE-India trade potential is slated to touch US$ 25 billion in 2010, according to a ASSOCHAM report. [33] Further, a recent economic study rooted in gravity model analysis points out that India's export basket is not diversified and is overtraded with some of the GCC countries. [34] While the free trade agreement is being touted as the much-needed stimulant, negotiations have taken longer than expected after the India-GCC framework agreement was signed in 2004. [35]

Moreover, Indian leaders are all over the world except in its 'neighborhood', which holds a strategic key to its economic growth. Despite several heads of GCC states visiting India in the last three years, no Indian prime minister has visited the GCC countries since 1993. Despite the Indian call for a 'look East' policy, it appears to be still stuck in a 'look West' mold. On the other hand, Chinese President Hu Jintao reciprocated the Saudi head of state's visit within fours months in 2006, and even made a brief stopover in the UAE in 2007, which was reciprocated by the UAE Vice-President and Prime Minister and Ruler of Dubai Sheikh Mohammed bin Rashid Al-Maktoum later in the year. [36]

Thus, India needs to replace its relatively passive approach towards the GCC countries with a far more proactive and innovative approach to sustain this vitally important relationship amid the Chinese inroads.

Factors that Could Condition India-China Role in Region

- US-China ties: For now, China says it has no vital "strategic" interests in the Middle East requiring protection.

The region is distant from China and is not an area from which hostile forces might threaten Chinese territory. Nor is it a traditional Chinese sphere of influence. China's interests in the Middle East are mainly commercial: oil and trade. And, China does not want to get entangled in any Middle Eastern conflicts. Beijing intends to free ride on Washington's efforts in the Middle East; if the United States fails to stabilise the region, China will not step in and is not concerned about who would. And, if China's energy interests are affected because of instability, China will go elsewhere for oil. [37]

China cannot supplant the United States in the Middle East as a military power. "Yet, Middle Eastern countries can use a relationship with China to supplement the bilateral relations with the United States and perhaps give those countries the freedom of greater distance from Washington. China is playing the game well. Unlike the Soviet Union, whose frequently heavy-handed reach in the Middle East prompted most countries to flee for the US security umbrella, all Middle Eastern states welcome China."

Whether or not China is interested in the region, the United States is worried about Chinese inroads in the Middle East, principally in terms of seeking access to its oil and gas reserves. "It is a fear for energy security -- rather than a concern over energy adequacy itself -- that could fuel Sino-American tensions in the Middle East." Some US analysts fear that a Chinese military build-up, especially the prospect of blue-water navy and power projection capabilities, could challenge US control of vital sea lanes. [38]

- China and Iran: One aspect of concern for the GCC countries is the relationship between China and Iran. The two countries share a special affinity that is too close for the comfort of the GCC countries given the lack of confidence between them and Iran; this is also true of the United States, the main powerbroker in the region. China and Iran have not only signed some major oil and gas deals in recent years, but have agreed to jointly build power plants, cement factories, shipping lines and even cooperated in the nuclear technology arena. [39]

China has also supplies arms to Iran, which makes it an even greater threat to regional stability and security; and given the strained American-Iranian ties, Chinese support to Iran's nuclear program is bound to put the interests of three parties plus the GCC bloc at loggerheads.

- India-Iran ties: While India has been under pressure from the United States about its ties with Iran, a certain section of the intellectual community in the GCC countries is attempting to pressure New Delhi into choosing between the two while deciding on Tehran's nuclear policy and the threat it poses to the region. How clear or ambiguous New Delhi's policy towards Tehran, especially on the nuclear issue, will shape the GCC's approach towards India. However, it is important for India to reiterate the strategic importance of both Iran and the GCC countries, which extend beyond energy interests.
- US-Iran ties: Some suggest that the future of US-Iran ties will determine whether or not Asia will have a security role in the Gulf. With US-Iran war and peace plans in a limbo, one could also argue that both scenarios open the doors for India and China. If any 'grand bargain' materialises following a new administration in Washington, it will encourage the GCC countries to look Eastward to protect their interests. However, if the tension persists, the GCC countries would be naturally encouraged to explore developing alternatives by involving India and China, among others, thus intensifying competition between the two.
- GCC-Iran ties: If there is any meaningful rapprochement between the GCC countries and Iran, then the US role naturally diminishes, clearing the decks for a more proactive Asian role in the region.
- US approach towards India and China: While Washington would desire "a unipolar world and a multipolar Asia, China would prefer a multipolar world and a China-centric unipolar Asia." On the other hand, India — which is growing closer to

the United States and which Washington wants to use to counter Beijing — "would like to see a multipolar world and a multipolar Asia," thereby intensifying Beijing-New Delhi competition. [40]

How the United States will reconcile with a new world – which has an emergent India and China – that is not "anti-US, but approaches it as if it were a post-US world" is important. [41] While economic growth enables countries to play around with existing structures to protect their interests, too many in the United States appear to be looking at dangers, rather than the opportunities of the Asian giants. The United States could be making a mountain out of a molehill while expressing long-term fears about China's intentions in the Gulf security architecture, and possibly India's in the future.

- US-India versus China: How successful will the US effort be to woo India in order to counter China and how will India's growing ties with the US be viewed by the GCC countries, especially at a time when the mood in favour of the United States and its policies is clearly at the lowest ever?
- India-China ties: Finally, and most importantly, though Sino-Indian ties have steadily improved, there is enough to keep their relations on tenterhooks. However, in spite of the overall challenges, which have not manifested in any way in the Gulf, it is important to stop viewing the Indo-Sino developments in mere India-versus-China terms and take an optimistic India-plus-China approach that guarantees a win-win situation. As the global economic balance shifts towards Asia, India and China could engage in cooperative as well as competitive, and not necessarily confrontational engagement.

Given the state of infrastructure in India and the realisation about its linkage with growth, China's success is acting as a catalyst for change in India. In the prevailing mood of competition, the Indian leadership has said: "We want to catch up with China," but doing so requires "greater political consensus" on reforms, which is an internal dilemma, without China in the picture.

While it is fashionable among common Indians to believe that India and China are engaged in a developmental race, New Delhi has reinforced that China's rise is an opportunity rather than a threat to India. It has clearly stated that Indians would do well to stop racing with the Chinese and start admiring — "We are not in a race...They have already won the race." [42]

In the foreign policy realm too, "China is a model for India in how to operate in the new world order and deal with the United States." [43] Analysts argue that India's new foreign policy diluting non-alignment is influenced by China's realism. Further, the 'look East' policy could also be a result of the "concern that a rising China might economically and politically isolate India from Southeast Asia." [44]

Energy has been the prime reason for competition in recent years, but has also witnessed cooperation. They have signed numerous pacts in the hydrocarbon sector, most notably the 2006 "Memorandum for Enhancing Cooperation in the Field of Oil and Natural Gas". Yes, India has lost out to China in US$ 10 billion of auctions for energy assets, among others, in Kazakhstan, Myanmar, as well as parts of Africa. At the same time, however, the two countries partnered successfully in Syria in 2005.

From about US$ 1 billion in 1995, the annual bilateral trade inched towards US$ 20 billion in little more than a decade. The two have pledged to double it by 2010 by signing agreements on science, space exploration, agriculture, education, tourism, nuclear energy, among others. China is already India's leading trade partner in the region and is expected to replace the United States as the top trade partner in a few years.

Since 2003, there has been a steady progress in security cooperation too. Starting with joint naval exercises, an agreement in 2004 facilitated exchanging military exercise observers; the following year, the two countries announced a deal to convert "bilateral engagements into a long-term and strategic relationship," pledging to resolve long-standing border disputes and boost trade and economic cooperation.

More recently, the two armies conducted their first-ever joint anti-terrorism military training exercise in China. Aptly termed 'Hand-in-Hand 2007', the drill was aimed at deterring the "three evil forces" of terrorism, separatism and extremism, and promote the development of a bilateral strategic partnership."

Of course, there are problems between Asia's "dragon" and "elephant", but they exist between India and Pakistan as well. In fact, the Indo-Pak dimension was, is and will remain more complicated than Indo-Sino relations can ever get. Yet, if India and Pakistan can stave off confrontation through efforts to cooperate, amid limited competition, then why not India and China? Again, unlike the Iran-Israel relationship, where ideology determines geostrategic interests, there are few or no ideological factors remaining to deter Indo-Sino ties, leaving them to just worry about geostrategic interests. [45]

Thus, while competition is inevitable, there is nothing stopping the two countries with "oversized egos" from cooperating and avoiding confrontation. Their cooperative relationship has significant implications not only for the future of the two countries, but also for the Gulf region, the Asian continent and the world at large.

Both countries have extremely good ties with the GCC countries, Iran and Israel. Apart from intensifying economic ties, they can serve as the honest peace brokers between the capitals of the GCC countries on one side, as well as Teheran and Tel Aviv on the other.

Conclusion

The GCC countries too need to take note of the fact that Indian and Chinese's basket of energy suppliers are widening. It is not impossible that India may follow the United Sates, which gets more oil from Africa than the Middle East, or China which gets more crude supplies from Angola than Saudi

Arabia. The Indian and Chinese quest to expand their sources of energy has even touched nuclear frontiers. With a view to strengthening and diversifying relations, it is imperative for the GCC countries to treat India and China in a manner that doesn't antagonise one against the other. In fact, the GCC countries must evolve fresh dimensions to consolidate their positions in a fast-changing world.

Further, while the GCC countries may be uncomfortable with India's or China's ties with Israel and Iran, there is no doubt that New Delhi and Beijing would not compromise on their own strategic interests and downgrade their relationship with Tel Aviv and Tehran to accommodate the GCC countries reservations. Instead, the GCC countries could use the India-China-Iran bonhomie to their advantage by in mending ties with Tehran.

The challenge is if the Asian security architecture, led by China and India, among others, will able to give rise to new institutions that foster stability, security, cooperation, and growth instead of being mired in suspicion and insecurities that others will take advantage of. Indications, so far, give rise to optimism. During the visit to India of Chinese President Hu Jintao in November 2006, the two governments seemed willing to cooperate. The goal of Asian architecture *figured in the Joint Declaration* with both sides agreeing "to expand their coordination within regional organizations and exploring a new architecture for closer regional cooperation in Asia." The two countries said they "positively view each other's participation in Asian inter-regional, regional and sub-regional cooperation processes."

If the 21st century truly has to be Asia's, the ties between and among India, China and the GCC counties have to be based on the development and security of all the countries and their people, as well as playing a constructive role in world affairs. And, as New Delhi has stressed: "The world is big enough for both countries and each is too big to be contained by the other," which lends hope against confrontation.

However, whether or not this developing triangle will end up being congruent or incongruent is contingent on several extraneous factors, which will pan out only in the medium term.

Notes

1. Conference draft.
2. *Gulf News* (UAE), 17 October 2008.
3. For more details, read N. Janardhan, "GCC-Asia ties: economy first; what next?" *Khaleej Times* (UAE), 31 January 2006.
4. N. Janardhan, "Chindia: Cooperate, compete or confront?" *Khaleej Times*, 18 June 2008.
5. Stephen Glain, "The Modern Silk Road," *Newsweek* (United States), 26 May 2008.
6. Lee Hudson Teslik, "China-Gulf Economic Relations," Council on Foreign Relations (Washington), 4 June 2008.
7. For more on Sino-UAE ties, read N. Janardhan, "UAE-Sino Ties: Full of energy for synergy," *Arab News* (Saudi Arabia), 12 November 2007.
8. Ziad Haider, "Oil fuels Beijing's new power game," *Yale Global*, 11 March 2005.
9. Dr Abdallah E. Dabbagh, President and CEO of Maaden, the Saudi National Mining Company.
10. *Financial Times* (London), 18 July 2007; Gulf Finance House has launched similar energy cities in Qatar and India too.
11. Press Trust of India, 6 November 2007.
12. India Ambassador to the UAE Talmiz Ahmad, *Xpress* (UAE) 25 September 2008.
13. Indo-Asian News Service, 25 June 2008.
14. These statements were part of Pranab Mukherjee's keynote address at the Emirates Center for Strategic Studies and Research in Abu Dhabi during an official visit to the UAE in May 2008.
15. Indian Minister of Commerce and Industry Kamal Nath's statement at a lecture in University College, Oxford, in May 2007.
16. The Indian embassy in Abu Dhabi estimated in 2006 that about 25 percent of the Indian working population could be categorised as unskilled, 50 percent as semi-skilled/skilled, and the remaining as professionals and businessmen.

17. For more on these issues, read Christian Koch, "Gulf Region Bakes Strategic Shift in New Global System," *Arab News* (Saudi Arabia), 22 October 2006; and "Gulf Needs More, Not Less, External Involvement," *Gulf in the Media* (UAE), 27 January 2006.
18. Julian Madsen, "China makes friends in the Gulf," www.asiasentinel.com, 30 October 2006.
19. Dan Blumenthal, "Providing arms: China and the Middle East," *The Middle East Quarterly*, Volume 12, No. 2, Spring 2005.
20. "China Becomes Increasingly Involved in the Middle East," *PINR*, 10 March 2006.
21. *Iran Daily*, 16 April 2005.
22. Edward Cody, "China Offers Glimpse of Rationale Behind its Military Policies," *Washington Post*, 30 December 2006; for more details of the Chinese Navy modernisation plan, see Bernard D. Cole, "The PLA Navy's Developing Strategy," China Brief, Jamestown Foundation (Washington), 25 October 2006.
23. "PM Keen on Building Strong Ties with Gulf States," Sify.com (India), 7 August 2005.
24. Part of a statement by former Indian defense minister Pranab Mukherjee at the Carnegie Endowment for International Peace, Washington, DC, 27 June 2005.
25. These views were part of his presentation titled "China and India: The Asian Rising Powers Debate–An Indian Perspective," at the third Global Strategic Review Conference of the International Institute for Strategic Studies in Geneva, 18 September 2005.
26. India's defense expenditure has more than doubled from $11.6 billion in 1998-99 to $26.4 billion for 2008-09. More details on India's military plans available in "India's Place in the US Strategic Order," Research Unit for Political Economy (Mumbai), December 2005.
27. For more on GCC-India tactical dimensions, see Khadija Arafah Muhammad Amin, "Need for Strategic Cooperation," *GCC-India Research Bulletin* (Gulf Research Center, Dubai, January 2006).
28. "Navy Chief Promises Technologically Fighting Fit Force," *Indo-Asian News Service,* 8 August 2006.

29. For more, see "US, China, India Flex Muscle Over Energy-critical Sea Lanes," *Freerepublic.com*, 10 June 2006.
30. "India as a strategic factor, in 21st century geopolitics," Lecture by Ambassador Ranjit Gupta, Gulf Research Centre, Dubai, March 2008.
31. Statement by Victor Chu, Chairman of First Eastern Investment Bank, the first Chinese bank authorised to do business in Dubai.
32. Opinion of Timothy Gray, CEO of HSBC Saudi Arabia.
33. *The Financial Express* (India), 25 March 2008.
34. Samir Ranjan Pradhan, "India's export potential to the Gulf Cooperation Council Countries: A gravity model analysis," (Research and Information System for Developing Countries, New Delhi, 2008).
35. China is also negotiating a free trade agreement with the GCC countries.
36. For more, read N. Janardhan, "UAE-India ties: Time to pull no punches," *Khaleej Times*, 20 March 2007.
37. Jon Alterman and John Garver, *The vital triangle: China, the United States, and the Middle East*, (Center for Strategic and International Studies, Washington, 2008).
38. Ibid.
39. Sharif Shuja, "Warming Sino-Iranian Relations: will China trade nuclear technology for oil?" Jamestown Foundation, Volume 5, Issue 12, 24 May 2005.
40. Gupta, no. 28.
41. Fareed Zakaria, "The Future of American Power: How America Can Survive the Rise of the Rest," F*oreign Affairs* (May/June 2008).
42. Indian Minister of State for Commerce Jairam Ramesh comment at a seminar sponsored by the Confederation of Indian Industry in New Delhi in November 2006.
43. Stephen Cohen, *India: Emerging Power* (Oxford University Press, New Delhi, 2001).
44. Stephen Blank, "Natural Allies? Regional Security in Asia and Prospects for Indo-American Strategic Cooperation" (Strategic Studies Institute, US Army War College, 2005).
45. Former Singapore diplomat and academic Kishore Mahbubani attributes the lack of regional conflict despite India and China's simultaneous emergence to Asia's geopolitical competence –

being innovative and creating new patterns of cooperation not witnessed by the West.

5

China as an Economic Rival of India in the Gulf

Javed Ahmad Khan

Introduction

Since the last two decades, the oil-rich Gulf States are much attracted to the Asian economic powers, particularly China and India. This has resulted into a massive scale of business and investment opportunities between these two regions. In fact, the process of economic integration of the world economies since the early 1990s has paved the ways for other developing countries to enter the Gulf market as a competitor to the US and other Western multinationals. This also provided new opportunities for India and China which they could not get despite their claim to having old trade and civilizational links with the Arab Islamic world.

Both China and India, with vast labor force, expanding skills bases that imply massive productive potentials at comparatively low costs, are currently attracting the Arab investors in order to boost their trade and technology inflows. However, the trade brings with it the competitions that occur naturally when two economies target the same goal; to attract the Arab funds for their economic growth. Keeping in view the current scenario, the basic questions raised in this paper are; how the recent Arab confidence is building up with two Asian giants in the Arab region? And why is it that India is facing a stiff competition with China to win over the Arab business and finance despite claiming to have a civilizational link to the Arab world?

China's entry in the Gulf is rather late as compared to India. However, China has gone far ahead in capturing the Gulf market. The Gulf investments have been flowing into China on three levels — industrial ventures, refinery joint ventures and investment in the capital market. Another significant aspect to be noted here is that China and India together account for a large portion (40-50 percent) of incremental global oil use, and for their current requirements, both depend heavily on the Gulf oil and gas. This is becoming another vital area for both to clinch the energy deals with the Gulf regimes.

This paper aims to focus on the China and India's entry into the Gulf region and in this context point out the nature of competitions and economic rivalry between these two Asian economic powers. Moreover, while analyzing the prospects of China and India in attaining their new world status, what we find is some basic similarity, in the process of attaining the status of economic power. Because, both are undergoing economic transition from a centrally planned system to a market economy. [1]

India and the Gulf

The gradual economic and political liberalization and opening up of financial markets in the GCC provide ample opportunities for Indian companies, organizations and investors in recent years. India's growing GDP and expanding market, as well as the Arab Gulf's 'Look East Policy' with their excessive oil revenue are now indicating that Arabs are in no mood to be wholly dependent on their traditional US/Western allies particularly after the 9/11 incident, and are seeking trustworthy partners in Asia with mutual respects and co-operations. Now, GCC has emerged as the third largest trade partner for India after the EU and the US. India's total trade with GCC countries is likely to go up to $40bn by 2010. India's trade basket with GCC is highly concentrated and its top five exports categories gems, jewellery, mineral fuels, copper articles, cereals and steel, which account for over 50 per cent of India's export basket to the bloc. India has started attracting Gulf investments to its food processing industry - a fast growing sector which will need Rs. 1000 billion over the next eight years to emerge as a world leader. The UAE and India have already agreed in February 2007 for boosting the food processing sector which has the potential to attract $33 billion in investments in 10 years. In November 2007, the launching of India Business Forum (IBF), at Riyadh, Saudi Arabia, with the support of the Indo-Arab Chamber of Commerce and Industry (IACCI), is set to enhance the business and investment in the region. The Arab World's investments into India are also worth watching as the real estate and petrochemicals sectors are attracting the Arab finance.

Energy Relations

In fact, the GCC and Asian energy ties took a new mould in early 2005, when energy ministers of the principal oil and gas importing and exporting countries in Asia gathered for informal discussions on energy security, stability and sustainability. The significance of this lied behind the massive oil consumption by the booming Asian economies especially in China and India. It is also noteworthy that India's energy relation with the Arab Gulf is not that of 1970s or of 1980s, the cold war era posing the supply threat. Now, in the de-controlled oil regimes, India and Gulf, as a consumer and supplier, are interdependent on each other. Though India still imports 75 per cent of its energy requirements and by 2020 India is estimated to import 90% of oil from other nations, out of which 85 would come from the Arab world. However, India and Gulf States are looking for partnership across the continent for refining and marketing investments. India, with its technological backup, is all set to participate in the petrochemicals projects in the Gulf countries.

The economic reform era and the deregulation of global oil markets have almost altered the conventional type of energy relations among the countries where the rule of game was not based on competition but on cold war rivalry. This can be understood more in the context of present GCC-India energy relations, where the former as energy supplier and latter one as its purchasers are in the process of building a new business and economic relations in 21st century. [2] The oil-rich Gulf States being not only the global petrochemical hub but also the main supplier of oil and gas to India are creating a climate where the Gulf's economic rent inherent in oil prices, have created more opportunities for the region's traders and investors who now foresee the prospects of more interdependence in the years to come. [3]

GCC Energy Investment in India

Many oil-producing developing countries have liberalized their FDI policies in the oil and gas sector as a way of modernizing technology and attracting equity capital from abroad. Foreign-owned companies operate under various arrangements, including direct ownership, joint ventures, and product-sharing arrangements. Compared to previous oil boom periods, a higher amount of the surplus now available to the oil-exporting Gulf countries is being channeled into project-based investments in the region. For example, the Saudi government is using its oil income to transform a relatively undeveloped, oil-based economy into that of a modern industrial state where the India and China, the new giants, were keen to enter the Saudi market and contribute to the non-oil trade. [4]

Similarly, Abu Dhabi National Energy Co. is eyeing Indian power generation and natural gas projects in a $6 billion spending spree. Also, Abu Dhabi National Energy Company (Taqa) signed a joint venture agreement with India's Infrastructure Leasing & Financial Services Ltd to build power plants across India with a total capacity of as much as 7,000 megawatts. Taqa's intention is to assume an equity stake in India's rapidly growing energy sector. These projects will require significant equity capital, and the intended partnership with Taqa and ONGC as a partner. [5] On other hand, the Gulf Finance House, in association with Gulf Energy already in process to develop India's first integrated Energy business district. The Energy City concept involves the master planning and construction of an integrated business centre that specializes in the provision of complete business infrastructure for leading oil and gas producers, both local and international, downstream refiners and producers, support services, shipping and energy trading businesses. India has also made joint venture project in Oman, LNG terminal in Qatar and investment of $1 billion in Great Nile project and the up gradation of a refinery and exploration of oil in Libya and Iraq. Kuwait has also shown interest in investing in existing refineries to cater the local market as most of new refineries being set up in India primarily aimed at the export market. Kuwait's oil firms are close to picking up a stake in oil asset as Indian Oil Corporation (IOC) had offered Kuwaiti oil firms the chance to invest in a new petrochemical plant at Panipat and a new refinery at Paradip on the eastern coast of India. [6]

The other advantage that the Gulf region has for India is the availability of cheaper refinery fuels. To heighten the competition with the Indian oil refining industry, additional refineries are proposed to be built in Saudi Arabia, Kuwait and Oman. The Gulf States have ample funds for such projects and also competent partners with technological expertise, along with access to the feed-stocks. India's ONGC Videsh has had a strong presence in Iran since October 2002, when it was earmarked for a major contract, worth $30 million to develop the offshore Farsi exploration field and it formed a new consortium, alongside the Indian Oil Company and Oil India Ltd. [7]

India is also courting the Gulf oil producers for a possible deal in which foreign companies can invest in state-run refineries in return for a secure long-term oil supply. The companies like Saudi Aramco and National Iranian Oil Co. (NIOC) are exploring the options of investments. [8] Reliance Industries, India's largest company by market value, plans to spend 24 billion dollars over the next ten years in setting up petrochemicals projects in the Gulf with each costing USD4-6 billion. Presently, Reliance import 30 billion dollars to 40 billion dollar worth of oil, including the bulk from the Gulf, refine it and export gasoline worth 80 billion dollars to Europe and the US. [9] Thus, under the new liberalized energy markets, the GCC States are investing their massive oil incomes into the emerging Asian economies in order to gain maximum profits and also to secure their energy exports markets in the region. This is an important development in recent GCC-Asia economic as well strategic relations where a new partnership between the investors from the both sides is emerging.

Perhaps, it has rightly been pointed out that the present GCC-Asia economic and energy relations is much in accordance to their aspirations, especially under the climate of interdependence. In this context, the two economic giants of Asia; China and India will finally compete with each other for securing the Gulf's energy and finance in the decades to come. But how far it would be reasonable to compare India and China in West Asian market? For the centuries both have forged strong linkages to the Arab world. The first Muslim settlers in China were Arab and Persian merchants who traveled via the sea routes around India and soon found the Chinese trade remunerative enough to justify their permanent presence in Chinese coastal cities. [10] Arab merchants developed a trade in spices as far as the Malabar Coast of India, the Spice Islands of Indonesia and even China. According to one recent historical survey, 'everything was in place for a flourishing trade'. [11]

India, China, and the Britain constituted a tightly-knit trading block in Asia in the period before 1880. After the 1870s, however, the picture begins to change. Almost like India's long and deep economic relations since the middle of 20th century, the primary motive for China's continued interest in the West Asia was to mobilize and encourage the local peoples and governments to resist imperialism, social-imperialism, or both. Even till the end of cold war period, when Arab-Israel tensions prevailed, and superpower pressure mounted on the Arab for a peaceful solution to the Arab-Israeli disputes over liberation of the occupied Arab lands and Palestine, China also seized this opportunity to declare its solidarity with the Arabs and succeeded in gaining some influence in West-Asia politics generally and Syria in particular. [12]

In fact, the Chinese interest in West Asia, which had long preceded the actual establishment of relations, has been closely associated with their perception of the world situation. Thus, like India, China's West Asia policy also reflected these considerations and particularly its sensitivity to external threats. Because of its rich oil resources and its strategic location at the cross roads of Asia, Africa and Europe, the Chinese sometimes regarded this area as one of the main keys for the control of the intermediate zone. China gained its first foothold in the West Asia in the mid-1950s. At that time China, which had been an outcast in the world community and rejected by the United Nations, was offered full diplomatic relations by only two West Asian countries, Egypt and Syria. [13]

Even China's trade with the West Asia, apart from its (limited) economic value, had an important dual political function. China concluded trade treaties and agreements in order to lay the groundwork for the establishment of diplomatic relations. China's diplomatic relations with Egypt and more recently, Kuwait, Lebanon and Jordan had maintained extensive trade relations with Beijing. The other function of China's West Asian trade, particularly imports, was to enlist Arab goodwill and support. Moreover, China's foreign policy has been implemented in the West Asia, as elsewhere, by many organizations and agencies. These include Friendship Associations; the Chinese People's Institute of Foreign Affairs; the Chinese People's Association for Friendship with Foreign Countries; the CCP International Liaison Department; the Foreign Affairs Bureau of the Ministry of National Defense; the New China News Agency; and so on. [14]

China's Entry in the Gulf Market

In April 2005, some more than 200 Arab businessmen took part in a conference mainly to seek business and investment opportunities in China and where the Secretary General of the Arab League, Amr Mousa has said that the Arab world needs to forge strong links with other global powers especially China which has become one of the biggest import and exports markets for the Arab countries. [15] In recent years, UAE is becoming a major trade partner of China in GCC. Trade relations between China and the Gulf Cooperation Council (GCC) countries have gathered pace over the past few years and in the year 2005, over $32 billion dollar worth of goods and services were traded. The UAE's share of this trade amounted to $10 billion, which makes the UAE — and Dubai as China's largest trading partner in the region. Also, the emerging links between Saudi Arabia and China increasingly points to a very strong bond between them. On the pattern of India, the Sino-Saudi economic relations had received a tremendous boost following the landmark visit of King Abdullah to Beijing. A major Chinese industrial project with investments exceeding $4 billion was planned in the Kingdom. [16]

The Kingdom of Saudi Arabia is in fact looking towards East to participate in developing its oil reserves, while at the same time transferring their know-how and expertise. China National Machinery Industry Corp. (Sinomach), and China

Nonferrous Metal Industries (NFC) have already signed a deal with Saudi-based Western Way for Industrial Development Co. (WWIDC) to invest in a $4 billion aluminum complex and a power plant to be built in Jizan Economic City. The Saudi Ministry of Transportation plans several railway and port contracts and Chinese players took part the bids. Already China Railway 18th Bureau was approved, for the second contract (CRW 200) worth $524 million of the North-South Railway. Aside from Saudi Aramco's oil refinery in Fujian and SABIC's Ethylene plant in Tianjin and petrochemical project in Dalian, Saudi Ajlan ibn Abdulaziz Aljalan & Brother got a stake in cotton spinning project in Xinjiang and Saudi Economic & Development Co. (SEDCO) acquired shares in a marble factory. Thus, in short time, Saudi Arabia has indicated how serious its ambitions are in the Chinese market. The Kingdom seeks to draw $50 billion of foreign cash into the petrochemical industry over the next 15 to 20 years as part of a campaign to make it one of the top three countries in the sector. Amr Al-Dabbagh, governor of the Saudi Arabian General Investment Authority (SAGIA), told Chinese investors in the Kingdom's petrochemical sector in November 2006 - "Don't' miss the boat'. [17] UAE Chambers of Commerce and Industry along with Arab and Chinese financial institutions and government representatives is now exploring economic cooperation between China and the Arab countries and means to enhance investments. In fact, Chinamex, the Chinese Investment and Trade Promotion Centre has planned to set up the largest Chinese logistics platform and manufacturing centre overseas in the UAE, to enhance trade turnover of more than $1 billion within next 3 to 5 years. [18]

Trade between China and Dubai jumped to US$19.4 billion in 2007 from US$13.18 billion in the previous year 2006. This reflects a very positive trend in the economic relations between Dubai and China over a growing area of investment in different sectors. China topped the list of countries from which Dubai imports goods, with imports valued at US$19 billion. Non-oil trade between Dubai and China, which has been increasing steadily over the past five years, has registered an increase by 47 percent at US$19.4 billion in 2008. China occupies the 12th position as Dubai's export destination, for a value of around AED 661.2 million. [19]

GCC Investment in China

Like India, the Gulf investments have also been flowing into China on three levels, industrial ventures, refinery joint ventures and investment in the capital market. Since both India and China have the low cost in production and skilled manpower, together with mounting energy needs, these Asian economic powers have always acted as a magnet for institutional investors from the Gulf States. For example, Saudi Arabia has in recent years shown much inclination towards the investment in China. This steady flow of Saudi funds into the Chinese economy not only underlines the strength of bilateral relations but also recognizes the geopolitical compulsions behind the dynamics of the "Look East" policy. Saudi investment in China's capital market is also growing. Al-Azizia Commercial Investment Corporation (ACIC) and a group of Saudi investors signed an agreement for a strategic offer for $2 billion in the Bank of China, the second largest state-owned bank in China and one of the largest banks in Asia. Figure 5.1, shows how the Gulf capital is increasingly being invested in China and India especially since the beginning of the 21st Century. Although both the countries are experiencing the steady growth of Arab funds but China is comparatively for ahead of India in attracting the Gulf finance.

Energy Cooperation – GCC and China

Thus, China and India together account for a large portion (40-50 percent) of incremental global oil use. [20] China's quest for energy and its ensuing rivalries with other major consumers like Japan and India have enormous potential and international repercussions. A rapid rise in energy demand is the key driving force for the development of an energy strategy in China. The range of energy demand in China in 2020 by resource is: coal, about 18.5 to 28.5 million tones; oil, 400 to 520 million tons, natural gas, 120 to 200 billion cubic meters. And the total energy demand is projected at 2.4 to 3.1 billion tce, but it is not certain that it will be starry lower than 3.1 billion. [21]

Figure 5.1

Capital Outflows from Gulf Oil Exporting Countries (US$ million)

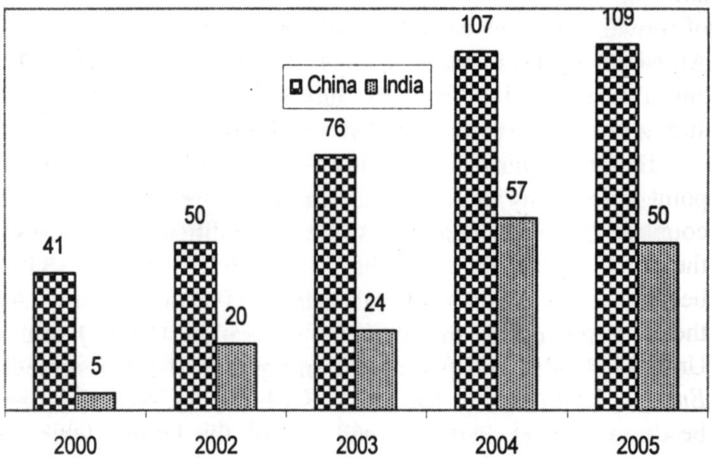

Source: *World Bank, MENA-China and India Report-2008*

While undermining Washington's ties with its allies, Iran is also creating stronger political links with American rivals such China, Russia and also India. In case of China and India, these links reflect the particularly important role that Iranian oil and gas is playing in feeding their rapid economic growth: China's relatively new commercial and political relation with Tehran, one that is still only in its relative infancy, has been created and sustained by an insatiable Chinese thirst for oil that is domestic production has failed to quench since the early 1990s. Like China and Pakistan, India's newly founded relationship with Iran is largely a product of its domestic energy crisis. India's industrial and consumer demand for oil and gas is growing fast and shows no sign of slowing down Iran's energy resources play a critical role in not only sustaining the present regime's grip on power but also in creating a more proactive threat to America's regional strategic interests. So by using these reserves to build alliances with countries like India and China, the Iranian regime has been able to take away the stigma of international isolation. China and Iran appear to have remarkably similar views on a number of foreign policy issues, such as the situation in the West Asia, Afghanistan and Central Asia, and advocated the need for a 'multi-polar' international community that would challenge the strength of America's global influence. [22]

The key driving force from the Chinese government's point of view is the desire to enhance the security of the country's petroleum supply through owing both the resource in the ground and, where relevant, the transport network. Beijing became a net importer of oil some 10 years ago and became the world's second largest oil consumer in 2002 following the United States, overtaking Japan in the process. As per the *Energy Development Report of China - 2007*, the country will be dependent on crude imports to meet more than half of its energy needs by 2010 and around 60 percent by 2020. China has also been stressing on inking long-term relationship with some of these oil-rich countries with more than $6 billion of investments there, mostly in energy and infrastructure projects. Chinese interest is growing in upstream investment in the oil-rich Gulf countries. Since 2003, China has signed supply and development contracts with Iran, and also Sinopec, China's state petroleum company, has signed a $300m deal with Saudi Arabia in 2004 to develop gas reservoirs close to the Ghawar field. Recently, in June 2005, the heads of the Chinese and Abu Dhabi state oil forms signed a MoU, calling for increased cooperation in the energy sector. It is increasingly impossible for Abu Dhabi to ignore China as it becomes the main driver of East Asian oil and gas demand. As China shifts its interest from marginal producers such as Sudan to more established exporters like Iran and Saudi Arabia, it is natural that it will wish to increase investment in Abu Dhabi. [23]

China imports a large quantity of oil and intends to import significant amounts of LNG from Iran. The two major projects of North Pars gas field exploration and Yadavaran oil field development are among the most important projects between the two countries. The project involves an investment of $16bn from the Chinese side. Another project worth $2bn, the Yadavaran project between Sinopec and NIOC, was finalized in 2007. Sinopec will develop it and buy 10mn tons of LNG over 25 years. The main rationale for cooperating with Iran is not only to secure the supply of oil and gas, but also to seek commercial opportunities for Chinese NOCs, as Iran is one of the few countries in the Gulf region that assigns China the right to conduct business in its upstream sector. China is the largest petroleum trade partner of Iran in 2007, and is one of the few countries to break US sanctions against Iran, which "penalizes foreign companies for investing more than $20mn. Also, the gas giant Qatar home to the world's third-largest gas reserves after Russia and Iran, started to look in mid 2005, to sell LNG to China's top offshore oil and gas producer, CNOOC Group. Qatar, planed to export 77 million tonnes of the super-cooled and compressed gas by 2012. Industry experts forecast China will import about 20 million tonnes of LNG a year by 2010, and may build up to nine new LNG terminals. [24]

Saudi Aramco is also planning a refinery investment in China, acquiring a 25-percent stake in Sinopec's planned $1.2-billion refinery at the port city of Qingdao, in the province of Shandong. [25] In July 2006, China approved a $5 billion domestic oil refinery joint venture with Kuwait. The project between China's Sinopec and Kuwait Petroleum Corp. became the biggest Sino-foreign joint venture in the petrochemical industry, marking another major development in the Asian nation's quest for energy. China's active strategy in the region is also welcomed by the oil producing countries in the interest of secure demand in the fastest growing market. China's energy strategy in the region seems to be effective so far. In an era where security of supplies is a crucial, top national objective for major crude importing nations, China's crude oil dependency is expanding rapidly and is now expected to exceed the 50 percent mark. China has been actively promoting energy ties with the Gulf States, driven not only by the security of supply concerns of the government, but also by the commercial interests of its national oil companies (NOCs). However, there are still many pitfalls and obstacles that remain to be solved for the Sino-West Asia cooperation to develop smoothly. [26]

However, being the economic rival, India and China now realize that in order to compete with other western dominating multinationals they must come together. In April 2005, these two Asian giants agreed to create a strategic partnership for peace and prosperity to promote diplomatic relations, economic ties and contribute to the two nations jointly addressing global challenges and threats. For example, these two energy-hungry Asian giants, are competing for stakes in foreign oil and gas projects to secure supplies. Indian and Chinese oil firms have already signed memorandums of understanding (MOUs) with Sinopec Corp, China National Petroleum and CNOOC, bidding jointly for foreign oil and gas projects and reducing cut-throat competition. China has also now sought to moderate its rivalry with India over bidding for foreign energy sources and in late 2005 filed a joint bid with ONGC for Syrian pipelines. The Indo-Chinese energy cooperation got more familiarized when the idea of an Asian energy association has been floated by India's former Minister of Petroleum and Natural Gas Mani Shankar Aiyar who pursued this as a matter of policy, connecting the China in the future to the projected Iran-Afghanistan-Pakistan-India pipeline. [27]

China and India as Economic Rivals

How far India is catching up with China? Or is China surpassing India in the Arabian Gulf market? Although, India is compared with China yet actual figures leave India far behind. Thus, while Indo-Chinese relations have improved recently and China may be interested in India's plans for an Asian structure that brings together consumers and producers of energy to reduce price fluctuations. The comparison between the two is normally made on the Gulf investor's attraction towards them. But when it comes to crucial areas such as infrastructure, compared to China, India hardly comes in the picture. For example, India spent just about $28 billion in 2005 compared to $201 billion spent by China. This means India spent 3.5 percent of its GDP for infrastructure development as against 9 percent of the GDP spent by China.

Further, how the recent growth of China and India is seen in the Arab Gulf region? This question is more relevant in the context of Arab world's 'Look East policy' and their greater inclinations towards these two economies. Another important aspect worth noting is that, India and China are among the top destinations for Foreign Direct Investments while the world's centre of power continues its "perceptible shift" from developed to developing markets. Keeping in view this scenario, Victor Chu, chairman of Hong Kong-based First Eastern Investment while addressing the Arab Strategy Forum December 2006, urged closer integration between China, India and the Arab world more because, 'we are culturally similar being family-oriented, value-driven and knowledge-focused. [28] Moreover, as the infrastructure spending across emerging markets is expected to reach $21.7 trillion over the next decade, with Asia representing 67 per cent of the total and the West Asia four per cent. Here China and India are expected to dominate this spending. [29]

In the mid-1990s, the World Bank Report had predicted that competition in the world commodity markets and manufactures markets in India and China will remain fierce. Given their overwhelming abundance of labor relative to other factors of production and assuming continued reforms, China and India are likely to retain their comparative advantage in labor manufactories for some time, especially given these country's large income disparities between regions and between urban and rural population. [30] In fact, the recent studies have already indicated that though the Asia and West Asian regions are likely to come economically closer, but both are facing terrorist's threat since the 11 September 2001. Whether Muslim capital and finance can be an alternative to capitalism or socialism, however, with new products in Islamic banking and finance, the GCC countries have started looking towards the East with their massive oil incomes for the acquisition of refineries, and other related petrochemical sectors. [31]

It is not that from the very beginning of its economic reforms, China was in any way different from India. The same political conflicts, regional income inequalities, threat of energy crisis, the bad debts, and also the problems of absorbing the increasing numbers of migrants and unemployed persons from the countryside already overcrowded the cities, as of India. However, since the late 1970s, China continues to move in the direction of markets and capitalism. It formally accepted the private sector in its constitution in 1999 and accepted new capitalists into the higher ranks of the Communist Party in 2002. [32] In fact, China's economy since 2001, when this country gained accession into the WTO, has experienced a new spurt of high growth with its GDP expanding at the average rate of 9.8 per cent for the period-2002-05. Such dynamic expansion of exports in recent years bears the best testimony to the positive 'WTO effects' on China, and now more closely integrated with the global economy, leading to a large influx of foreign direct investment, FDI. [33] Figure 5.2 below shows the average percentage of increase of FDI into the Gulf countries from China and India. Here, it can be seen that both these Asian economic power are competing to each others. However, the volume of their investments, from country to country differ. For example, in the Gulf states of Iran, Oman and UAE, India is more successful than China in penetrating these countries. On the other hand, China is more aggressively entering into Saudi Arabia and Iran, the two major oil exporting and expanding economies in the region.

Figure 5.2

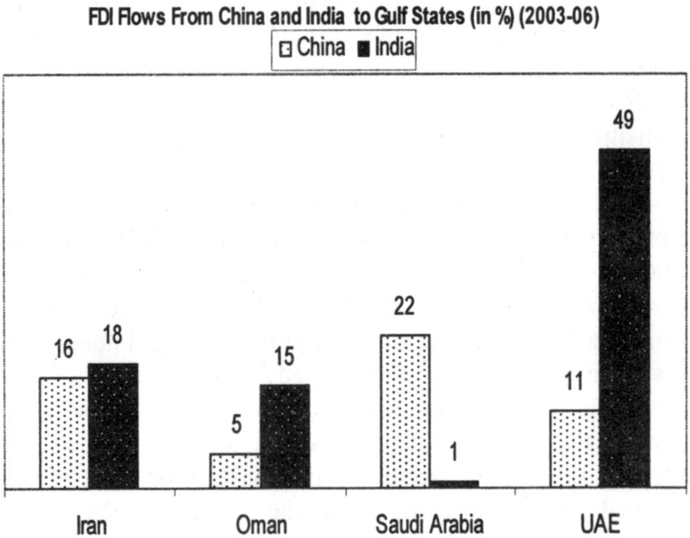

Sources: *China Statistical Bulletin 2007* and *Investment Division, Department of Economic Affairs, Ministry of Finance, India*

As a fastest-growing emerging economy in the world since the 1990s, the growth story begins with economic liberalization and policy reforms, an ideology that India adopted rather late as compared to China. However, India's high growth performance since the 1980s is a direct result of purposive investments for building human capital, accumulation of capitals, creating institutional capabilities to support functioning of markets. India's manufacturing exports are poised to reach US$ 300 billion by 2015. This amounts to a surge of 650 per cent in manufacturing exports in various skill-based industries such as specialized automotive parts, electrical and electronic parts, chemicals and pharmaceuticals products, and so forth. [34] It is possible to admire China's various achievements and to learn from them, but the Chinese experience convincingly demonstrates that, if properly supplemented, a thriving market economy can transform their living conditicns. China's supportive public intervention, especially in fields such as education, health care, social security, and the mechanism are an essential part of effective trade and production arrangements to penetrate in the global market. [35] Both China and India, with their vast labour forces and expanding skills bases imply massive productive potential, especially if they continue (China) or start (India) to invest heavily in the emerging Gulf markets. The growth of these two giant economies will affect not only goods markets but also flows of savings, investment, and even people in West Asia. [36]

Conclusion

The business and commercial relations bring with it the competition that naturally occurs when two economies exchange goods and services for money. Each side hopes to maximize their benefit. As trade grows, national economies become concerned about their status in the global economy and the long-term effects on their domestic well-being. What was at first seen to be mutually beneficial trade programme between two friendly nations, can suddenly be viewed by either side or both as a pernicious attempt to take advantage or even subjugate. [37] While the markets are integrating, the competition among countries, their firms and workers are also increasing. Developing countries, once at the periphery of the global economy, are now moving to center state and are becoming serious competitors in the markets of high-income countries and in each other's markets.

While the phenomenal success that China has enjoyed in expanding its world market share since the introduction of market reforms has increased competitive pressure on both developing and developed countries. The expansion of developing country's commerce means that these countries are increasingly becoming privileged destinations for FDI, both as an export platform for multinational companies and because they represent the fastest-growing market segment. [38] This naturally makes the sense that under such a scenario both China and India would be economic rival to each other in the Gulf region. Since the pace of economic change in India has been much slower than in China, all that can be envisaged is the latter replacing Japan and the European Union, and perhaps ultimately the United States, as the dominant force ultimately shaping the economic future of the Indian Ocean region including the GCC where India is the natural hub of the region. [39] In January 2008, the Gulf States took serious note to conclude some Free Trade Agreements (FTAs) with China and India besides European Union in order to boost their industrial cooperation, trade and business. Due to the huge oil revenue, the Gulf's state-owned investment companies are now looking at Asia to diversify their assets. [40] It has been rightly pointed out that India is not yet in China's league, and it is at some distance from becoming a major economic power. However, the rise of China as a major economic power has rekindled old anti-Chinese fear in New Delhi. [41]

Notes

1. See, Haishun Sun and Ashok Parikh, 'Exports, Inward Foreign Direct Investment and Regional Economic Growth in China', in: *Trade Liberalization: Impact on Growth and Trade in*

Developing Countries, By Ashok Parikh, World Scientific, 2007, p. 84.

2. Arne Walther, 'A New Asian Energy Identity', *Middle East Economic Survey*, VOL. XLVIII, No 4, 24 January 2005.
3. Paul Stevens, 'The Changing Dynamics of OPEC and Non-OPEC Relations: Present Status and Future Prospects', in: *Gulf Oil in the Aftermath of the Iraq War: Strategies and Policies*, Abu Dhabi, UAE: The Emirates Center For Strategic Studies and Research, 2005, pp. 127-55.
4. Gawdat Bahgat, 'Energy Partnership: Pacific Asia and the Middle East', *The Middle East Economic Survey*, VOL. XLVIII, No 33, 15 August, 2005.
5. *Khaleej Times*, 30 November 2006.
6. *The Financial Express*, June 17, 2006.
7. Roger Howard, *Iran Oil: The New Middle East Challenge to America,* I.B.Tauris, 2007, p. 115.
8. As for NIOC, it already holds about 14 per cent of the equity in Madras-based Chennai Petroleum Corp Ltd. (CPCL) which was initially a joint venture between NIOC, US group Amoco and the government of India, but in 1985 the American firm sold its equity and in 2001 state-run Indian Oil Corp bought the government's 51.8 per cent stake in the firm. See, *Khaleej Times*, 29 January 2005.
9. *Gulf News*, December 13, 2007.
10. Raphael Israeli, 'Islam in the Chinese Environment', in: Annemarie Schimmel, *Islam in India and Pakistan,* E.J. Brill, 1982, p. 34.
11. Chris Caldicott, *The Spice Routes Recipes and Lore*, Frances Lincoln ltd, 2004, p. 22.
12. Hafizullah Emadi, *Politics of the Dispossessed: Superpowers and Developments in the Middle East*, Greenwood Publishing Group, 2001, p. 5.
13. Yitzhak Shichor, *The Middle East in China's Foreign Policy, 1949-1977: 1949-1977,* Cambridge University Press, 1979, pp. 1-5.
14. Ibid. pp. 203-204.
15. *Arab News* 17 April 2005.
16. *Arab News*, 2 November 2006.
17. *Arab News,* 3 November 2006.
18. *Khaleej Times* 21 February 2005.

19. *Arab News*, 24 March 2008.
20. L Alan Winters, Shahid Yusuf, *Dancing with Giants: China, India, and the Global Economy,* World Bank Publications, 2007, p. 146.
21. Donat-Peter Häder, Adrian J. Bradbrook, Ruth Hemmersbach, *The Law of Energy for Sustainable Development,* Cambridge University Press, 2005, p. 53.
22. Roger Howard, *Iran Oil: The New Middle East Challenge to America,* I. B. Tauris, 2007, p. 98.
23. *Emerging Abu Dhabi 2006,* Oxford Business Group, 2006 p. 126.
24. *The Khaleej Times,* 13 May 2005.
25. Under the deal, Aramco will supply 80 percent of the refinery's oil needs. The project is expected to start up in early 2009. It will be owned by Sinopec (55 percent), ExxonMobil China Petroleum and Petrochemical Company Limited (22.5 percent) and Saudi Aramco Sino Company Limited (22.5 percent). See, Syed Rashid Husain, 'Oil Scene: Oil Takes Center Stage in China's Diplomacy', *Arab News* 31 March 2007.
26. Xin Ma, 'China's Energy Strategy in the Middle East', *Middle East Economic Survey,* vol. LI, No 23, 9 June 2008.
27. Stephen Blank, *Russo-Chinese Energy Relations: Politics in Command,* GMB Publishing Ltd, 2006, p. 9.
28. *Arab News,* 7 December 2006.
29. *Khaleej Times* 16 January 2008.
30. *Global Economic Prospects and the Developing Countries 1996,* World Bank Publications, 1996, pp. 29-30.
31. Swee-Hock Saw, *Asian-China Economic Relations,* Institute of Southeast Asian Studies, 2006, p. 3.
32. John Barkley Rosser, Marina V. Rosser, *Comparative Economics in a Transforming World Economy,* MIT Press, Comparative economics, 2007, p. 418.
33. John Wong, 'China's Economy in Search of New Development Strategies', in: *Asean-China Economic Relations,* By Swee-Hock Saw, Saw Swee Hock, Institute of Southeast Asian Studies, Institute of Southeast Asian Studies, 2006, pp. 12-13.
34. Baldev, Raj, 'India's Economic Growth Miracle in a Global Economy', in: *India and South Asia: Economic Developments in the Age of Globalization,* by Anjum Siddiqui, M.E. Sharpe, 2007, p. 61.

35. Jean Drèze, *India: Development and Participation*, Oxford University Press, 2002, p. 140.
36. Marcus Noland, Howard Pack, *The Arab Economies in a Changing World*, Peterson Institute, 2007, p. 221.
37. Jeffrey E. Curry, *A Short Course in International Economics,* World Trade Press, 2000, p. 129.
38. *Global Economic Prospects 2007: Managing the Next Wave of Globalization,* World Bank Publications, 2007, p. 11.
39. Rodney Wilson, 'Economic Relations between the GCC and South and South East Asia', in: *The Middle East's Relations with Asia and Russia,* by Hannah Carter, Anoushiravan Ehteshami, Routledge, 2004, p. 103.
40. *Gulf News* May 06 2008.
41. Stephen P. Cohen, *India: Emerging Power,* Brookings Institution Press, 2001, p. 200.

6

India and the GCC-Trade and Geopolitical Engagements

Faisal Ahmed

Introduction

The Gulf Cooperation Council (GCC) is a regional trade agreement between Bahrain, Kuwait, Oman, Qatar, Saudi Arabia and the United Arab Emirates (UAE) to enhance cooperation in trade and other strategic areas among the member nations. [1] These member countries clearly stated that 'the GCC was established in view of the special relations between them, their similar political systems based on Islamic beliefs, joint destiny and common objectives'. [2] The Kingdom of Saudi Arabia (KSA) has been the main force in mobilizing the gulf opinion for forming such a regional trade agreement. GCC is not only a trading agreement but its genesis also reflects the power of geopolitical inertia. This is evident from the fact that their immediate concern was to protect themselves from the threat arising out of the Iran-Iraq war. It was during the early eighties that the GCC countries, through their initiatives in joint defence exercises, started preparing themselves to face the realities and consequences of regional geopolitical instability in West Asia. Oil has helped the GCC countries position themselves well on the global arena. However, their worth in the global market is still to be attained as they now seem to be destined to become the hub of energy and regional security solutions across the globe. Herewith, India's engagements with GCC countries as well as some crucial areas of potential cooperation between India and GCC countries have been outlined and discussed.

India's Engagements with GCC

The Gulf Cooperation Council (GCC) has emerged as a major trading entity for India and offers tremendous potential for cooperation in the areas ranging from trade and investment to energy and manpower, amongst others. Whereas, the GCC constitutes more than 12 percent of India's total exports and supplies nearly two-thirds of India's energy needs; it also hosts the largest expatriate Indian Community which is nearly four million in numbers. [3] There have been several instances of interactions between India and GCC as well as between India and the individual GCC countries. Table 6.1 presents a series of interactions that took between India and GCC since 1984. Moreover, there have been three India-GCC business conferences till date. The Third India-GCC Business Conference (Industrial Forum) was held at Mumbai (India) on May 29-30, 2007. India and GCC are also heading to sign a FTA agreement between them which is expected to open avenues for more strategic collaborations in trade and other areas. India's demand for oil is witnessing a rising trend, and is likely to remain so in the future; and therefore, the GCC has positioned itself as a source of geo-economic strength for India. Traditionally, the GCC countries have been west-oriented, but after 2001, there has been noticeable change with India being looked at as an alternative. [4] A report suggests that GCC countries have invested around $406.3 million constituting around one percent of total FDI received by India. [5] Among the GCC countries, UAE is the largest investor in India, accounting for around 79.0 percent ($321.1 million) of the total investment made by the GCC countries, followed by Bahrain ($32.7 million), Oman ($24.51 million), Saudi Arabia ($19.18 million), Kuwait ($8.87 million) and Qatar ($0.09 million)". The Global Investment House, [6] in one of its report mentioned that the 'GCC investors have started focusing on India as an investment destination'. [7]

The urge for cooperation between India and GCC is not only dependant on trade but also involves investment and security issues. A strong reinforcement to this effect has been put forth by Dr. Manmohan Singh, Indian Prime Minister who remarked that 'the Gulf region is a part of our natural economic hinterland.

Table 6.1: India-GCC Engagements in a Retrospect

Year	Events
1984	A Round Table conference was organized by ICRIER (New Delhi).
1989	Talks were held between the visiting GCC Assistant Secretary General for Economic Affairs and the Indian Commerce Minister. Some of the military installations in India were inspected by a joint GCC Defence Team.
1992	GCC Secretary General visited India and met the Prime Minister and other ministers and dignitaries including FICCI officials.
2003	A structured annual political dialogue at Foreign Ministers' level in lines with the UNGA was proposed and accepted.
2004	First India-GCC Industrial Conference held in Mumbai on February 17-18. It issued the 'Mumbai Declaration'. India and GCC enter into an agreement in the month of August to explore the possibility of a Free Trade Area (FTA) between them. A GCC negotiating team comprising 3-members visited India in November to discuss bilateral issues, chiefly including, amongst other, (i) initiating negotiations towards FTA, and, (ii) the issue of NTB's affecting Indian exports to the GCC region.

2006	Second India-GCC Industrial Conference hosted by the Government of the Sultanate of Oman at Muscat on March 25-26. Popularly known as the "Muscat Declaration", its motto was highlighted as "GCC and India – Cooperation and Partnership" The declaration recommended initiation of JVs and private investments in the field of industry, energy, petrochemicals, biotechnology and tourism.
2007	Third India-GCC Business Conference (Industrial Forum) held at Mumbai on May 29-30. The underlying theme of this conference was "India-GCC Investment Opportunities". It concluded with adoption of 'Mumbai Declaration', which called for 'facilitating and expediting projects in the field of agriculture and food processing' besides enhancing bilateral cooperation in the areas of real estate, energy, petrochemicals and infrastructure.
2008	Interaction between India and GCC happened on September 9-10 on the sidelines of the FTA in which GCC proposed a tariff liberalization schedule incorporating three categories of goods.

Source: Compiled from the web sites of the MEA (Gulf Division) and MENAFN.

We must pursue closer economic relations with all neighbors in our wider Asian neighborhood'. [8] In this light, it is imperative to understand that the first requirement for a strategic Gulf-India dialogue in the post-cold war security environment is to ensure interaction between India on the one side and all GCC countries, as one unit, on the other. [9] This would broaden India's horizon of trade and strategic relations with the gulf.

India and Qatar signed a defence pact on joint maritime security; joint naval exercise and law enforcement in 2008 which has been has been seen as a step toward establishing closer ties. Qatar is also playing a major role in the Indian Ocean Rim for enhancing maritime security. India and UAE have also undertaken several defence exercises and strategic dialogues since they agreed to form a Joint Defence Cooperation Committee in the year 2003. India and Oman have also signed a Memorandum of Association (MoA) on defence cooperation in December 2005 for exchanging military training and expertise in the field of information technology. The collaboration in the field of geo-strategic concerns is also witnessed in the patterns of trade in relevant commodities and equipments between India and GCC. Commodities with HC Code 84 (including nuclear reactors, boilers, machinery and mechanical appliances; parts thereof) have occupied the place among the major trading items between India and GCC. Therefore, in order to strengthen their trade diplomacy, both India and GCC possesses the potential for mutual cooperation in geo-strategic affairs.

The endowment of hydrocarbon resources including oil and natural gas has helped the GCC countries position themselves well on the global arena. Their worth in the global market is yet to increase as they are destined to become the hub for both global energy and security solutions. Through a passage of time, the GCC has emerged as a major trading partner for India and offers tremendous potential for cooperation in the areas ranging from trade and investment to energy and manpower, amongst others.

The GCC countries also collectively host the largest expatriate Indian community. GCC countries gained prominence in India's foreign trade in the post-liberalization trade policy regime initiated in 1991; which duly helped in the culmination of enhanced export performance amidst easily accessible and implementation-oriented procedures. The bilateral trade relationship between India and GCC has witnessed astounding growth in recent years thereby making GCC as India's second largest trading partner with India being the GCC's ninth largest partner. The GCC economies are traversing the trajectory of growth because of being endowed with hydrocarbon resources (especially oil) whose prices are again showing increasing trend, if not consistently so, after the huge oil price inflation which affected the whole world during the 2008/09 global recession. In order to understand the relation between India and individual countries, it is imperative that both the geo-economic as well as the geo-strategic pursuits be discussed.

India-Bahrain Engagements

The Kingdom of Bahrain is an archipelago of 33 low-lying islands located in the central southern shores of the Arabian Gulf between 25°32' and 26° 20' North latitudes and 50° 20' and 50°50' East longitudes. Bahrain was the political headquarter of the British Empire in the Gulf in the nineteenth century till it gained independence on 15 August 1971. It became a constitutional monarchy in February 2002. Bahrain has a sizeable private sector; but oil refining and production, water & electricity, among others are wholly owned by Government. Banking and financial sector contributes around 24% of the GDP. As per 2007, Bahrain's top export destinations (non-oil) includes Saudi Arabia, USA, UAE, India and Qatar while it top sources of import include Australia, Japan, Saudi Arabia, China, and USA (web site of MEA, Govt. of India). Bahrain has proven oil reserves of 125 million barrels while its proven natural gas reserves accounts for 3.25 trillion cubic feet. [10] Bahrain's oil sector accounts for about two-thirds of total Government revenues.

Indian nationals form the largest expatriate community in Bahrain ranging from blue-collar workers to professionals including doctors, engineers, chartered accountants, bankers and managers. In order to enhance cooperation in geo-economic areas the two countries have signed bilateral agreements, namely, Agreement on the Promotion and Protection of Bilateral Investment and the other for Executive

Program on Cooperation in Culture Agreement for Media Cooperation between Prasar Bharti and Bahrain Radio and TV Corporation. [11] Moreover, India's export to Bahrain was US$ 251.82 million in 2007-08 as compared to US$ 183.59 million in 2006-07; with the following commodities comprising the top three positions (in terms of value) in India's exports to Bahrain as per the 2007-08 figures: Nuclear Reactors, Boilers, Machinery and Mechanical Appliances, parts thereof (HS Code: 84); Iron And Steel (HS Code: 72); and, Natural or cultured pearls, precious or semiprecious stones, premetals, clad with premetal and articles thereof, imitation jewellery; coin (HS Code: 71).

India's import from Bahrain in 2007-08 accounted for US$ 829.71 million as compared to US$ 470.97 million in 2006-07. The following commodities comprises the top three positions (in terms of value) in India's imports from Bahrain as per the 2007-08 figures: Mineral fuels, mineral oils and products of their distillation; bituminous substances; mineral waxes (HS Code: 27); Aluminium and articles thereof (HS Code: 76); and, Ores, slag and ash (HS Code: 26). [12] Table 6.2 shows India's major engagements with Bahrain.

The Gulf region has a tri-continental location and the Kingdom of Bahrain occupies a place of immense strategic importance. The political and diplomatic ties between the two countries have been fairly good including their bilateral cooperation in the Non-Aligned Movement conferences. India and Bahrain, in order to boost up their geo-strategic ties have entered into the following agreements, namely, Memorandum of Understanding on cooperation between Ministries of Foreign Affairs, Agreement on Juridical and Judicial Cooperation in Civil and Commercial Matters, Extradition Treaty, Agreement on Mutual Legal Assistance in Criminal Matters and Air Services Agreement.

India-Kuwait Engagements

Kuwait was found in the early 1700s by tribes from Central Arabia and became a British protectorate in 1899 and remained so until it became independent in 1961. Later, Kuwait also remained under the Iraqi occupation from 2 August 1990 to 26 February 1991.

Table 6.2: India-Bahrain Major Engagements in Retrospect

Year	Events
1981	India and Bahrain signed an Economic and Technical Cooperation Agreement during the visit of Amir of Bahrain, Shaikh Isa Bin Salman Al Khalifa to New Delhi. The Instruments of Ratification were exchanged in 1983.
1986	First session of Indo-Bahrain Joint Economic and Technical Committee (JCETC) held in New Delhi.
1991	Second session of Indo-Bahrain Joint Economic and Technical Committee held in Bahrain.
1998	Third session of Indo-Bahrain Joint Economic and Technical Committee held in New Delhi on November 11-12. Several areas of cooperation in economic, commercial, educational, training and cultural fields were identified.
2007	Third session of Indo-Bahrain Joint Economic and Technical Committee held in Bahrain on November 14-15. For the first time, the delegations were headed at Ministerial level and private sector was also associated with the committee.
1994	A Joint Business Council (JBC) was set up on October 12 with Bahrain Chamber of Commerce & Industry (BCCI) on the one hand, and, FICCI and ASSOCHAM, on the other.
2001	A 15-member delegation led by the Electronics and Computer Software Export Promotion Council (ESC) from India visited Bahrain and

	signed a MoU with the Bahrain's Economic Development Board (EDB) in May.
2006	A delegation led by Dr. Zakaria Hejres, Deputy Chief Executive of Bahrain's Economic Development Board visited India in July
2007	An NTPC (India) five member delegation led by Mr. Harish Chandra, Special Advisor, Ministry of Power visited Bahrain from April 11-12
2007	The Minister for Industries, Government of State of Kerala, Mr. Elamaran Kareem, visited Bahrain with a four member delegation on May 4 to attract investment specifically from non-resident Keralites in infrastructure sector through Infrastructure Kerala Ltd. (INKEL)
2008	Federation of Indian Chambers of Commerce and Industry (FICCI), New Delhi hosted the Indo-Arab Investment Conclave on April 18-19

Source: Compiled from web site of Ministry of External Affairs (MEA), Government of India.

The State of Kuwait occupies an immensely important geo-strategic location and has a geo-economic significance too. It is located between 29° and 30° North latitudes and 47° and 48° East longitudes. Kuwait has an estimated oil reserve of about 101.5 billion barrels, which accounts for almost 10% of the world reserves. It has a natural gas reserve of 56 trillion cubic feet. Petroleum accounts for nearly half of its GDP, 95% of export revenues, and 80% of the Government income. Oil was discovered in Kuwait in 1938, and the first shipment was exported in 1946. Besides GCC, Kuwait is also a member of ESCWA, FAO, G-77, IAEA, ILO, IMF, NAM, OPEC, UN and WIPO. The geo-economic and geo-strategic relation between India and Kuwait has been discussed further.

India's geo-economic relation with Kuwait has been traditional and reflects a gradually developing initiative. The

India-Kuwait Chamber of Commerce (IKCC) has also been functioning to help in the revitalization of the economic relations and trade diplomacy between the two countries. An account of India's major engagements with Kuwait has been given in Table 6.3 starting with the trade agreement between the Government of India and the Government of the State of Kuwait signed on 13 February 1974. Moreover, India's export to Kuwait was US$ 682.12 million in 2007-08 as compared to US$ 614.35 million in 2006-07; with the following commodities comprising the top three positions (in terms of value) in India's exports to Kuwait as per the 2007-08 figures: Cereals (HS Code: 10); Meat and edible meat offal (HS Code: 02); and, Nuclear reactors, boilers, machinery and mechanical appliances; parts thereof (HS Code: 84). Whereas, India's import from Kuwait in 2007-08 accounted for US$ 7693.63 million as compared to US$ 5992.15 million in 2006-07; with the following commodities comprising the top three positions (in terms of value) in India's imports from Kuwait as per the 2007-08 figures: Mineral fuels, mineral oils and products of their distillation; bituminous substances; mineral waxes (HS Code: 27); Organic chemicals (HS Code: 29); and, Iron and steel (HS Code: 72). Besides, there are several Indian companies in Kuwait including TCIL, LIC (International), LIC Housing Finance, New India Assurance Company, Oriental Insurance Company and Indian (including Air India and Indian Airlines), L&T, Bridge & Roof, Punj Lloyd and Kalpataru, among others (Source: MEA web site, GoI).

India and Kuwait have shared a fairly good geo-strategic relation. The Ministry of External Affairs (India) and Ministry of Foreign Affairs (Kuwait) signed the Memorandum of Understanding on the Conducting of Bilateral Consultations signed on 09 July 2000. Further, in the year 2004, the extradition treaty was signed between the two country followed by a MoU for the establishment of an Indo-Kuwait Strategic Consultative Group. Recently in the year 2008, India and Kuwait held the second meeting of the India-Kuwait Joint

Ministerial Commission in New Delhi on July 1-3. Major decisions reached during his meeting included the forming of a Joint Working Group on Hydrocarbons and setting up of a technical level mechanism to review the implementation of the decisions.

Table 6.3: India-Kuwait Major Engagements in a Retrospect

Year	Events
1974	Trade Agreement between the Government of India and the Government of the State of Kuwait signed on February 13.
1992	Cooperation Agreement between India and Kuwait signed on February 15. An MOU on cooperation in the field of telecommunication was also signed on February 19.
1995	Protocol between India's Council of Scientific and Industrial Research (CSIR) and Kuwait Institute for Scientific Research (KISR) for Scientific and Technical Cooperation signed on June 16.
2000	Memorandum of Understanding between the Ministry of External Affairs (India) and Ministry of Foreign Affairs (Kuwait) on the Conducting of Bilateral Consultations signed on July 9.
2001	Agreement between the Kuwait and India for the Encouragement and Reciprocal Protection of Investment signed on November 27.
2003	Academic Agreement between Jamia Millia Islamia, New Delhi and Faculty of Arts, Kuwait University signed in December.
2004	Extradition Treaty between signed on August 25.
2004	MOU for Establishment of Indo-Kuwait Strategic Consultative Group signed on August 25.
2005	Agreement on Juridical and Judicial Cooperation in Civil and Commercial Matters signed on August

	16.
2006	First meeting of the India-Kuwait Joint Ministerial Commission for Trade and Economic Cooperation held in Kuwait on November 25-27. It included discussions on four Working Groups dealing with Labor and Employment; Trade, Investment and Finance; Energy, Petroleum, Petrochemicals and Fertilizers; and Science & Technology, Information Technology and Communications, Health and Education.
2006	Avoidance of Double Taxation Agreement and for the Prevention of Fiscal Evasion with respect to Taxes on Income (DTAA) between India and Kuwait signed on June 15. This has been implemented from 01 April 2008.
2006	The Kuwait Chamber of Commerce & Industry (KCCI) signed a MoU with the Associated Chambers of Commerce & Industry (ASSOCHAM) during the State Visit of HH Sheikh Sabah Al-Ahmad Al-Jaber Al-Sabah, the Amir of the State of Kuwait to India from June 14-19. The MoU aspired to promote trade, investment and scientific and technical cooperation between the India and Kuwait.
2006	MoU between the Public Authority for Industry (PAI) of Kuwait and Indian Importers Association (IIA), New Delhi signed in May. This was aimed to help IIA will promote the export, re-export and sales of Kuwaiti manufactured non oil industrial products in its appointed territory for the Kuwaiti manufacturers introduced to it by PAI.
2007	MoU on Labor, Employment and Manpower Development signed on April 10. It came into effect from 18 October 2007.

2008	Second meeting of the India-Kuwait Joint Ministerial Commission held in New Delhi on July 1-3. Major decisions reached during his meeting included the forming of a Joint Working Group (JWG) on Hydrocarbons and setting up of a technical level mechanism to review the implementation of the decisions.
2008	MoU on Cooperation between the Comptroller and Auditor General of India and Kuwait's State Audit Bureau signed on July 15.

Source: Compiled from web site of Ministry of External Affairs (MEA), Government of India.

India-Oman Engagements

Most of the Oman's foreign policy is aligned with the GCC. Oman joined WTO in 2000. Even though its economy is quite dependant on oil, Oman is not a member of OPEC. Oman has proven oil reserves of around 5.5 billion barrels and proven natural gas reserves of 30 trillion cubic feet. Its annual production of natural gas is estimated at around 1070,736 million standard cubic feet. LNG processing and industries to utilize the natural gas are priorities for the country; and India shares with Oman one of the largest ventures in this field (OMIFCO) in Sur city. Oman's total export in 2007 accounted to US$ 24.5 billion of which the share of oil & gas was US$ 18.6 billion. The major Omani export destinations include UAE, India, Saudi Arabia, Qatar and China. Whereas, Oman's major import items include machinery, transport equipment & vehicles, food, beverages and other manufactured goods from principal importing sources like UAE, Japan, India, USA and Germany, among others. As far as India's relation with Oman is concerned, Table 6.4 shows major engagements between the two countries.

Oman has been well-known for its open market policies and an investor-friendly economy for several years. The agreements between India and Oman incorporate both the areas of geo-economic and geo-strategic concerns. Some of the major geo-economic agreements include: Cultural Agreement, Agreement on Economic, Trade and Technical Cooperation, Agreements on Avoidance of Double Taxation, Promotion and Protection of Bilateral Investments, MoU on Cooperation on Audit Services, and MOU on cooperation in field of Higher Education.

Table 6.4: India-Oman Major Engagements in a Retrospect

Year	Events
1993	The Agreement on Economic, Trade and Technical Co-operation, signed during the visit of the then Indian Prime Minister Mr. P.V. Narasimha Rao, which proposed the setting up of an India-Oman Joint Commission (JCM) at the Commerce Ministerial level.
1995	Joint Business Council (JBC) set up with an agreement between FICCI & ASSOCHAM and OCCI (Oman Chamber of Commerce and Industry) during the JCM meeting in April.
1997	An agreement on Avoidance of Double Taxation and Prevention of Fiscal Evasion, an MOU on Scientific & Technical Cooperation in Agriculture, Bilateral Investment Promotion and Protection Agreement, an MOU on Civil Aviation, Agreement on Joint Venture in a Fertilizer project in Oman and a Cultural Exchange Program were signed during the visit of His Majesty Sultan Qaboos of Oman to India in April.
2003	Fourth Meeting of the India-Oman Joint Commission held in Muscat on October 20-22.
2004	Visits of two Indian Ministers to Oman including Mr. E. Ahmed, Minister of State for External Affairs in November and External Affairs Minister,

	Mr. K. Natwar Singh in December.
2005	Omani Minister for Defence visited India in December.
2006	Fifth Meeting of the Joint Commission held in India on September 5.
2006	OMIFCO fertilizer plant in Sur, one of the largest Indian Joint Ventures abroad inaugurated in January
2006	Second India-GCC Industrial Conference held in Muscat in March. The Indian Minister for Commerce and Industry Mr. Kamal Nath, led the delegation.
2007	H.H. Sayyid Fahd bin Mehmoud Al Said, the Deputy prime minister for the Council of Ministers of Oman led a high level delegation including ministers and business representatives for a three-day official visit to India from December 12-14.
2008	A new Chancery-cum-Embassy Residence in Muscat jointly inaugurated during the visit of India's External Affairs Minister, Mr. Pranab Mukherjee to Oman during 13-14 January.

Source: Compiled from web site of Ministry of External Affairs (MEA), Government of India.

Moreover, India's export to Oman was US$ 937.75 million in 2007-08 as compared to US$ 630.43 million in 2006-07; with the following commodities comprising the top three positions (in terms of value) in India's exports to Oman as per the 2007-08 figures: Articles of iron or steel (HS Code: 73); Copper and articles thereof (HS Code: 74); and, Nuclear reactors, boilers, machinery and mechanical appliances; parts thereof (HS Code: 84). Whereas, India's import from Oman in 2007-08 accounted for US$ 1134.13 million as compared to US$ 460.19 million in 2006-07; with the following commodities comprising the top three positions (in terms of value) in India's imports from Oman as per the 2007-08 figures: Mineral fuels, mineral oils and products of their distillation; bituminous substances; mineral waxes (HS Code: 27); Fertilisers (HS Code: 31); and, Salt; sulphur; earths and stone; plastering materials, lime and cement (HS Code: 25).

Further, several Indian companies have a sizeable presence in the Omani market in the field of infrastructure development, oil & gas related engineering works, IT, banking and financial services and education, among others. [13] And even Omani companies are increasing their presence in India. [14]

Oman has a promising advantage in terms of its geographical location owing to its geo-strategic position working as a bridging link between the trade routes of the East and the West. [15] Oman has been a good example of establishing interface between trade and geopolitics when it registered itself as a founding member of the Indian Ocean Rim Association in 1997 for the purpose of trade facilitation and investment in the region. India and Oman have signed several treaties and agreements pertaining to the strengthening of their geo-strategic ties. These include Air Services Agreement; Extradition Treaty; Treaty of Friendship; Commerce and Navigation; MoU on Joint Cooperation for Combating Crime; and MOU on Defence Cooperation. The geo-strategic relations was further strengthened by the visit of two Indian Ministers to Oman including Mr. E. Ahmed, Minister of State for External Affairs in November and External Affairs Minister, Mr. K. Natwar Singh in December, 2004. The Omani Minister for Defence also visited India in December, 2005. In a relatively recent development, a new Chancery-cum-Embassy Residence in Muscat was jointly inaugurated during the visit of India's External Affairs Minister, Mr. Pranab Mukherjee to Oman in January, 2008.

India-Qatar Engagements

Qatar is one of the most important members of the Gulf Cooperation Council (GCC) owing to its huge endowment of natural gas and oil, which accounts for more than 60% of its GDP. Oil and gas contributes around 85% of its export earnings and 70% of the government revenue. It is surrounded the Persian Gulf. Qatar is also a member of G-77, WTO, OIC and OPEC. It has a proven natural gas reserve of approximately 25 trillion cubic meters, which accounts for about 15% of the world's total. Oil and gas contributes around 85% of its export earnings and 70% of the Qatari government revenue. Qatar has proven oil reserves of 15.2 billion barrels. Its proven natural gas reserve is 910.5 trillion cubic feet, which accounts for about 15% of the world's total. As far as India's relation with Qatar is concerned, Table 6.5 shows major engagements between the two countries.

India and Qatar have good geo-economic ties. The two countries have entered into the following agreements: Bilateral Investment Promotion and Protection Agreement, Double Taxation Avoidance Agreement, Agreement on Cultural Cooperation, Agreement on Economic and Technical Cooperation and Agreement on Organization of Manpower Employment. The India-Qatar Joint Committee for Economic and Technical Cooperation which held its meeting at New Delhi on 10-11 March 1999 identified several new areas for cooperation such as petrochemicals, civil aviation, science and technology, environment, education and culture. An Industrial-cum-Business Mission of Confederation of Indian Industries visited Qatar on 29-30 May 2002 and had wide ranging interactions with Qatari Government and businesses.

Moreover, India's export to Qatar was US$ 538.13 million in 2007-08 as compared to US$ 331.36 million in 2006-07; with the following commodities comprising the top three positions (in terms of value) in India's exports to Qatar as per the 2007-08 figures: Electrical machinery and equipment and parts thereof; sound recorders and reproducers, television image and sound recorders and reproducers, and parts (HS Code: 85); Salt; sulphur; earths and stone; plastering materials, lime and cement (HS Code: 25); and, Nuclear reactors, boilers, machinery and mechanical appliances; parts thereof (HS Code: 84).

Table 6.5: India-Qatar Major Engagements in a Retrospect

Year	Events
1980	Agreements on Cultural and Technical Cooperation signed.
1984	Agreement on Economic and Technical Cooperation signed.
1985	Agreement on Organization of Manpower Employment signed.
1999	The India-Qatar Joint Committee for Economic and Technical Cooperation met in New Delhi on 10-11 March 1999, after a gap of 11 years. It identified several new areas for cooperation such as petrochemicals, civil aviation, science and technology, environment, education and culture.
1999	CII (India) established institutional links with QCCI (Qatar).
1999	The Emir of Qatar, H.H. Sheikh Hamad bin Khalifa al Thani visited India in April.
2002	An Industrial-cum-Business Mission of CII visited Qatar on May 29-30 and had wide ranging interactions with Qatari Government and business.
2002	The first meeting of the Joint Business Council took place in January when a QCCI delegation visited Delhi and Mumbai. The delegation had meetings with representatives of major industrial houses, hosted by FICCI, as well as a one to one interaction with Indian business leaders.
2005	Qatari Minister of State for Foreign Affairs visited India in June.
2005	The Emir of Qatar, H.H. Sheikh Hamad bin Khalifa al Thani paid his second official state visit to India May.
2006	Qatari Prime Minister and Minister for Foreign Affairs H.E. Sheikh Hamad bin Jassim al Thani

	visited India in April.
2006	H.E. Mr. Abdullah bin Hamad al Attiyal, Deputy Premier and Minister of Energy and Industry of Qatar visited India in November
2006	The Chief of Staff of Qatar Armed Forces visited India in August .
2007	The Qatari Minister of Civil Services and housing visited India.
2008	India and Qatar signed a defence pact on joint maritime security; joint naval exercise and law enforcement.

Source: Compiled from web sites of Ministry of External Affairs (MEA), Government of India and the Embassy of India in Doha (Qatar).

Whereas, India's import from Qatar in 2007-08 accounted for US$ 2457.42 million as compared to US$ 2068.33 million in 2006-07; with the following commodities comprising the top three positions (in terms of value) in India's imports from Qatar as per the 2007-08 figures: Mineral fuels, mineral oils and products of their distillation; bituminous substances; mineral waxes (HS Code: 27); Organic chemicals (HS Code: 29); and, Plastic and articles thereof (HS Code: 39).

Some of the major Indian companies in Qatar include L&T, Dodsal, Canara Bank, Essar Global Services, Punj Lloyd, Voltas, Simplex, ONGC, ONGC Videsh Limited, Simplex concrete Piles (India) Ltd., Ranbaxy Laboratories, Tata Projects Limited, Bank of India and NIIT among others. India and Qatar have been evolving their geo-strategic relations and continues to do so. The two countries have already signed an MOU on Foreign Office Consultations. The Qatari Minister of State for Foreign Affairs visited India in June 2005 following the visit of the Emir of Qatar, H.H. Sheikh Hamad bin Khalifa al Thani to India in May. The Chief of Staff of Qatar Armed Forces also visited India in August,

2006 to discuss issues of regional and international security. In a recent development in the year 2008, India and Qatar have signed a defence pact on joint maritime security; joint naval exercise and law enforcement.

India-Saudi Arabia Engagements

The Kingdom of Saudi Arabia is the largest country in the Middle East, occupying 4/5th of the Arabian Peninsula. It is bordered by the Red Sea on the west, and the Persian Gulf on the east. To the south, it shares borders with Yemen and the Sultanate of Oman and in the north, it shares borders with Kuwait, Iraq and Jordan. Its economy is primarily dependant on oil, which forms a major chunk of its revenue. Saudi Arabia's proven oil reserve is 269.25 billion barrels which accounts for almost one-fourth of the world's known reserves. Besides, it also has a vast endowment of natural gas reserves which is 253 trillion cubic feet accounting for four percent of the world's total gas reserves. Saudi Arabia is also endowed with other natural resources including industrial raw materials and minerals such as bauxite, limestone, gypsum and phosphate and iron ores. It has a strategic location which makes it easy accessible from Europe, Africa and other parts of Asia. Besides GCC, Saudi Arabia is also a member of UNO, OIC, OPEC and WTO. Its major trading partners include USA, Japan, South Korea, China, India, Holland, Italy, Taiwan, UAE and France, among others; besides also being a hub of attracting Foreign Direct Investments. [16]

The Kingdom of Saudi Arabia has been one of the most prominent trading partners of India. Reports say that India is seeking 'larger participation in exploration, exploitation and development of gas-based and petrochemical-based industry in Saudi Arabia'. [17]

India's esteemed effort in acquiring energy security has also been seconded by Saudi Prince Saud wherein he invited Indian companies to explore the possibilities of joint projects and consultancy with Saudi Aramco. [18] India and Saudi

Arabia signed the following accords in the presence of Prime Minister Manmohan Singh and Saudi King Abdullah, the Agreement on Avoidance of Double Taxation, Bilateral Investment Promotion and Protection Agreement, and, Agreement for Cooperation in the field of Youth and Sports.

Moreover, India's export to Saudi Arabia was US$ 3708.30 million in 2007-08 as compared to US$ 2588.18 million in 2006-07; with the following commodities comprising the top three positions (in terms of value) in India's exports to Saudi Arabia as per the 2007-08 figures: Cereals (HS Code: 10); Mineral fuels, mineral oils and products of their distillation; bituminous substances; mineral waxes (HS Code: 27); and, Copper and articles thereof (HS Code: 74). Whereas, India's import from Saudi Arabia in 2007-08 accounted for US$ 19410.63 million as compared to US$ 13383.90 million in 2006-07; with the following commodities comprising the top three positions (in terms of value) in India's imports from Saudi Arabia as per the 2007-08 figures: Mineral fuels, mineral oils and products of their distillation; bituminous substances; mineral waxes (HS Code: 27); Organic chemicals (HS Code: 29); and, Plastic and articles thereof (HS Code: 39). Table 6.6 shows India's major engagements with Saudi Arabia.

The history of the evolution of geo-strategic ties between India and Saudi Arabia may be finely observed through the year 1955 when the King Saud of Saudi Arabia visited India. This was followed by visits of Indian Prime Ministers Pt. Jawaharlal Nehru in 1956 and Smt. Indira Gandhi in 1982. Further, H.E. Mr. Abdulrahman bin Hamad Al-Attiyah, Secretary General of the Gulf Cooperation Council (GCC) visited India from 15-18 February 2004 leading to the landmark 'GCC-India Political Dialogue', of which Saudi Arabia is a key player. India and Saudi Arabia also entered into a MoU on Combating Crime. In the year 2007, the special Envoy for West Asia and the Middle East Peace Process,

Ambassador C.R. Gharekhan visited Jeddah (Saudi Arabia) on September 8-9 to discuss areas of geo-strategic concerns.

Table 6.6: India-Saudi Arabia Major Engagements in a Retrospect

Year	Events
1955	Visit of King Saud to India.
1956	Indian Prime Minister Pt. Jawaharlal Nehru visited Saudi Arabia.
1982	Prime Minister of India, Smt. Indira Gandhi visited the Kingdom.
1981	Saudi Foreign Minister Saud Al Faisal visited India from April 13-15.
1981	The Joint Commission for economic, trade, scientific, technical and cultural cooperation (JCM) was established between India and Saudi Arabia.
1993	CSIR (India) and the Saudi Arabian Standards Organization (SASO) started a program of technical cooperation (POC) in June.
1994	Indo-Saudi Joint Commission meeting held in December.
1997	CSIR (India) and the King Abdulaziz City for Science and Technology (KACST) signed a MoU for bilateral cooperation with focus in the fields of space science, remote sensing and installation of internet.
2003	A MoU relating to SMEs/SSI cooperation between India's National Small Industries Corporation (NSIC) and Jeddah Chamber of Commerce and Industry (JCCI) was signed.
2004	H.E. Mr. Abdulrahman bin Hamad Al-Attiyah, Secretary General, Gulf Cooperation Council (GCC) visited India from February 15-18. This followed the landmark 'GCC-India Political Dialogue'.

2005	First Round Table of Asian Ministers on Regional Cooperation in the Oil and Gas Economy held in New Delhi. This occasion was attended by the Saudi Minister of Petroleum and Mineral Resources, Ali Al Naimi who visited India on January 6.
2005	A MoU between IOC (India) and Saudi Aramco (Saudi Arabia) was signed during March 28-31.
2005	An MoU on the establishment of Joint Business Council between Council of Saudi Chambers of Commerce & Industry (CSCCI) and Federation of Indian Chambers of Commerce & Industry (FICCI) was signed on April 12.
2006	Saudi King Abdullah visited India on a four-day state visit from January 24 to 27 as the Chief Guest on India's Republic Day celebrations. India and Saudi Arabia signed four accords.
2006	Memorandum of Understanding on Scientific and Educational Cooperation between the two countries was signed on November 6.
2007	The Special Envoy for West Asia and the Middle East Peace Process, Ambassador C.R. Gharekhan visited Jeddah (Saudi Arabia) on September 8-9 to discuss areas of geo-strategic concerns.
2008	India's External Affairs Minister visited Saudi Arabia on April 19-20 during which the agreement concerning Encouragement and Reciprocal Protection of Investments (BIPPA) was ratified.
2008	Mr. Montek Singh Ahluwalia, Deputy Chairman, Planning Commission of India, visited Saudi Arabia from May 3-4 to invite Saudi investors to invest in India in various sectors.

Source: Compiled from web site of Ministry of External Affairs (MEA), Government of India and Embassy of India, Saudi Arabia.

India-UAE Engagements

The United Arab Emirates (UAE), situated in the southeast of the Arabian Peninsula is a federation of seven emirates (states) which includes Abu Dhabi, Dubai, Sharjah, Ajman, Umm al-Quwain, Ras al-Khaimah and Fujairah. The competitiveness of UAE in international trade can best be adjudged by its emergence as the third largest entrepot centre in the world after Singapore and Hong Kong. [19] UAE has a proven oil reserve of 97.6 billion barrels and natural gas reserves of 214 trillion cubic feet.

UAE is the second largest destination for India's exports after USA. UAE has shown consistently good progress in trade with India. Various Indian companies have gone to the extent of maintaining their warehouses in the UAE which has gradually led to the increase in India-UAE trade in particular and also the India-GCC trade, at large. It may be mentioned herein that a blueprint of future two-way trade between India and the UAE submitted by then ASSOCHAM President Venugopal Dhoot, projects that the India-UAE two-way trade is likely to exceed US$ 25 billion by 2010 with trade balance remaining in India's favor in view of rising bilateral relations between the two nations. [20]

Moreover, India's export to UAE was US$ 15634.56 million in 2007-08 as compared to US$ 12032.17 million in 2006-07; with the following commodities comprising the top three positions (in terms of value) in India's exports to UAE as per the 2007-08 figures: Mineral fuels, mineral oils and products of their distillation; bituminous substances; min. waxes (HS Code: 27); Natural or cultured pearls, precious or semiprecious stones, pre-metals, clad with pre-metal &articles thereof; imitation jewelry; coin (HS Code: 71); and, Nuclear reactors, boilers, machinery and mechanical appliances; parts thereof (HS Code: 84). Whereas, India's import from UAE in 2007-08 accounted for US$ 13477.10 million as compared to US$ 8657.54 million in 2006-07; with the following commodities comprising the top three positions (in terms of value) in India's imports from UAE as per the 2007-08 figures: Mineral fuels, mineral oils and products of their distillation; bituminous substances; mineral waxes (HS Code: 27); Natural or cultured pearls, precious or semiprecious stones, pre-metals, clad with pre metal &articles thereof, imitation jewelry; coin (HS Code: 71); and, Electrical machinery and equipment and parts thereof; sound recorders and reproducers, television image and sound recorders and reproducers, and part (HS Code: 85). Table 6.7 shows India's major engagements with the UAE.

India's geo-strategic relation with the UAE can well be defined as that of evolving nature. From 1-5 January 1975, the UAE President, H.H. Sheikh Zayed bin Sultan Al Nahyan visited India and discussed bilateral issues ranging from trade to regional security and cooperation.

Table 6.7: India-UAE Major Engagements in a Retrospect

Year	Events
1975	UAE President H.H. Sheikh Zayed bin Sultan Al Nahyan visited India on January 1-5. India-UAE Joint Commission for Economic, Scientific and Technical Cooperation set up in January at EAM level.
1976	Indian President H.E. Dr. Fakhruddin Ali Ahmed visited UAE in November.
1981	Prime Minister of India, Smt. Indira Gandhi visited UAE on May 11-13.
1989	Civil Aviation Agreement which provided for establishing air services between and beyond India and the UAE signed in March.
1992	UAE President H.H. Sheikh Zayed bin Sultan Al Nahyan visited India on April 28-30.

1999	India and UAE signed three landmark Treaties providing for cooperation in Extradition, Mutual Legal Assistance in Criminal Matters and Juridical and Judicial Cooperation in Civil and Commercial Matters. The Instruments of Ratification of these three Treaties were exchanged at Abu Dhabi on 29 May 2000 and thus entered into force as on 29 May 2000. The three Treaties constitute the first set of agreements entered into by India on these matters with any country in the Gulf.
2000	Information Cooperation Agreement was signed in New Delhi in April between the Emirates News Agency (WAM) and the Press Trust of India (PTI) for cooperation and exchange of news.
2003	President Dr. A.P.J. Abdul Kalam, accompanied by a high-level delegation, paid a State visit to UAE from October 18 – 20.
2003	Defence Cooperation Agreement was signed in June in New Delhi for the purpose of enhancing cooperation between the two countries in matters related to security and defence and for annual meetings of 'Strategic Dialogue'.
2004	A Joint Business Council agreement was signed on February 19 at Mumbai between Federation of UAE Chambers of Commerce & Industry and Federation of Indian Chambers of Commerce & Industry. In furtherance to the same, the first meeting of the JBC was held at Abu Dhabi on March 8.

2006	Minister for Overseas Indian Affairs, Government of India, Mr. Vayalar Ravi, visited UAE on May 4-6, 2006 and again on May 10-13, 2007 to discuss measures for welfare of Indian labor that included proposals like payment of salary through banks, a compulsory health insurance scheme for workers and better housing facilities.
2006	MoU on Manpower Sourcing signed between India and UAE.
2006	FICCI-IIFA Global Business Forum was held in Dubai on June 15- 16.
2007	A Session of the India-UAE JCM took place in New Delhi on June 5-6.
2008	ETA Star International (UAE based company) entered into an agreement with The Energy and Resources Institute (TERI) of India on September 2 to explore areas of cooperation in sustainable development.

Source: Compiled from web site of the Embassy of India, Abu Dhabi (UAE.)

In the year 1999, India and UAE signed three landmark Treaties providing for cooperation in Extradition, Mutual Legal Assistance in Criminal Matters and Juridical and Judicial Cooperation in Civil and Commercial Matters. The three Treaties constitute the first set of agreements entered into by India on these matters with any country in the Gulf. Another important landmark in the evolution of India-UAE geo-strategic relations came in the year 2003 when the Defence Cooperation Agreement was signed between the two countries in New Delhi for the purpose of enhancing cooperation between the two countries in matters related to security and defence and for annual meetings of the strategic dialogue.

Crucial Areas of Potential Co-operation

Major current areas and also areas with potential for cooperation in the emerging economic order between India and GCC includes: Energy and Petroleum Products, Food and Cereals, Medicines, Tourism, Manufacturing, Small and Medium Enterprises, Defence, Investments and Services and Project Exports.

a) Energy and Petroleum Products: The endowment of hydrocarbon resources like oil and natural gas has helped many states in evolving and strengthening their bilateral ties with the GCC. Saudi Arabia, Kuwait and UAE are among the major oil producers and exporters with Qatar being rich in natural gas. As per the recent data, GCC's oil production in 2007 was US$ 1769.579 mn b/d [21] while India's oil production in the same year was 0.801 mn b/d [22]; whereas, on the other hand, India's oil consumption was 2.748 mn b/d in 2007 as compared to whole of Middle East's (including GCC) consumption which was 6.203 mn b/d [23]. This shows the importance of Gulf oil in India's foreign trade policy thereby asserting the fact that items under HS Code 27 occupies the place among the top Indian imports (in terms of values) from the GCC countries. [24] Besides, India's competitiveness in petroleum products is also increasing and both India and GCC can mutually investment to secure advantages of capital flows, desired infrastructure and cost-advantage.

b) Food and Cereals: India is one of the world's major food producers. While, on the other hand, the GCC countries are suffering from the problem of food insecurity and huge food price inflation. The gulf is becoming heavily dependant on food imports as FAO also (in one of its document paper of the 27th FAO Regional Conference for the Near East held in Doha on March 13-17, 2004) projected that the Arabian Peninsula's production of food will be 17.754 million tons; whereas, the demand will be 41.811 million tons by the year 2010 thus accounting for a deficit of 24.057 million tons. This implies that the average dependence of the gulf on food imports would cross 60 percent by 2010. A news-item in commodityonline.com dated July 21, 2008 mentions that GCC's food imports amounted to US$ 10 billion in 2007 with Saudi Arabia being the largest food importer. In this wake, India has the potential to cater to the Gulf requirement of food and thereby an opportunity to enhance its international food trade which at present accounts for less than 1.5 per cent of the world's total. In an interesting development occurring on 30 June 2009, GCC and ASEAN have expressed desire to form FTA for food and oil. [25] This is an opportunity that India can also explore as part of its FTA with GCC and follow the 'food for oil' and 'oil for food' diplomacy.

c) Medicines: The Indian pharmaceutical industry has developed strong competitiveness in quality researches and R&D costs; production technology and drug development; and clinical trials. It is estimated to be worth US$ 6 billion and is growing at a rate of more than 13 percent per annum. The Indian pharmaceutical industry ranks 4th in terms of volume and 13th in terms of value globally thereby producing 20-24 percent of the world generic drugs in terms of value. According to Pharmexcil, India's pharmaceutical exports were US$ 6.68 billion in 2007-08 as compared to US$ 5.73 billion in 2006-07; thereby showing a growth rate of 16 percent. Moreover, IBEF notes that 15 of the 20 largest pharmaceutical companies in the world have their presence in India; and that, during April 2000 to October 2007, drugs and pharmaceuticals have been the tenth largest FDI attracting sectors in India. Whereas, the pharmaceutical and bio-medical research is the GCC is still evolving, GCC can get the advantage of low-cost medicines and higher accessibility if they enhance cooperation with India in this sector.

d) Tourism: One of the major chunks of revenues in the services sector in both India and GCC countries comes from tourism; for instance, it forms around 18 percent of the GDP of the United Arab Emirates. Though the events like the global recession and H1N1 flu have caused recent drop in tourist traffic to North America, Latin America and Europe, the intra-regional tourism in West Asia and the Gulf region has shown an increase, thereby making them a preferred destination both for internal tourism as well as for tourists from other Asian countries. Indian tourism industry has a remarkable growth trend owing to its culture, heritage, historical importance, beaches and scenic landscapes. According to the United Nations World Tourism Organization (UNWTO), the Indian tourism industry may witness a growth of 200 percent in 2010. It is estimated that by the year 2012, medical tourism itself can bring in revenue US$ 2 billion a year into India. [26] The Ministry of Tourism, Govt. of India has been taking several steps including the 'Incredible India' campaign to boost tourism.

e) Manufacturing: India has high competitiveness in the manufacturing and OEM sector coupled with huge growth potential. The manufacturing industry has grown by three times in 2008-09 as compared to 2005-06. The Automotive Component Manufacturers Association of India (ACMA) reveals that more than 60% of Indian auto component exports go to the EU and North America. India competitiveness in manufacturing and OEMs is attributed to the following factors: cost of castings and forgings, established production lines, full service supply capability, increasing domestic and international demand. It is also evident from the Export Import Data Bank (Govt. of India) that as per India's 2007-08 exports, items with HS code 85 (including electrical machinery and equipment and parts thereof; sound recorders and reproducers, television image and sound recorders and reproducers, and parts) have occupied among the top three places for most GCC countries. Also, the GCC countries are investing heavily in industrial manufacturing and countries like Saudi Arabia, UAE and Qatar have huge potential for foreign investments in the manufacturing sector. The total value of all non-oil and gas industrial projects in the GCC is very high and this implies that both India and GCC countries can explore the possibilities of mutual investments in the manufacturing sector based on advantages in cost, quality and efficiency.

f) Small and Medium Enterprises: The Mumbai Declaration as part of the Third India-GCC Business Conference in 2007 focuses on India-GCC mutual investment opportunities in SME and SSI sectors. India has a higher degree of competitiveness in terms of cost, manpower and export market in SME/SSI sector as compared to the GCC countries; and, therefore, a mutual sharing on this front could be beneficial for both. According to an EXIM Bank (India) Research brief, the sectors that contribute to SME exports include readymade garments (27%), engineering goods (14.5%), chemicals and pharmaceuticals (11%), electronics and computers (11%) and processed foods (11%). In terms of export orientation, the areas in the SME sector include sports goods with a 100% orientation, readymade garments (90%), leather (70%), marine products (47%) and chemicals and pharmaceuticals (44%). SMEs are also on the rise in GCC and constitute a large chunk of market. Mutual cooperation between India and GCC can help boost each others competitiveness in SMEs.

g) Defence: The regional instability in the Middle East as well in South Asia is a matter of concern for both India and the GCC as such insecurities affect the possibilities of smooth trade flows. India and Qatar recently signed a defence pact on joint maritime security; joint naval exercise and law enforcement in 2008 which has been has been seen as a step toward establishing closer ties. India and UAE have also undertaken several defence exercises and strategic dialogues since they agreed to form a Joint Defence Cooperation Committee in the year 2003. India and Oman have also signed a Memorandum of Association (MoA) on defence cooperation in December 2005 for exchanging military training and expertise in the field of information technology. The collaboration in the field of geo-strategic concerns is also witnessed in the patterns of trade in relevant commodities and equipments between India and GCC. Commodities with HS Code 84 (including nuclear reactors, boilers, machinery and mechanical appliances; parts thereof) have occupied the place among the major trading items between India and GCC. Therefore, in order to strengthen their trade diplomacy, both India and GCC possesses the potential for mutual cooperation in geo-strategic affairs.

h) Investments: FDI in India is increased from US$ 5.55 billion in 2005 to US$ 7.23 billion at the end of November 2006, which account for 30.3 percent. Mauritius and USA are the biggest investors in India, accounting for 40.8 percent and 13.8 percent respectively of the total FDI in India. In 2007-08, India received FDI inflows of US$ 24.57 billion. [27] Moreover, the FDI Flow in GCC has almost doubled in US$ 41.5 billion in 2007 as compared to US$ 21.8 in 2006. Also the GCC countries have invested around US$ 406.3 million constituting around 1.1 percent of total FDI received by India. Among the GCC countries, UAE is the largest investor in India, accounting for around 79.0 percent (US$ 321.1 million) of the total investment made by the GCC countries, followed by Bahrain (US$ 32.7 million), Oman (US$ 24.51 million), Saudi Arabia (US$ 19.18 million), Kuwait (US$ 8.87 million) and Qatar (US$ 0.09 million). [28] India and GCC can enhance mutual investment in the fields of energy infrastructure, real estate, Islamic Banking, biotechnology, agriculture, biotechnology and services.

i) Services and Project Exports: India has a huge potential to engage with GCC in terms of services. The major services category in which India has immense potential includes higher education and training; management consulting; telecommunication services; software services; engineering services; and, financial services. Recreational services can also be enhanced but it has certain limitations in few GCC countries like Saudi Arabia. Moreover, GCC has also emerged as a major destination for India's project exports. It accounted for Rs. 85.34 billion (that is 42.5%) of the total value of contracts secured by Indian project exporters during the period 2000-01 to 2004-05, with the support of Exim India. Some of the projects under execution by Indian project exporters in the region include: Marinascape Development Project, chilled water cooling plant for Conference Palace Hotel, and turnkey contract for high voltage overhead transmission line project in UAE; construction of three super specialty hospitals, consultancy contract for operating and managing cement plants of Yanbu Cement Company, construction of dams and branch sewerage line network in Saudi Arabia; setting up of gas turbine stations, high voltage transmission network project, and water transmission network project in Oman; setting-up of high voltage sub-stations and power distribution network, turnkey package comprising heating, ventilation, air-conditioning, electrical and plumbing works for Defence Project, and engineering, procurement and construction contract for coffer dams in Qatar; construction of Electricity and Water Training Institute and ancillary facilities, and engineering consultancy services for provision of effluent water disposal plants in Kuwait; and consultancy services for Bahrain National Gas Company in Bahrain. [29]

Conclusion

India's trade with GCC cannot be studied in isolation and therefore, its confluence with geopolitical factors becomes inevitable. The signing of the Comprehensive Economic Cooperation Agreement (CECA) between India and GCC which happened in the year 2004 reflects the strong conviction followed by the GCC in their urge for 'Look East'. Moreover, the India-GCC FTA is also being negotiated. The proposed FTA between India and GCC would bring about following benefits including more intensive economic engagement between the two entities, removal of restrictive duties, reduction of tariffs on traded commodities and increase in trade and FDI, amongst others. The FTA shall also help in larger engagements in the crucial areas of potential cooperation outlined herein.

Notes

1. The agreement was concluded on May 25, 1981 in Riyadh, Saudi Arabia among the members.
2. See details on Ministry of External Affairs (Gulf Division), Govt. of India, http://mea.gov.in/onmouse/gcc2.pdf.
3. 'An in-depth look at the GCC-India Web Portal'; Gulf Research Center – GCC-India Research Bulletin, Issue No. 1, January 2006, p. 2.
4. See Patankar, A. C. (2006), "Economic and Industrial Cooperation: Future Challenges", *GCC-India Research Bulletin*, Issue 2, pp. 17-19.
5. "India—Attractive Destination for GCC Investments", (MENAFN-Arab News) Jeddah, published online on MENAFN Web Site; 12 February 2007.
6. The Global Investment House is a Kuwait-based investment company licensed by the Central Bank of Kuwait. It envisions becoming the preferred investment bank in the Middle East.
7. 'India—Attractive Destination for GCC Investments' (MENAFN - Arab News) Jeddah; published online on MENAFN Web Site; 12 February 2007.
8. 'GCC-India FTA Talks Give Fillip to Asian Community'; N. Janardhan; Arab News; January 5, 2006.
9. See Amin, Khadija Arafah M. (2006), "Need for strategic cooperation", *GCC-India Research Bulletin*, Issue No. 1, pp. 8-9.
10. The data estimates for proven oil reserves and proven natural gas reserves of each of the GCC country have been taken from Energy Information Administration (EIA) Country Analysis Briefs (2008) for respective countries.
11. The information on various bilateral agreements and Memorandum of Understanding (MoU) signed between India and any GCC country and as mentioned under geo-economic and geo-strategic relations in this chapter have been taken from the web site of the Ministry of External Affairs, Govt. of India.
12. The data for the values of India's exports and imports as well as the particulars relating to the major commodities (in terms of value and pertaining to the year 2007-08) to all the GCC

countries have been taken from Export Import Database, Ministry of Commerce and Industry, Govt. of India. The values of India's exports and imports to all the GCC countries have also been mentioned in Tables 6.2 and 6.3.

13. The Bank of Baroda, State Bank of India, New India Assurance Co. Ltd, Life Insurance Corporation of India, ICICI Bank and Syndicate Bank have operations in Oman.
14. Oman International Bank has two branches in India, at Mumbai and Cochin, since 1985. Bank Muscat opened a branch in Bangalore in September 1998 and took 33% stake in the Centurion Bank in India by merging its Bangalore branch in the venture in 2003.
15. See "The Souk of Oman – Foreign Investors upbeat on Investments in Oman". Accessed on February 12, 2008; http://www.soukofoman.com/forinuponini.html.
16. The Saudi Arabian General Investment Authority (SAGIA), the nodal agency for licensing all foreign investment proposals in Saudi Arabia has since its establishment in April 10, 2000, licensed 3608 projects amounting to the value of SR 292.657 billion(US$78.041 billion). Foreign investors, from 82 countries contributed 38.331%, i.e. SR 112.137 billion (US$29.903 billion) of total licensed investments, whereas the Saudi share amounted to SR 180.414 billion (48.110 billion), i.e. 61.669%. The major investing countries in Saudi Arabia include U.A.E, Japan, British Virgin Islands, Bahrain, France, Germany, Lebanon, Cayman Island, Canada and Bermuda.
17. See Pranab Mukherjee Boosts Energy Ties with Saudi Arabia'; April 20, 2008;
    Web link: http://www.india-server.com/news/pranab-mukherjee-boosts-energy-ties-406.html.
18. See 'India, Saudi Arabia initiate key economic measures to boost relations'; Reported by Atul Aneja;
    Web link:
    http://www.hindu.com/2008/04/21/stories/2008042160521700.htm.
19. See 'India-UAE Bilateral Relations' at http://www.indembassyuae.org/induae_bilateral.phtml.
20. See 'India-UAE trade likely to exceed $25 bn by 2010'; March 25, 2008; Accessed: March 30, 2008; Available:

http://www.thaindian.com/newsportal/business/india-uae-trade-likely-to-exceed-25-bn-by-2010_10031091.html.

21. Energy Information Administration (EIA), March 2008.
22. BP Statistical review of World Energy, 2008.
23. Ibid.
24. Items classified under HS Code 27 include mineral fuels, mineral oils and products of their distillation; bituminous substances; mineral waxes.
25. See http://www.bilaterals.org/article.php3?id_article=15474 to read "GCC, ASEAN eye new trade bloc based on food, oil", Posted on 1 July 2009.
26. See the web link www.holidayiq.com/visit-india-2009.php.
27. See "Centre looks at Gulf countries for FDI"; http://www.financialexpress.com/news/centre-looks-at-gulf-countries-for-fdi/375746/2; 21 October 2008.
28. See the World Investment Report, 2008 for further information.
29. See Exim Bank Research Brief No. 23, March 2006, http://www.eximbankindia.com/op110.pdf.

7

Resurgent Russia and the Gulf

Prasanta Kumar Pradhan

Introduction

The disintegration of the Soviet Union and the emergence of several new republics in the region in 1991 brought out new challenges for the Russian foreign policy. An economically and politically weakened Russia was suddenly found to focus on its new neighbours of Central Asia and its regional political dynamics. During this period, Russia lost its previous Cold War political influence all over the world and searched for solutions to its own new found problems. In this period, Russian foreign policy in the Gulf region also witnessed a weakening and the United States emerged as the sole external power and the security provider in the region.

During the Soviet era, Soviet Russia exercised enormous influence over the Gulf region because of the geographical contiguity, economic interests and for the strategic reasons as well. [1] The breakdown of the Soviet Union left it pondering over its own security and strategic interests in its immediate neighbourhood. Russia's over indulgence in its new found neighbourhood and the changed international balance of power led to its abstinence from the Gulf region. Though formal political and diplomatic relations continued along with bilateral visits of the leaders from both the sides, a strong ground could not be built for a Russian policy in the region. The coming in to power of Vladimir Putin in the year 2000 brought in a change in the Russian approach towards the Gulf region. The changing political and strategic environment in its neighbourhood may also have influenced the Russian decision to engage the Gulf region more constructively. Russia has now emerged with a vision for its engagement with the Gulf countries. Russia's security concerns keeping in mind the advancement of North Atlantic Treaty Organisation (NATO), American presence in the Central Asian region, long term economic interests associated with the Gulf region, issues related to Islamic terrorism, and other international political and strategic issues have shaped the Russian new policy of seriously engaging the Gulf States.

Strategic Interests

After a long hiatus, Russia is trying to give shape to its strategic interests in the Gulf region. There are, clearly, a number of them. One of the important Russian interests to engage the Gulf countries is the secessionist movement it is facing from the Islamic Chechen rebels in its territory. There are apprehensions that the Chechen rebels are getting support from some elements in the Gulf region and the Gulf countries have substantial ideological and religious influence over these groups. And now, as Russia wants stability in its Chechnya region, engaging the Gulf countries becomes prudent for her. Russian security officials suspect that the Chechen rebels who seized a Moscow theatre in October 2002 had wealthy Arab sponsors in Saudi Arabia and other Gulf states. They also claim to have traced a series of telephone calls from the gunmen to their sponsors in Saudi Arabia, the UAE and Qatar. [2] During his visit to Moscow in the year 2003, Saudi Crown Prince Abdullah informed Putin that Russia's wish to enter the Organisation of Islamic Conference (OIC) would not be granted because of the continued conflict in its Chechnya region. [3] As the region is vital for Russia and it carries further importance because of the Islamic terrorism, Russia has initiated diplomacy with the countries from which the rebels get their support. Russia has also been successful in engaging with some of the Gulf countries over the issue and has tried to neutralize the rebels.

Geographically, Russia has been virtually encircled by the

American and the NATO forces who have reached its boundaries and are actively engaging the former Soviet allies. The USA has also established its military bases in Uzbekistan and Kyrgyzstan in Central Asia which also increases the Russia's threat perception of the situation. USA has also signed a missile defence deal with Poland in early 2008. Under the deal, America will help bolster Polish air defences in return for permission to place 10 interceptor missiles on the country's Baltic seaboard. Though the USA says that the weapons are meant to defend Europe and Israel against missile attacks from Iran and other emerging threats from rogue states or terrorists, Russia sees the move as an attempt to undermine its own nuclear deterrent. [4] It does not represent any immediate physical threat at this moment, but it would certainly make the Russians think about their national security. To come out of the trap, Russia needs to break the barrier being set by the USA and create her own security zone. Thus, coming out of the dragnet and engaging the Gulf countries would clearly mean defying the American strategic trap and setting up their own security discourse.

Moscow now wants to play its part in the Gulf intending to reduce the hegemony of the USA in the region. Taking a cue from the US policy in the region, Russia also intends to strike a delicate balance in its relationship between Iran and the Arabs. It wants to reassert and strengthen its strategic interests and political influence in the Gulf and maintain the balance of power in the region in her favour. Russia's relationship with Iran through the period of intense political turmoil challenging the American and Israeli antagonism with Iran, and the emerging relationship with Saudi Arabia and other Gulf countries, is certainly a huge political and strategic gain for Russia in the Gulf.

Iran remains the most important strategic partner for Russia in the Gulf at the moment. Iran has been a major foothold for Russia in the Gulf region. Russia's ties with Iran solidify the Russian presence in the region and at the same time pose a strategic and diplomatic challenge for the USA. To strengthen their relationship further in this regard, Russia has been diversifying its engagement with Iran. For Iran, Russia's support for it in the face of opposition and hostility it faces from the regional neighbours and the USA and Israel has flowed in the appropriate time. Iran has fought a long war with its neighbour, Iraq, and has soured its relationship with the Arab Gulf monarchies over a number of issues like boundary issues, radical Shia Islam and struggle for regional supremacy and the nuclear weapons issue. Since the fall of Shah and coming of power of the Islamic regime in power in Tehran, its relationship with the USA has taken a U-turn. In such circumstances, for Iran, the support from Russia would have not come at any better time. There have remained a number of contentious issues between the two countries like Russian support to the UNSC resolutions on Iran, Russian support to build Bushehr nuclear reactor, Uranium enrichment and Russia's offer to share Gabala radar station in Azerbaijan with the USA among others. [5] Similarly, Putin's decision to join the US-led war on terror in the aftermath of the September 11, 2001 attacks on the USA put Russian foreign policy to a test. Russian dilemma centred around how to support the American war on terror and at the same time support the Iranian nuclear weapons programme. Russia pledged to continue support to the Bushehr nuclear reactor and at the same time it urged Iran to sign a protocol to the NPT that would allow more aggressive inspection of its nuclear programme by the IAEA. Thus, Russian diplomacy has managed to balance its interests with United States and its support for the Iran and maintain its presence in the region.

Iraq has been of particular importance for the Russians because of its geographical proximity to its near abroad, strategic location, arms sale and oil reserves. Russia's relationship with Iraq has moved in a zigzag manner and has witnessed many ups and downs. Since the soviet era, their relation with Iraq has been guided by the treaty of friendship and co-operation with Iraq which was signed in 1972. Soviet Russia enjoyed a very cordial relationship with Iraq when Saddam Hussain was in power, mainly, because of his socialist ideological predilections. But trouble started when on 6 January 1980 Saddam Hussain strongly criticized the Soviet invasion in Afghanistan. In the same year in September, Iraq attacked Iran, a war which went on for eight long years. The Soviet Union did not openly condemn the attack but it immediately stopped military support to Iraq only to be resumed few years later. Again in 1990, Iraq invaded Kuwait. This time Soviet government condemned it as an act of aggression and demanded immediate and unconditional withdrawal of Iraqi forces from Kuwaiti territory and "the re-establishment of the sovereignty, national independence, and territorial integrity of Kuwait." The USSR also voted for the United Nations' Security Council resolution 678 which called for "all necessary means" to be used to end the occupation of Kuwait. [6] Since the disintegration of the Soviet Union, the Russian leaders have tried to improve their relationships with Iraq with no ideological strings attached.

The American invasion of Iraq posed a fresh challenge for Russia. President Putin declared that there is no justification for such an action. For him, neither had Iraq supported international terrorism nor did it pose any danger to its neighbours or any other countries. [7] According to a Western perspective, Russia opposed the American intervention in Iraq because it felt that the USA should not completely take over the fight against terrorism, since that would threaten the status quo in world politics. [8] They also allege that, apart from the strategic calculations Russia had a considerable stake in the post-Saddam regime. The total value of the Russian oil contracts with the former regime was estimated at about 30 billion dollars, Iraqi debt to Russia amounted to an estimated 8 billion dollars, and Russia had apparently been making 1-2 billion dollars a year from the UN's Oil-for-Food programme. [9] Whatever might be the intentions and dynamics, Russia has now established good relationship with Iraq and in also involved in oil drilling in some oil fields there. At this point, Russia's interests clearly lies with the status quo and with allowing Iraq to regain its normal standing in the international community. [10] American interference in Iraq has, probably, added more legitimacy for Russia to make a comeback in the region.

Similarly, Russia has also moved ahead to improve its relation with Saudi Arabia. President Putin visited Saudi Arabia in 2007 and signaled stronger ties with the kingdom. Both the countries agreed to sign a military-technical cooperation while at the same time, Saudi Arabia agreed to support Russia joining the WTO and more importantly, Riyadh agreed to support Russian policy in Chechnya. [11] In the same year, Saudi Crown Prince Sultan visited Moscow and in the very next year Foreign Minister Prince Saud Al Faisal also visited Russia. With increased interaction, the Russian complain of Saudi support for the Chechen rebels has come down.

Trade and Business

Strengthening trade and business ties with the Gulf countries is also a main priority of the resurgent Russia. In past one decade Russia has made tremendous headways in establishing trade ties with the Gulf countries. Russia's trade relations with Saudi Arabia serve as the best example of it. Prior to the 1990s, trade between Russia and the Kingdom was virtually non-existent. It was only from the mid-nineties onwards that a significant trade between the two countries began. Russia's exports to Saudi Arabia in 1998 were valued at 85.6 million USD. By 2006 it went up to 272.6 million USD. [12] Iran has remained the largest trade partner of Russia (total trade of 2141 million USD in 2006) in the Gulf region followed by UAE and Saudi Arabia, with the total trade volume of 648 million USD and 279 million USD, respectively. Qatar remains Russia's smallest trading partner in the region followed by Kuwait and Bahrain.

Apart from the usual mercantile trade Russia has also been involved in a number of projects and joint collaborations in the region. Russian company, LUKoil was awarded a tender (LUKoil Saudi Arabia) to develop the 11,200- square-mile 'Zone A' natural gas field in the Rub Al-Khali, signing a 40-year contract with Saudi Arabia to explore and develop the field. Similarly, Stroitransagaz, the engineering arm of Russia's state-controlled gas monopoly Gazprom, has established a joint venture with construction company Saudi Oger to bid for contracts with Saudi ARAMCO. [13]

Russia has signed Economic, Trade, and Technical Cooperation Agreement, with Oman in November 2005. They have also signed a Cooperation Agreement between Oman Chamber of Commerce and Industry and the Russian Chamber of Commerce and Industry, in August 2005.

In November 2008, Russia organised a two day investment Roadshow in Dubai which was attended by a number of investors and companies. It was the largest ever Russia-focussed business event to be held in the UAE, opening the door to a wide range of new cooperation between Russia and the Gulf. Plans are already underway for a follow-up event in Dubai in 2009, and for taking the Roadshow to other destinations around the world. Appreciating the event, Hamad Buamim, Director General of the Dubai Chamber of Commerce and Industry, said: "In a time when it is more important than ever to continuously seek opportunities to beat the global market trends, Russia is proving to be a haven for investors who are keen to explore new markets. The Russia Investment Roadshow provided such opportunity, being held here in Dubai - the commercial capital of the region." [14] A delegation of Russian businessmen and politicians participated in the Roadshow to urge Emiratis to divert investments from the West to the East called on the UAE as well as other Gulf countries to invest in Russia's infrastructure. While some Emirati investors complained that they were concerned about corruption and a lack of transparency in Russia, Stanislav Voskresensky, Russia's Deputy Minister for Economic Development assured them by explaining that, "There is a new package of laws being discussed and one of the main reforms is tackling corruption and the reintroducing confidence in our courts and justice system. Law and reinforcement is one of the Russian president's main priorities." [15]

In March 2007, a delegation from the Russian Railways Public Joint Stock Company visited Bahrain. It was understood that developing transportation infrastructure tops the company's strategic objectives, particularly in the GCC countries and the West Asian region. The company is also bidding for a string of tenders in Saudi Arabia, Iran among others. [16]

In an effort to economically engage the Gulf countries, a delegation of Russian business circles headed by Vladimir Evtushenkov, the Chairman of Russian-Arab Business Council (RABC), visited the Kingdom of Bahrain in April 2007 and met their counterparts there. During the meeting, Essam Fahro, the Chairman of the Board of the Bahrain Chamber of Commerce and Industry, expressed his interest in widening the financial and banking cooperation with Russian companies which was to benefit both the parties. [17] The same delegation then visited Kuwait where it held negotiations with the Kuwaiti Oil Minister, Ali Al Jarrakh, heads of some of the Government agencies and a number of Kuwaiti companies. The parties expressed their interest in the development of the commercial, economic and investment cooperation and, in particular, setting up contacts in the financial and banking spheres. Both Russia and Kuwait also signed a Protocol on Cooperation between the Russian and Kuwaiti Chambers of Commerce and Industry. [18]

Another reason of Russian engagement of the Gulf countries is its ambitious plan of the construction of the North-South International Transport Corridor (ITC). According to Russia, when complete, North-South ITC will offer a highly competitive alternative to the sea route via the Suez Canal, slashing costs by around 30 percent and shipment times between Russia/Northern Europe and the Persian Gulf/Indian Ocean/South Asia/South-East Asia. The North-South ITC will allow Russian Railways to alter the existing routes for container cargo transportation and reduce delivery times, thus providing for delivery of cargo from India, Pakistan and Persian Gulf countries to Russia via Iran, as well as transit to North, East and Central Europe. [19] Russia understands that to achieve this objective, the cooperation of the Gulf countries is necessary. Completion of the ITC project will not only boost Russian trade and relations with other countries but also will have implications for the future relationship between the two regions.

Energy

In recent times Russia has expressed its desire to work more closely with the Organisation of the Petroleum Exporting Countries (OPEC). Russia being a non-OPEC member does not have any production quota obligation like the member countries and thus sometimes even produces more than Saudi Arabia. Traditionally, Russia has always favoured a higher oil price in the market to meet its revenue expenditures whereas Riyadh sees its interests as best being served by moderate oil prices. [20] At the same time Russia also appeals the OPEC to reduce their production. This Russian double standard has annoyed the OPEC members, particularly, Saudi Arabia. While the Saudis would like Russia to join the cartel and follow the quota restrictions on oil production, Russia on its part would like not to come under such quota regulations and would cooperate to the extent of coordination and market stability. But Russia wants to further its clout in the international energy market by engaging with the OPEC. As Igor Sechin, Russia's Deputy Prime Minister who led the Russian observer delegation at the 149th meeting of the OPEC Conference in Vienna in September 2008, said that Russia is interested in a "mechanism for regular coordination, information exchange and market analysis and forecasting" with OPEC and added that, "We are putting forward an initiative to establish regular energy dialogue between Russia and OPEC, the main goal of which will be to contribute to providing sustainable stability on the oil market in the interests of all participants." [21]

Russia is reportedly proposing a gas joint venture equivalent of the OPEC which is to be called 'Gaspec' along with two other major gas suppliers in the Gulf region - Iran and Qatar. This "gas troika" would build a pipeline to pump gas from Iran's South Pars deposit, the world's largest, to be processed at a plant in Qatar. Russia's Gazprom, Iran's National Oil Company and Qatar Liquefied Gas Company would hold 30 percent each in the venture and another 10 percent stake will be reserved for other interested clients. [22] Russia being the largest owner and producer of the natural gas, wants to control the international gas market. Building joint venture with other major gas producing countries would help her influence the production and supply of gas to the international market.

Cooperation in the field of peaceful nuclear energy with the Gulf countries is also an important agenda for Russia. Apart from Iran, Russia has offered supplying peaceful nuclear energy to countries like Bahrain and Saudi Arabia. In a recent meeting in December 2008 Russia's President Dmitry Medvedev and King of Bahrain Sheikh Hamad Bin Isa Al Khalifa discussed the issue of cooperation in the field if civilian nuclear energy between the two countries. Both sides agreed to set up bilateral working teams which will deliberate on training the personal for the use of civil nuclear energy. [23] Russia has also started talks with Saudi Arabia over a possible cooperation in nuclear energy program.

Arms Sale

An important reason behind Russia's re-emergence in the

Gulf is the lucrative arms market it finds because of the continuing tensions in the region. Traditionally, United States has been the major arms supplier to the Gulf countries. But the resurgent Russia has now decided to venture into the Gulf to sell its arms in the Gulf market.

Among the Gulf countries, Iran has been the main importer of arms from Russia in the Gulf region. Russia emerged as the main supplier of arms to Iran only after the fall of Shah in 1979. In 1989, following the death of Ayatollah Khomeini, Moscow and Tehran negotiated their first major arms deal along with agreements on scientific-technical cooperation, which included pledges of non-interference in each other's domestic affairs. Relations continued to improve and by the end of the 1990s, Russia emerged as Iran's main supplier of conventional arms. According to the SIPRI arms transfer database, the value of weapons supplied by Russia to Iran from 2000 to 2007 stands at 1427 million dollars. [24] Russia has sold Iran hundreds of major weapons systems, including twenty T-72 tanks, air-to-air missiles, and a handful of combat aircraft like the MiG-29, surface-to-air missile defense system (SA-15 Gauntlet) along with TOR M-1 air-defense missile systems, ostensibly to defend its Russian-built nuclear reactor at Bushehr. [25]

Russia has, in recent times, been able to build up friendly relationship with Saudi Arabia, probably, the wealthiest arms customer in the Gulf. During his visit to Saudi Arabia in February 2007, which was the first ever visit by any Russian leader to the kingdom; Russian President Vladimir Putin discussed the issue with authorities in Riyadh. It was reported that Putin offered to sell Saudi Arabia 'peaceful' nuclear reactors, T-90 tanks, helicopters, air-defence systems and other weapons, expanded satellite launches and an opportunity to join the Russian satellite navigation system, GLONASS. [26] According to reports, the value of the arms deal between the two countries may reach around 2.2 billion USD. [27] In a return visit by the Saudi Crown Prince Sultan to Russia in

November that year the issue was also discussed at length. It is also understood at some quarters that Saudi Arabia has offered the lucrative arms deal to Russia instead of its traditional arms supplier, the USA, to reduce its cooperation with Iran. Though Russian authorities denies any link with Iran over their deals with Saudi Arabia, the possibilities of Iran factor playing a role in the deal cannot be denied keeping in view the longstanding political and ideological rivalry between the two major Gulf powers. Whatever may be the intentions of Riyadh in signing the deal; Moscow would immensely gain from this move and strengthen its foothold in the region.

Apart from Iran and Saudi Arabia, Russia is also supplying arms to other Gulf countries like UAE and Yemen. According to the CRS report to the Congress, from 2000 to 2007, Russia has supplied arms worth 200 million dollars to Iraq, 1000 million dollars to UAE and 900 million dollars to Yemen. [28] Yemeni President Ali Abdullah Saleh visited Moscow in February 2009 and signed a deal to buy $1 billion worth of weapons from Russia, including purchase of MiG-29 planes, helicopters, T-80 and T-72 tanks, and armored vehicles.

UAE has been continuously receiving Russian arms and military technologies. According to a new report from SIPRI, UAE accounted for 6.0 percent of the world's arms imports between 2004 and 2008; and Russia supplied 25 percent of the arms to the country. In February of 2007, Rosoboroneksport, the Russian state arms trade agency, signed a contract to deliver a batch of infantry armaments for over $50 million, including small arms, ammunition, RPG-29 Vampir antitank rocket launchers and several Kornet-E ATGW systems. From the year 2001 to 2004, UAE received 1,000 KamAZ-4326 double-axis all-wheel trucks for its armed forces which amounted to around $40 million. [29] Though there were a number of arms deals between Russia and Kuwait in the 1990s, there have not been any significant contracts between the two countries primarily because the threat of Iraq has now subsided with the US-led invasion and subsequent execution of

Saddam Hussain.

Challenge to American Hegemony?

During the Cold War the Arab monarchies of the Gulf along with Turkey and Iran allied with the United States and the Soviet Union supported the socialist regimes of Egypt, Libya, Syria and Iraq. In the post Cold War era, with the disintegration of the Soviet Union, Russia failed to challenge the USA in the region and thus leaving it to be the sole superpower in the region.

Russia's muscle flexing in the Gulf is, certainly, a challenge for the USA in the region. In recent times Russia has been vocal in its ambitions and strategies in the Gulf which may clash directly with the interests of the USA. Given that situation, Russia's rise in the Gulf would not be easy and peaceful as its leaders in Kremlin have imagined. It would have to face tough competition and hostility from the United States in maintaining the desired delicate balance of power in the region and keeping their interests in tact. Though none of the big powers would like to let the situation go out of hand to revert back to the hostilities of the Cold War era, they certainly, would not intend to compromise on their respective standings and vested national interests in the region. While Russia has moved all out to strengthen its existing relationship with its friendly countries and to woo the Arab Gulf countries, the USA would be trying hard to maintain the balance of power in her favour and not to let loose her traditional Arab friends. In this context, the behaviour of the Arab countries and their response towards Russia would largely determine the balance of power in the Gulf.

Russia has also taken the opportunity to enter into the Gulf during the eight year rule of President Bush when the USA got militarily involved in Iraq and Afghanistan. The same period also witnessed the shrinking of the American image in the Islamic world. Thus, Putin took it as the right moment to initiate political and strategic ties with the Gulf countries.

Russia's entry into the Gulf would largely undermine the American interests so far as the sale of American arms in the Gulf market is concerned. The USA has been the principal supplier of arms to the oil-rich Gulf monarchies which it would certainly like to continue. But the entry of Russia has, to some extent, diluted the hegemony of the USA in this regard as some Arab Gulf monarchies have opted for Russian arms to diversify their weaponry.

Similarly, Russia's cooperation with the OPEC countries in balancing oil production to keep prices higher has irritated the USA as well the Europe. They feel insecure as Russian intimacy with the OPEC may lead Russia to influence the decision making of the cartel. Again, American hostile nations in OPEC like Iran and Venezuela may support for a bigger Russian cooperation with the cartel. Though America's biggest ally Saudi Arabia would act to safeguard her interest in this regard, Russia's direct involvement in talks with OPEC and the Saudis pose a challenge for the USA in the Gulf in the times to come.

Keeping in view the United States' current position in the Gulf region and in the whole world as well, it seems difficult for Russia to be able to challenge its hegemony though it can to a large extent damage the American interests in the region. In the foreseeable future, it seems, the USA would virtually remain the dominant power in the region. The present Russian challenge is not military or ideological in nature as it used to be during the Cold War era; rather it is a political, strategic and economic one posed by a resurgent Russia.

Implications for India

There are a number of common areas of cooperation possible between India and Russia in the Gulf region. Russian presence in the region does not seem to pose any serious threat to the interest of India. As discussed earlier in the paper the resurgent Russia aims at reviving its lost glory in the region and emphasizes increasing its political, economic and strategic interests. Thus, there remains a scope for cooperation between the two in the region. India follows a policy of political non-interference in the domestic and foreign affairs in the Gulf. India is primarily interested in increasing trade with the Gulf countries, energy security, protecting interests of the five million strong Indian Diaspora in the region, building a strategic cooperation etc. Thus both countries should take it an opportunity to seek cooperation with each other in the region.

Cooperation in the field of terrorism would be important for both India and Russia as both the countries have been victims of terrorism since long and some radical Muslim terrorists get ideological and financial support from their counterparts in the Gulf region. Thus, sharing of intelligence and information over the issue can lead to further cooperation.

India and Russia can be partners in the Gulf region to check the growing Chinese power in the region. The growth of china in the West Asian region has been a matter of deep concern for both Russia and India. For much of the history, India's policy in the Gulf has been determined by the Cold War between USA and USSR that independent India had to deal with. After the end of Cold War India have had to deal with the USA in the region. But in recent years the rise of china has been a major challenge and concern for India in the fields of trade, investment and markets. Thus India and Russia can be natural partners in dealing with China in the Gulf.

Another area of cooperation between India and Russia is in the field of fighting against piracy in the Gulf of Aden. The Russian Navy has deployed its naval ships in the Gulf of Aden. The Russian Navy has maintained a presence off the Horn of Africa with warships operating on a rotation basis. Russia joined international anti-piracy efforts off the Somali coast in October 2008. India has also deployed naval ships in the Gulf of Aden to check piracy. As the interests of both the countries lie in a secure sea lane communication in the high seas in the India Ocean, India and Russia can cooperate with each other in this regard.

But in the fields of trade and commerce India will have to face some competition from countries like Russia particularly in the fields of marketing, business and acquiring contracts. Russia has taken big strides in strengthening its business interests in the region. It has been doing so by actively reaching to all the countries and by holding road shows to attract the attention of the people in important business centres in the Gulf region. Though India has huge oil and non-oil trade and business with the Gulf countries, it has been struggling to acquire big contracts. In such a situation, rise of countries like Russia would pose further challenges to India.

Conclusions

Russia has a number of interests to engage with the States of the Gulf region. While long term economic interests drive Russian ambitions in the Gulf, there are a number of political and strategic factors which dictate its moves. But this is only a beginning of it. As Russia moves ahead with its goals it may face numerous hurdles on its way. Clash with the American interests is one of the most important challenges Russia would face in the future. There is no doubt over the fact that Russian advance in the Gulf region would substantially damage American interests, in economic as well as strategic calculations. The probability of confrontation with the American interest increases as the Russian engagement with the region becomes more serious and broad-based. Similarly, in a region of diverse interests and conflicts over ideology, resources and boundaries, simultaneously accommodating expectations of all the parties concerned would remain an uphill task for Russia. Nevertheless, Russia's venture into the Gulf would give it a renewed sense of self-confidence and standing in the international arena.

To conclude it can be said that the new Russian policy in the Gulf has also achieved some success – though not as high as the policy makers at Kremlin would have imagined. By engaging countries like Saudi Arabia, UAE and Qatar, Russia has managed to reduce the Arab support for the Chechen rebels. Russia has diversified its trade basket with the Gulf countries and at the same time is attracting more and more Arab investment into the country. The policy arms sale to the Gulf countries has also proved to be beneficial for Russia. Though the USA remains the most powerful external player in the region and the Gulf sheikhdoms remain the staunch allies of it, the entry of Russia into the scene would certainly threaten the existing strategic balance of power.

Notes

1. For an analysis of the Soviet policy and involvement in the Gulf region see A. Yodfat and M. Abir, *In the Direction of the Gulf: The Soviet Union and the Persian Gulf* (London: Frank Cass and Company Limited, 1977); Carol R. Saivetz, *The Soviet Union and the Gulf in the 1980s* (Boulder: Westview Press, 1989); Arey Y. Yodfat, *The Soviet Union and the Arabian Peninsula: Soviet Policy towards the Persian Gulf and Arabia* (New York: St. Martin's Press, 1983).
2. Nick Paton Walsh, "Chechen rebels phoned Gulf during siege", *The Guardian*, December 5, 2002.
3. Robert H. Donaldson and Joseph L. Nogee, *The Foreign Policy of Russia: Changing Systems and Enduring Interests* (London: M.E. Sharpe, 2005), p. 325.
4. Angus McDowall, "Poland 'agrees' to US missile defence deal", *The Telegraph*, February 3, 2008.
5. See Mark Katz, "Russian-Iranian Relations in the Ahmadinejad Era", *Middle East Journal*, Vol. 62, No. 2, Spring 2008.
6. For an analysis of the Russia-Iraq relations see, Tareq Y. Ismael, "Russian-Iraqi Relations: A Historical and Political Analysis", *Arab Studies Quarterly*, Fall 2001.
7. Stephen white, "Russia: Diminished Power", in Rick Fawn and Raymond Hinnebusch (eds.), *The Iraq War: Causes and Consequences* (Delhi: Viva Books Private Limited, 2007), p. 74.
8. Charlotte Wagnsson, "Russia's Choice: Preserve the status Quo", in Jan Hallenberg and Hakan Karlsson (eds.), *The Iraq War: European Perspectives on Politics, Strategy and Operations* (London: Routledge, 2005), p. 69.
9. White, n. 10, p. 75.

10. Roland Dannreuther, "Russia and the Middle East", in Hannah Carter and Anoushiravan Ehteshami (eds.), *The Middle East's Relations with Asia and Russia*, (London: RoutledgeCurzon, 2004), p. 30.
11. Mark N. Katz, "Saudi-Russian Relations since the Abdullah-Putin Summit", *Middle East Policy*, Vol. 16, No. 1, 2009, pp. 114-120.
12. United Nations Commodity Trade, COMTRADE Database.
13. John Sfakianakis, "Saudi-Russian Trade Relations Deepen" *The Arab News*, November 21, 2007.
14. http://www.russiaroadshow.com/eng/2008_DUBAI/
15. Rym Ghazal, "Russia seeks investment from UAE", *The National*, November 10, 2008.
16. http://www.eng-forum.com/News/Mar07/020307a.htm
17. See the website of the Russian-Arab Business Council, Russian Delegation visits Bahrain and Kuwait, April 12, 2007, available at http://www.russarabbc.ru/en/about/detail.php?ID=1315&PHPSESSID=5a93adb00e8b363c88983d2f44812c6
18. Ibid.
19. See the details at the website of Russian Railways, available at http://eng.rzd.ru/wps/portal/rzdeng?STRUCTURE_ID=86
20. See Mark Katz, "Saudi-Russian Relations in the Putin Era", *Middle East Journal*, Vol. 55, No. 4, Autumn 2001, pp. 603-622.
21. *RIA Novosti* "Russia seeks closer ties with OPEC" September 10, 2008, available at http://en.rian.ru/russia/20080910/116666199.html.
22. http://www.topnews.in/russia-iran-qatar-form-gas-export-joint-venture-287900.
23. "Russia Cements Relations with Bahrain", *Kommersant*, December 02, 2008, available at http://www.kommersant.com/page.asp?id=-13676.
24. SIPRI Arms Transfer Database [figures in US dollar Constant (1990) Prices]
25. Lionel Beehner, "Russia-Iran Arms Trade", Council on Foreign Relations, November 1, 2006, available at http://www.cfr.org/publication/11869/russiairan_arms_trade.html.
26. Ariel Cohen, "Putin's Middle East Visit: Russia is Back", The Heritage Foundation, March 5, 2007

available at
http://www.heritage.org/research/russiaandeurasia/wm1382.cfm.

27. http://www.reuters.com/article/worldNews/idUSL1541793320080715.
28. CRS Report for Congress, Conventional Arms Transfers to Developing Nations, 2000-2007, October 23, 2008, (figures in current US dollars).
29. Mikhail Barabanov, "Russian Arms Deliveries to Arab Countries of the Persian Gulf Region", *Moscow Defence Brief*, Vol. 2, No. 16, 2009, available at http://mdb.cast.ru/mdb/4-2008/item4/article1/

8

India's Energy Requirements, Natural Gas and the Persian Gulf

Pranav Kumar

India is one of the fastest growing economies in the present world. It faces the critical challenge of meeting a rapidly increasing demand for energy. With over a billion people, more than 16 percent of the World, India ranks fifth in the world in terms of energy demand, accounting for 3.75 percent of world commercial energy demand in 2006. [1] Despite overall energy consumption is very high India's per capita energy consumption is abysmally low. Its economy is projected to grow over eight percent during the next two decades, and there will be a substantial increase in demand for oil and natural gas to fuel land, sea, and air transport. India's Energy concern is very similar to the global energy concerns and is heavily centered around reliance on the hydrocarbons. Even though her domestic hydrocarbon production has been expanding, more than two third of her total demand is being fulfilled by exogenetic sources. [2] The substantial part of India's hydrocarbon supply has always been imported and on basis of the present level of technological development this trend is supposed to continue for the next few more decades. India's energy consumption is expected to more than double by 2020. The Hydrocarbon resources would continue to play vital role in it because of structural changes in the economy [3], transformation in demographic composition [4], shifts in the governmental policy for power generation [5], increasing defence and space related fuel requirements. Hence India's Energy Security needs are directly linked with the external supply of hydrocarbons. As the geopolitical realities of the world march into the 21st century, Oil as a source of energy continues to baffle and haunt the economic prosperity and national security of the states, both rich and powerful alike, India, being no exception. The first step for India to get energy security is to get rid of the supply side constraints. This means evaluating the available options of supply and choosing the most secure option out of them.

India possesses a large variety of energy resources and is almost self sufficient in the solid energy resources. India is relatively far better placed in the coal production. India's position in nuclear [6] ore reserves is also comfortable and a large amount of thorium is available, which is more than sufficient for her medium and long-term needs. The recently concluded nuclear deal is a substantial move to provide much required Uranium for its existing thermal nuclear reactors. Similarly it possesses immense amount of hydroelectric resources [7] and her Gross capacity in tangible terms is 2638,000 trillion Watt Hour/years. Nevertheless, her installed Hydro Electric Capacity (HEC) is lees than satisfactory and it accounts for only 24 percent of total installed plant capacity of utilizable electricity in 2004-05. [8] Furthermore, its contribution to generated energy is as low as 15 percent of the total development. Moreover, HEP is restrained by high installation cost and its related environmental [9], social [10] and political [11] ramifications.

India's Energy Mix and the Natural Gas

The non-commercial sources of energy, like fuel wood, dung cake and agricultural waste constitute over 30 percent of total energy supply in India. These sources have been progressively substituted, over the period, by commercial sources of energy to meet the ever-increasing needs of developing economy. In India too, the non-commercial consumption is being replaced with various commercial sources of energy. Increasing use of LPG, [12] and Kerosene for fuel and lighting in rural areas is reflective of this trend.

Hydrocarbon (i.e. oil and natural gas) constitutes forty three percent of Indian commercial energy consumption. Consumption of oil has grown at the rate of 4.6 percent in India during the decade ending 2002, which is much higher in comparison to that of most of the countries in the Asia Pacific. By 2000-01, India's estimated natural gas reserves would be 763 billion cubic meters According to the Petroleum Ministry data, gas demand in the financial year 2001-02 amounted to 81.3 million standard cubic meters per day (mmscmd), compared with domestic production of 65 mmscmd. Consumption is expected to grow significantly, rising to 130 mmscmd in 2006-07, 170 mmscmd in 2011-12 and finally to 391 mmscmd in 2024-25). [13] Contrary to the world trend, Indian consumption of coal is substantially low and farther less when it comes to petroleum products. Coal provides more than double the share of energy in India as against the world average. This trend is similar to that of China, where 66.5 percent of primary energy is provided by coal as against the world average of 25 percent. [14] Both countries have large coal reserves. But coals fuels have low calorific value and are not environment friendly. The other major sources of energy have a limited potential. The energy scene before us warrants research and discussion on the concerns of energy security in which the oil and gas would play the most dominant role at least in the short and medium term. The hydrocarbon vision has been converted into prioritized action agenda for implementation in the medium and long term. The vision emphasizes on one of its goal to pursue projects to meet the deficit in demand and supply of natural gas, and facilitate availability of LNG.

Anil Kakodkar, Chairman of Atomic Energy Commission points out "for a large country like India with its over one billion population and rapid economic growth rate, no single energy resource or technology constitutes a panacea to address all issues related to availability of fuel supplies, environmental impact, particularly, climate change, and health externalities."

[15] Despite the fact that the non conventional energy sources and nuclear energy will get prominence in the coming years, hydrocarbon energy seems to be the most important component of India's Energy Mix in the coming decades and so. As worldwide demand for energy continues its relentless rise, and as the sources for oil become riskier, the energy economy is shifting inexorably towards fuel that will reconfigure the world energy mix. Just thirty years ago, oil dominated the energy economy utterly, accounting for nearly 50 percent of global demand, and leaving just 31 percent to coal and barely 20 percent to natural gas. Since then, the natural gas- or simply "gas", in industry parlance- has emerged as the fuel of choice for everything. Gas's share of the world energy mix now matches that of coal and by as early as 2025, gas, not oil, could be the world's dominant energy source [16] As at the beginning of the twentieth century petroleum oil became most important future commodity, at the beginning of the twenty first century Natural Gas begin to grasp the limelight of energy thirsty international community. Often it is termed as the energy of this century. With the discoveries of new gas fields, most Asian countries, which are heavily dependent on oil, realize that NG not only diversifies energy sources but also contributes to security of supply. Besides that, gas is a cheap, efficient and environmentally clean source of energy. Gas is incredibly versatile. It can be used in everything from power plants to gas-powered buses and taxis. It can be converted to liquid fuels and compete directly with oil. Gas also contains less carbon and more hydrogen than either oil or coal does, so not only does it emit less pollution and climate-harming carbon dioxide, but it is also refined into pure hydrogen to power fuel cells and other energy technologies of the future. [17] It is important to note that demand for natural gas is projected to account for one third of world primary energy production by 2020, and that it is estimated to grow at three times the average rate of the overall demand for all type of energy. [18]

The gas industry seeks to play an important role in the growth of the energy sector in India. Natural gas is being increasingly used as fuel by the transport sector and has major usage in the industrial sector as eco-friendly fuel. At present, gas based power projects account for 11 percent of power generation and are expected to double their share in energy supply by the year 2011-12. Hydrocarbon Vision - 2025 projects a natural gas demand of 313 million metric standard cubic meters per day (mmscmd) and 391 mmscmd by the years 2011-12 and 2024-25 from the existing demand and supply of 115 mmscmd and 65 mmscmd respectively. However, as per a recent GAIL (Gas Authority of India limited) estimate, demand for gas will grow in the country form 110 mmscmd in 2001-02 to 145, 225 and 325 mmscmd in 2006-07, 2011-12 and 2019-20 respectively.

The Global Reserves, Distribution and the Gulf

Unexploited reserves of natural gas are immense in Russia, Iran and the Arabian Peninsula. The former USSR has 38.8 percent of the world reserves, with 85 percent of it in Russia and most of the rest in the republics surrounding the Caspian Sea. Table 8.1 depicts the global spatial distribution of proven gas reserve and gas production.

Table 8.1: Top Twenty Countries with Maximum Natural Gas Reserve (as on January 1, 2009)

Gas Producing Country	Proven reserve Trillion cubic feet (tcf)	Percent Of Total World's Reserve
Russia	1680	26.9
Iran	992	15.9
Qatar	892	14.3
Saudi Arabia	258	4.1
USA	238	3.8
United Arab Emirates	214	3.4
Nigeria	184	2.9
Venezuela	171	2.7
Algeria	159	2.5

Iraq	112	1.8
Indonesia	106	1.7
Turkmenistan	94	1.5
Kazakhstan	85	1.4
Malaysia	83	1.3
Norway	82	1.3
China	80	1.3
Uzbekistan	65	1.0
Kuwait	63	1.0
Egypt	59	0.9
Canada	58	0.9
Rest of the World	581	9.3
Top Twenty Countries	5,674	90
The Gulf Region	2581	41.3
World	6,254	100

Source: "Worldwide Look at Reserve and Production", Oil and Gas Journal, Vol. 106, No. 48 (December 22, 2008), pp. 22-23.

Table 8.2: The Gulf Countries' Natural Gas Reserve

Country	**Proven reserve (tcf) 2009**	**Percent of Total World's Reserve**	**Percent of Total Gulf's Reserve**
Iran	992	15.9	38.4
Qatar	892	14.3	34.5
Saudi Arabia	258	4.1	10.0
United Arab Emirates	214	3.4	8.3
Iraq	112	1.8	4.4
Kuwait	63	1.0	2.4
Oman	30	0.5	1.1
Yemen	17	0.3	0.6
Bahrain	3	0.05	0.1
The Gulf	2581	41.3	100
The World	6,254	100	--

Source: Compiled on the bases of "Worldwide Look at Reserve and Production", Oil and Gas Journal, Vol. 106, No. 48 (December 22, 2008), pp. 22-23 and http://www.eoearth.org extracted on 22nd August 2009.

Figure 8.1: Natural Gas Reserve in the Gulf (in TFC)

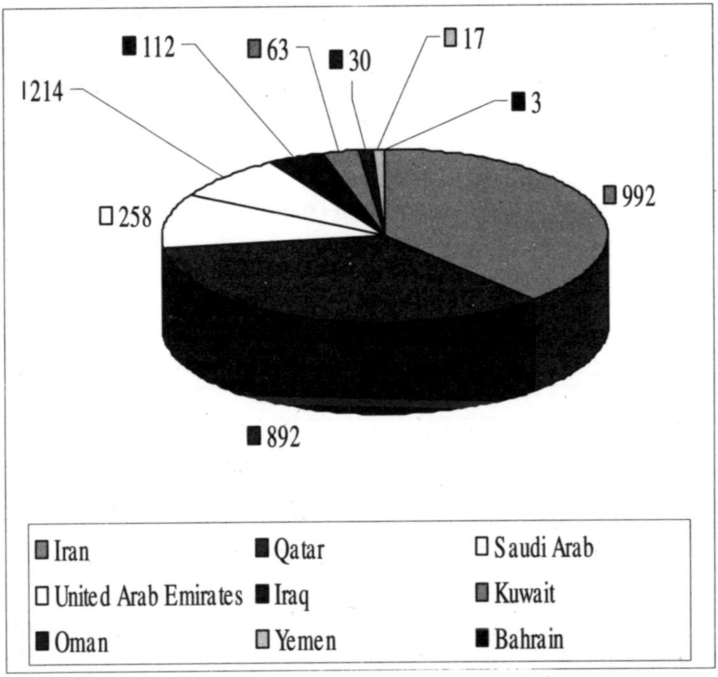

Source: Based on the facts Compiled on the bases of "Worldwide Look at Reserve and Production", Oil and Gas Journal, Vol. 106, No. 48 (December 22, 2008), pp. 22-23 and http://www.eoearth.org extracted on 22nd August 2009.

The West Asia excluding Turkey holds more than 41 percent of the proven world gas reserves (Table 8.1 and Table 8.2). Among the Gulf countries Iran, Qatar, Saudi Arab and United Arab Emirates are the most important countries as far as the Natural Gas Reserve is concerned accounting for as much as 91 percent region's Gas reserve. Country-wise, Iran, Qatar, Saudi Arabia and the UAE have the second, third, fourth and fifth largest natural gas reserves in the world. Further more their Natural Gas reserves remained largely under exploited and reserve/production ratio of these countries is such that they are capable of providing long term answer to

India's requirements (Table 8.3). It is estimated that 51 percent of the world's gas reserves, primarily from this region, are exportable surpluses. [19]

Table 8.3: World's Natural Gas Production

Gas Producing Country	Gross Gas Production (Bcm) 2004	Reserve / Production Ratio
Russia	589.1	81.5
USA	542.9	9.8
Canada	182.8	8.8
UK	95.9	6.1
Iran	85.5	321.6
Algeria	82.0	55.4
Norway	78.5	30.4
Indonesia	73.3	34.9
Netherlands	68.8	21.7
Saudi Arabia	64.0	105.5
Uzbekistan	55.8	33.3
Turkmenistan	54.6	53.1
Malaysia	53.9	45.7
UAE	45.8	132.3
Argentina	44.9	13.5

Source: BP Statistical Review, 2005.

Iran

Iran is a bonafide superpower in natural gas, all the more so because its potential has barely been tapped. With the present rate of extraction the gas resources of Iran will last for more than 320 years. Despite the friction over nuclear issues, Iran forges ahead on the gas front, with plans to develop the huge Pars field (first the south, then the north); the Khuff reservoir of the Salman oil field; the Zireh field in Bushehr province; the Homa field in southern Fars province; the Tabnak in southern Iran; the onshore Nar-Kangan fields; the Aghar and Dalan fields in Fars province; and the Sarkhoun and Mand fields. Most of Iran's attention has focused on the giant

South Pars offshore field, which is being developed in 28 phases. [20] The South Pars is Iran's largest energy project, and over US$ 15 billion in investment has been committed. The participant list is a virtual "Who's Who" of the international energy business, including many countries whose governments are occasionally at odds with Iran. [21] Iran signed a US$ 1.2 billion contract with a consortium of two foreign and two domestic companies to gather associated gas, previously flared or re-injected, from the Nowruz, Soroush, Hendijan, and Behregansar fields. This is an attempt to monetize "stranded gas." In addition, BG and NIOC have plans to develop a US$ 2.2-billion LNG plant at Bandar Tombak on the Persian Gulf. [22] Iran, besides being an important and potential gas supplier from the Gulf region, is also placed in a unique geo-strategic location, as a corridor for trans-shipment of Central Asian-Caspian oil transiting through Pakistani coastal, areas.

Iran presents bright prospect for India in the Gulf owing to former's anti-west sentiment emerging out of USA's animosity towards it. Tehran is carefully building an alliance with Moscow — an alliance that could control more than half the world's gas supplies. India on account of its good relationship with these countries can leapfrog in Iran vis-à-vis other gas hungry countries including USA and China. However, increasing interest of the Obama regime in Iran could add new dimension to the Geo-politics of Natural Gas in the country

Qatar

Qatar, a small Middle Eastern country with no oil production to speak of, contains 910 Trillion Cubic Feet (TCF) of proven natural gas reserves, third only to Russia and Iran. Qatar's offshore North Field is the largest natural gas field in the world. The country has other relatively large fields, but none comes close to the size of the North Field. Qatar is an obvious source of LNG, and two consortia are already exporting LNG, with many new additions on the way. [23]

Through these projects Qatar has already become a substantial natural gas exporter. It is expected that in a few years Gulf countries will be achieving significant successes in production and export of gas. The Qatari government firmly believes that this is where the country's economic future lies, and is currently developing an integrated natural gas pipeline grid that will connect Qatar, the UAE and Oman, with the possibility of a sub-sea connection linking Oman , Pakistan and India .

Saudi Arabia

Along with crude oil, Saudi Arabia has very large reserve of natural gas. Most of this gas is associated gas, produced jointly with the crude oil. Until recently, Saudi has not been a large natural gas producer, and is still not a large exporter of gas. It has exported natural gas liquids since 1962 but exporting large quantities of gas has proved uneconomical due to the distance to the western consumption centers. [24] According to the *Oil and Gas Journal*, Saudi Arabia has the fourth largest proven natural gas reserves in the world, estimated at 253 trillion cubic feet (Tcf). Over the last decade and a half, Saudi Aramco has added around 75 Tcf of non-associated reserves, including the fields: Mazalij, Manjura, Shaden, Niban, Tinat, Al-Waar, and Fazran in the deep Khuff, Unaizah and Jauf reservoirs. However, around 57 percent of Saudi Arabia's proven natural gas reserves consist of associated gas at the giant onshore Ghawar field and the offshore Safaniya and Zuluf fields. The Ghawar oil field alone accounts for approximately one-third of the country's proven natural gas reserves. Both associated and non-associated natural gas has also been discovered in the country's extreme northwest, at Midyan, and in the Empty Quarter (Rub al Khali) in the country's southeastern desert. The Rub al Khali is believed to contain natural gas reserves potentially as high as 300 Tcf, although these are not proven. The area remains under exploration. [25]

The UAE

The UAE possesses nearly 10 percent of the world's total reserve, and there is no doubt that oil will continue to provide the income for both economic growth and the expansion of social services for several more decades at least. In the coming years, natural gas will play an increasingly important role in the UAE's development. The UAE is estimated to have natural gas reserves that will last for anything up to 170 years.

Apart from above mentioned major countries having natural gas recourses, Oman's proven natural gas reserves stood at 30 trillion cubic feet (Tcf) as of January 2007. Expanding natural gas production has become a chief focus of Oman's strategy to diversify its economy away from the oil sector. Nearly two-thirds of Oman's LNG exports went to South Korea, while the remainder went to Japan, Taiwan, Spain, France, and the United States. [26] Bahrain has natural gas reserves of about 3.25 trillion cubic feet (Tcf), much of it associated gas from the Awali oil field. According to the 2008 BP Statistical Energy Survey, Yemen had 2007 proved natural gas reserves of 0.48 trillion cubic metres, the bulk of which are concentrated in the Marib-Jawf fields. Despite Yemen's longstanding plans to develop an export-based natural gas industry, Yemen has yet to produce any natural gas. Yemen is eagerly looking to exports of super chilled gas to help offset the impact of falling oil output on state revenues, despite obstacles ranging from domestic unrest to piracy in the Gulf of Aden. [27]

Emerging Geopolitics for Natural Gas

The importance of the region's gas reserve is likely to grow in coming years mainly because increase in domestic consumption and export of gas to East and South Asia, while gas exploitation by oil companies and transportation costs are becoming increasingly competitive. Political relations in the gas sector matter even more than in the oil sector, since gas network are much more vulnerable to political and economic disruption than oil. [28] Since gas networks increase the interdependence of the societies they connect, they create a pressure on all the countries along the transaction route to minimize their political differences and cement their economies together. Once the network is paid for, the benefits of stable gas supplies provide strong incentives for countries to cooperate. [29] At the regional level, in the recent years, as relations inside the GCC improved and regional demand for gas increased, some elements of the GCC regional gas pipeline network have moved ahead. [30] The UAE has taken the initiative in developing an intra- Gulf gas network that could eventually link up with the Indian subcontinent. [31] Throughout the region, vastly increased domestic consumption of electricity, linked to growing demand for domestic hydrocarbons for power generation, petrochemicals and desalination are the incentives for increased usage of natural gas - Saudi Arabia, as an example, has made increased natural gas production a priority, aiming to triple output to 15 billion cubic feet a day by 2009. Growth in the gas sector is taking place in the domestic market, where the use of natural gas has increased dramatically (in Abu Dhabi, for example, gas consumption has doubled over the last decade to its current level of 4 billion cubic feet a day), as well as in the highly lucrative export market, with global natural gas demand on a steep upward curve. [32] Governments throughout the Middle East region are therefore committing substantial investment to ensure that their natural gas infrastructure is in shape to take full advantage of the growth in the sector.

As far as involvement of external payers is concerned, the USA, guided by 'the Rimland Theory' has always been important player in the region. There have been frequent tensions and dilemmas both within and between USA administration and corporate interests. Since the fall or the weakening of its regional allies (principally Iran under the Sah and Saudi Arabia), US state policy entailed the support of each of its allies- in part because of tensions within and between them- and the 'dual containment' and weakening of regional challenges, mostly Iran and Iraq (which included supporting both sides during the Iran-Iraq war, and since redefined as 'rogue' states). In terms of stability, this policy has prolonged regional tension by preventing the emergence at the regional level of hegemony or effective co-operative partnership. [33]

A report commissioned by the European Union has found that a gas pipeline linking the GCC to Europe would be economically viable, and could become a reality by 2025. Part of a much larger plan to link the power grids and water systems of the GCC countries, the projected pipeline would have huge economic benefits for the region, particularly with natural gas consumption throughout the EU expected to double over the next 15 years. [34] Despite their economic importance and dependence on Gulf hydrocarbon, the European states played a limited rol^ in recent decision making process with in the region. Incapacity to forge a common foreign policy towards the middle East was most clearly demonstrated by the divergence of views on the USA-led War in Iraq, with the UK actively participating while France threatened to use its UN veto against the use of force. [35] Russia is probably the country with the most immediate stakes in the reshaping of the Persian Gulf. From the perspective of a strategic security planner in Moscow, the vulnerabilities of Russia's energy-export corridors are a source of significant concern. [36]

India in the Region

In recent year India is particularly considered as the most important new buyer of liquefied natural gas (LNG). India has been exploring avenues to strengthen relations with West Asian countries. India needs natural gas and is negotiating with several countries, including Qatar. Since mid 1990s, India's gas market has mainly attracted the Gulf States such as Qatar, Iran, Oman and UAE. Qatar's state-owned energy company RasGas wrapped its biggest-ever contract with two deals to supply LNG to supply LNG to India's government owned

Petronet Company, which made a firm order in July 1999 for 7.5 million tone of LNG per year, over a period of 25 years, starting at the beginning of 2004. India's private company Reliance is also holding talks with these countries for the initial purchase of 5 million tones per year of LNG over a 25years period beginning in 2004. This also points towards India's growing inter-dependency on the Arabian Gulf countries.

Pipeline Diplomacy

India has an ever-growing appetite for natural gas which is to some extent met by LNG. Pipelines are vital for carrying the gaseous form of hydrocarbon from these regions to India as this is cost effective, efficient and easy to carry. In this regard, the ongoing pipeline transportation network proposals may not be too expansive as the massive plan to import LNG from the countries like Qatar, Oman, Iran and UAE. Iran and Pakistan have signed an MOU for a possible 1,600-mile, US$4-billion gas pipeline from Iran to Pakistan and potentially, on to India. SAGE, an Indian private sector initiative, is working with a global consortium to create a US$3 billion natural gas transportation infrastructure linking the Gulf region with India. Its first phase would bring 31 MMcf/d to the Indian west coast. The SAGE energy corridor, with completion planned by early 2014, would allow suppliers from West Asia to deliver natural gas to buyers in India, at market price, after payment of SAGE's transit tariff. Plans are to source the gas from Qatar, Iran and Iraq which hold reserves of about 2,000 Trillion Cubic Feet (Tcf.) [37] Each pipeline would deliver about 8 Tcf natural gas to India over 25 years. The project features an upstream West Asia natural gas-gathering system connecting multiple gas sources to the coast of the Arabian Peninsula. From there, the deepwater pipelines would cross the Arabian Sea to the south of the territorial waters and economic exclusion zones of all third party countries and would mainly follow a route, reaching a depth of 3,500m, which was extensively surveyed 15 years ago. [38]

Conclusion

Large quantities of natural gas essentially involve costless production in the Gulf region because much of the natural gas is associated with the oil production. Until recently a large part of natural gas was simply flared as downstream activities related to it, had been perceived uneconomic. This Euro-Atlantic perception was mainly caused by the remoteness of the western countries from the region as. But the fossil fuel based environmental concerns have forced the west to rethink over the importance of the natural gas. In this context the Persian Gulf is increasingly becoming critical to India's vital interests. India is one the most proximate countries from the region. Nevertheless the Gulf can put challenge to India as the regions have been characterized by turbulence and ideological tensions. The Straits of Harmuz remain the critical choke point for gas flow; and the offshore installations in the Arabian Sea require protection on potential scenario relates to the geo-political and military-technology factors. Similarly, optimistic predictions regarding oil and gas availability in the region has created a situation where global players started to show renewed interest. Emerging domestic, regional and transnational geopolitics in the region could pose challenges to India's interests but could also provide opportunities for India to feed its long term natural gas requirements.

Notes

1. India's primary annual energy consumption is 17.677 British Thermal Unit (Btu). The USA (99.856 Btu), China (73.808 Btu), Russia (30.386 Btu) and Japan (22.786 Btu) occupies first four places. For Detail see, Table E.1, International Energy Annual 2006, Energy Information Administration, extracted from http://www.analyst-network.com/article.php?art_id=3113, on 22 August 2009.

2. Calculated on the basis of *Annual Report 2004-05*, Ministry of Petroleum, Government of India.
3. As structure of economy changes from primary to secondary and then tertiary this leads to change in per capita energy consumption in a big way.
4. At the one hand change in pattern of economy, rising contribution of service sector and whooping rate of urbanization have expanded the purchasing capacity of a large section of people at the other hand this scenario has also led to enlargement of middle class which is not only prone to consumerism is also increases the number of buyers.
5. Increasingly the government is keen to replace the existing coal based thermal power stations by less polluting petroleum and natural gas based thermal power stations. At the same time during the last a few years the government is aggressively pursuing a strategy of three pronged nuclear power plants development. Existing nuclear reactors are Uranium based Thermal reactors, however India, with help of Russia, is also developing Thorium Based Fast Breeder Reactor and is a part of Consortium of countries developing Fusion based thermonuclear reactor.
6. Nuclear fuel is any material that can be consumed to derive nuclear energy, by analogy to chemical fuel that is burned to derive energy. By far the most common type of nuclear fuel is heavy fissile elements that can be made to undergo nuclear fission chain reactions in a nuclear fission reactor; *nuclear fuel* can refer to the material or to physical objects (for example fuel bundles composed of fuel rods) composed of the fuel material, perhaps mixed with structural, neutron moderating, or neutron reflecting materials. The most common fissile nuclear fuels are ^{235}U and ^{239}Pu.
7. Hydroelectricity is electricity obtained from hydropower. Most hydroelectric power comes from the potential energy of dammed water driving a water turbine and generator. Less common variations make use of water's kinetic energy or undammed sources such as tidal power. Hydroelectricity is a renewable energy source.
8. *Economic Survey 2004-05*, Government of India. p. 78.
9. Dam sites are prone to deforestation, mass wasting and submergence of vast area of useful land.

10. All major dam sites are witnessing strong resentment and anti-dam movements.
11. Rivers are either interstate or international water bodies leading to interstate and international conflicts.
12. Liquified petroleum gas (also called liquefied petroleum gas, liquid petroleum gas, LPG, LP Gas, or autogas) is a mixture of hydrocarbon gases used as a fuel in heating appliances and vehicles, and increasingly replacing chlorofluorocarbons as an aerosol propellant and a refrigerant to reduce damage to the ozone layer. Varieties of LPG bought and sold include mixes that are primarily propane, mixes that are primarily butane, and mixes including both propane and butane, depending on the season—in winter more propane, in summer more butane. Propylene and butylenes are usually also present in small concentration. A powerful odorant, ethanethiol, is added so that leaks can be detected easily. LPG is manufactured during the refining of crude oil, or extracted from oil or gas streams as they emerge from the ground.
13. Malakar, S. N. (ed.), India's Energy Security and the Gulf, (New Delhi: Academic Excellence, 2006), p. 322.
14. Ibid.
15. Anil Kakodkar, Energy in India for the Coming Decades, extracted from http://www.dae.gov.in/iaea/ak-paris0305.doc, on 23rd Auq, 2009.
16. Roberts, Paul, *The end of oil: On the edge of a perilous new world*, (New York: Houghton Miffin, 2005), p. 166.
17. Ibid, p. 167.
18. Cordesman, Anthony H., *Saudi Arabia Enters the Twenty-First Century: The Political, Foreign Policy, Economic, and Energy Dimensions*, (Westport: Praeger Publishers, 2003), p. 512.
19. Markaz al-Imārāt lil-Dirāsāt wa-al-Buḥūth al-Istirātījīyah, *The future of natural gas in the world energy market,* (Abu Dhabi: The Emirates Centre for Strategic Studies and Research, 2001), p. 14.
20. Kumar, Pranav, "Oil Geopolitics in the Persian Gulf and India's Energy Security", in abhyankar, R. M (ed.), *West Asia and the Region: defining India's Role*, (New Delhi: Academic Foundation, 2008), p. 633.

21. The Energy Tribune, Posted on June.12, 2006, http://www.energytribune.com/articles.cfm?aid=152, accessed on 21st August 2009.
22. Ibid.
23. Kumar, n.xiv, p. 634.
24. Johany, Ali D, Michel Berne and J. Wilson Mixon, *The Saudi Arabian Economy*, (Beckenham: Croom Helm, 1986), p. 46.
25. http://www.eia.doe.gov/emeu/cabs/Saudi_Arabia/NaturalGas.html accessed on 02nd August 2009.
26. http://www.eoearth.org/article/Energy_profile_of_Oman accessed on 22nd July, 2009.
27. http://www.mbendi.com/indy/oilg/as/ye/p0005.htm accessed on 2nd Aug, 2009.
28. Billon, Philippe Le, ed., *Geopolitics of resource wars: resource dependence, governance and violence,* (New York: Frank Caas, 2005), p. 116.
29. Ibid.
30. Victor, David G., Amy Jaffe and Mark H. Hayes, *Natural Gas and Geopolitics from 1970 to 2040* (Cambridge: Cambridge University Press, 2006), p. 259.
31. Butt, Gerald, "Oil and Gas in the UAE", in Ibrahim Al Abed, and Peter Hellyer, eds, (London: Trident, 2001), *United Arab Emirates: A New Perspective,* p. 231.
32. http://www.ameinfo.com/60285.html accessed on 13th June, 2009.
33. Billon, n. 28, p. 117.
34. http://www.ameinfo.com/60285.html accessed on 24th July, 2009
35. Billon, n. 28, p. 125.
36. Ibid, p. 124.
37. "India Mulls Deepwater Natural Gas Pipeline System", *Pipeline and Gas Journal*, July 2009, vol. 236, no. 7, p. 56.
38. Ibid.

9

US-Iran Rivalries in the Region and its Implications for India

M. Mahtab Alam Rizvi

Introduction

The overthrow of the Shah in 1979 has been considered as a turning point in Iran-West relations. The US has played a vital role in shaping the western orientation toward Iran. Iran with its oil and gas resources, its geopolitical and strategic location and its unique place in the region and the Islamic world has been viewed as an important regional and international player. Meanwhile Iran's domestic process is a central and incorporated part of social and political change in West Asia, the whole Islamic world and developing countries. Iran is located at the centre of the world's largest resource of energy; it includes prominently the global oil and natural gas checkpoints at the Strait of Hormuz. It provides the cheapest and the shortest transit route at the heart of the ancient Silk Road for the transport of energy resources from the Caspian Sea basin to the world markets through the Persian Gulf; and it is the most populated country with one of the largest industrial bases in the vast region stretching from the Caspian Sea to Eastern Mediterranean.

Over the past several decades, history, geography and natural resources have contributed to the rise of Iran as a prominent regional power. With a population approaching 72 million people by 2008, [1] the Islamic Republic is by far the most populous country in the Persian Gulf. This has given the country with a large pool of labour, a sizeable middle-class. Iran is world's fourth oil producer and Organisation of Petroleum Exporting Countries (OPEC) second largest exporter and around 10 percent of the world's proven oil reserves and 15 percent of world natural gas proven reserves. Finally, Iran is considered an important gate way to the energy rich Central Asia region. Given all these facts, it can be said that the stability of Iran has been crucial for the all over the world in general and west Asia in particular. [2]

During the Shah regime the US enjoyed close and warm relations with Iran at political and economic level. [3] The US was an ally of the late Shah of Iran, Mohammad Reza Pahlavi, who ruled from 1941 until his ouster in February 1979. The Shah was anti-Communist, and the US viewed his government as a bulwark against the expansion of Soviet influence in the Gulf. In 1951, he appointed a popular nationalist parliamentarian, Mohammad Mossadeq, as Prime Minister of Iran. Mossadeq was widely considered left-leaning, and the US was wary of his policies, which included his drive for nationalization of the oil industry. Mossadeq's followers started a rebellion in August 1953 when the Shah endeavoured to dismiss Mossadeq, and finally the Shah fled. The Shah was restored by a Central Intelligence Agency (CIA) supported coup, and Mossadeq was arrested. [4]

The post revolutionary Islamic Iran appears to have two governments: a state structure with an "elected" president and parliament, and Expediency Council and an unelected religious-ideological structure with a Supreme Leader (who is designated for life and has total control over foreign policy of the country and all aspects of government and the institutions of the republic), Council of Guardians that contest each other. These are in turn supported by numerous intelligence centres, security organizations, and militias competing with one another. Iran's foreign policy is based on sometimes competing objectives. Iran's pragmatic foreign policy goals include, not surprisingly, protecting itself from external threats and building trade ties with foreign countries in general and its neighbouring countries in particular. Due to Iran's strategic location on the north side of the Gulf, it is in a position to intimidate oil fields in Saudi Arabia, Kuwait, Iraq, and the United Arab Emirates, which together possess more than half of the world's known oil reserves. Iran also sits crossways the Strait of Hormuz, the narrow waterway through which, daily, around 40% of the world's oil exports pass.

Iranian Elections and the Western Responses

Soon after the fall of Baghdad, Iran was made a controversial case by the western powers on two major pretexts—free and fair elections and uranium enrichment/nuclear programme. It is a fact that western powers neither approved Iranian presidential election (2005) nor expressed confidence in the government headed by President Mahmoud Ahmadinejad. The West also denounced the June 2009 Presidential election and victory of Ahmadinejad. Though, recent Iranian election broke all previous records. Reports suggest that 85 percent of the eligible voters (46.2 million) turned out to vote. Besides, people used modern technologies such as blogs, website and text messages for election campaign. In some places voting hours were extended for several hours to accommodate the flow of voters. The election was marked by televised debates of the candidates, in one-on-one format. President Mahmoud Ahmadinejad won this 10th presidential election by a surprisingly wide margin. He secured 62.63 percent votes. His nearest rival and former Prime Minister (1981 to 1989), Mir-Hossein Mousavi got only 33.75 percent. Mousavi supporters responded to the result with the most serious unrest in the capital in a decade and charges that the result was the work of manipulation and fraud. US President, Barack Obama stressed after the election result that he was deeply troubled by post-election violence in Iran and urged the Islamic republic to investigate voting irregularities in a way that would not result in bloodshed. [5] Other Western countries like Britain and France also joined with the US. French President Nicolas Sarkozy said his country stands by Britain amid tensions with Iran over the post-election unrest.

British Prime Minister Gordon Brown also pointed out that "the Iranian regime must be clear that we will act together with our European partners". [6]

In response, Iran's supreme leader, Ayatollah Ali Khamenei's warned Western governments saying that "some leaders of Western countries at the level of president, prime minister and foreign minister openly intervened in Iran's internal affairs that had nothing to do with them. Then, they said they don't intervene in Iran's internal affairs". [7] He also added that Iran will pay attention to the remarks and behaviors of Western governments and it will definitely have a negative impact on future relations with Iran.

Iran's Nuclear Programme and the US Standoff

On November 4, 1979, Iranian students occupied the United States (US) Embassy in Tehran and fifty-two Americans were held hostage for 444 days. On April 7, 1980, the US broke diplomatic relations with Islamic Republic. However, the US has held discussions with Iranian representatives on particular issues of concern over the years. The US and Iranian diplomats cooperated during operations to overthrow the Taliban in 2001 and during the Bonn Conference in 2002 that established a broad-based government in Afghanistan under the leadership of President Hamid Karzai. The Secretary of State, her Iranian counterpart, and others met at talks on Iraq in Sharm El Sheikh, Egypt, on May 3, 2007. The US and Iranian ambassadors to Iraq took part in face-to-face talks in Baghdad, with Iraqi officials in attendance, on May 28, 2007. Representatives from the three countries also engaged in a second round of talks on July 24, 2007. Ambassadors met for a third discussion on August 6, 2007. The US considers, however, that normal relations are impossible until Iran's policies change.

Although, one of the most complex security challenges for the US administration is undoubtedly Iran's quest for nuclear weapons. Iran's defiance of international opinion over its nuclear programme has led to a situation where the US has indicated that were diplomacy to fail, recourse to military options might be pursued. [8] The United States (US), the European Union (EU) and the IAEA (International Atomic Energy Agency) collaborated against Iran on its nuclear programme. Despite being signatory to be NPT both the IAEA and the United Nations Security Council (UNSC) have raised their doubts and questions over Iran's nuclear issue. Tensions over Iran's nuclear programme commenced in November 2003, when an IAEA [9] report detailed evidence of Iran developing a secret nuclear enrichment programme, even as it remains a signatory to the Nuclear Non-Proliferation Treaty (NPT). Under international pressure, Iran signed the Additional Protocol to the Safeguards Agreements on December 18, 2003, agreeing to suspend all uranium-enrichment as well as cooperate fully with the IAEA in resolving questions regarding nuclear programme. This commitment was not to last as Iran accelerated its nuclear programme. On June 6, 2006, the five-plus-one powers (China, France, Russia, UK, the US and Germany) offered Iran a substantial package of economic cooperation and assistance if Iran abandoned its nuclear enrichment process. Iran rejected the offer saying that it was developing a nuclear enrichment programme for purely 'civilian purposes' and not for nuclear weapons. The US and European countries are not convinced about Iran's claim that its nuclear programme is only for civilian purposes as Iran's quest for energy security through the nuclear route seems odd considering the fact that it is the world's fourth largest oil producer and also has the world's second largest reserves of natural gas. [10]

However, the recent two reports on Iran's nuclear activities, submitted by IAEA Chief El Baradei on November 15, 2007 and February 22, 2008 acknowledge the progress being made regarding Iran's nuclear programme, and Iran's cooperation with IAEA teams is considered positive. [11] Despite IAEA positive reports and Iranian cooperation with the agency, the UNSC moved towards third set of UNSC sanctions. The UNSC imposed third set of economic and trade sanctions against Iran on March 3, 2008 for refusing to halt nuclear programme. Now the West is seeking more pressure and fourth set of UNSC sanctions [12] that was imposed in June 2010.

However, recent Obama's landmark appeal to the Iranian people for a shift away from decades of confrontation was a significant move in the right direction. Obama's videotaped message on March 20, 2009 (on the occasion of Nowruz) stated that "the US wants the Islamic Republic of Iran to take its rightful place in the community of nations but it comes with real responsibilities..." Obama's offers came 30 years after the US broke off diplomatic relations with Iran. The President had promised in his election campaign to negotiate with Iran directly with a fresh approach and reach out to the Iranian people. At the same time Obama also warned Iranian leaders that 'this process will not be advanced by threats or terror or arms…we seek instead engagement that is honest and grounded in mutual respect.' Although, Iranian officials appear cautious given the Supreme Leader Ayatollah Ali Khamenei's statement that Iran does not see any change in US policy towards its government. Khamanei asked how Obama could wish the Iranian people and leaders even as he continues to blame Iran of supporting terrorism and seeking nuclear weapons. [13] He also added that there would be no change in relations between the two countries unless the president brought an end to US hostility towards Iran and brought "real changes" in foreign policy. Khamenei detailed a long list of Iranian grievances against the US over the past 30 years, saying it was continuing to interfere in Iranian internal affairs. He mentioned US sanctions against Iran, its support for the Iraqi dictator Saddam Hussein during his 1980-88 war against Iran and the shooting down of an Iranian airliner over the Persian Gulf in 1988. He also accused the US of provoking ethnic tension in Iran and said Washington's accusations that

Iran was seeking nuclear weapons were evidence of hostility. "Have you released Iranian assets? Have you lifted oppressive sanctions? Have you given up mudslinging and making accusations against the great Iranian nation and its officials? Have you given up your unconditional support for the Zionist regime? [14] Although, this is undoubtedly a welcome departure from past trends in Iran-US relations. The US has taken a positive step forward. It is now Iran's turn to create the best of the opportunity provided to it.

The Iraq Factor in Iran-US Relations

The US continues to allege that the Iranian government threatens peace and security, through production and export of ballistic missiles and backing of Shi'ite insurgents in Iraq. The annual US terrorism report released on April 30, 2008 declared Iran the 'most active state sponsor of terrorism.' It also silently raised the official number of US and Iraqi soldiers allegedly killed by Iranian actions in Iraq from 'hundreds' to 'thousands', which surprised even the most skeptical of observers. Iranian officials categorically rejected US allegations of supporting insurgent groups in Iraq. The US also alleged that Iran was encouraging a public campaign in Iraq against the proposed US-Iraq security agreement, popularly known as Status of Forces Agreement (SOFA). Despite, Iran and the anti-US Shi'ite cleric Muqtada al-Sadr, who has close ties with Tehran opposition, the security agreement was approved by Iraq's government as well as its parliament on November 27, 2008. The SOFA lays down the terms under which the foreign military is allowed to operate within Iraq. It is more concerned with the legal issues associated with military personnel and their operations. Under the agreement, the US is not only permitted to maintain military bases in Iraq, but it also has the right to carry out military operations from those bases against other countries without consultation with the Iraqi government after the United Nations mandate expires at the end of 2008. The SOFA would establish a long-term security relationship between Iraq and the US and the latter is quite upbeat about it. [15]

The major question of 'what to do with Iran' remains at the top of the agenda for the US and Western policy makers. Iran's multiple pronouncements and defiance of international opinion has had the effect of generating varied western opinion. Yet, three decades after the creation of the Islamic Republic of Iran, the US has not developed a clear policy to deal with it. With multiple centres of power in Tehran, no political (or religious) leader in Iran can directly engage in dialogue with the US without being immediately accused by rivals of straying from the anti-US line defined by Khomeini. However, Iraq's government appeared to back away from its claims of Iranian interference in the internal affairs of Iraq, to convey a message of friendship and amity to Iran. Iraq's willingness to back Iran shows the closeness between the two that further expanded when Iranian President, Mahmoud Ahmadinejad visited Iraq in March 2008 – this was the first visit of an Iranian President to Iraq since 1979. Iraqi Prime Minister Nouri al-Maliki also paid a reciprocal visit to Iran on June 7-9, 2008. Both countries also signed a memorandum of Understanding (MoU), to boost bilateral defence cooperation. Iraq is Iran's largest export market with Iraq importing an estimated $ 1.3 billion in goods from Iran in 2006. Estimates for non-oil trade since 2006 have reached as high as $ 2 billion, some 97 percent of which is one way from Iran to Iraq. Iran expects trade to rise to $ 10 billion over the next five years. [16]

Though, Iran supports the principle of universal suffrage in Iraq to secure a Shiite political majority, but Iran is not sure whether a Shiite dominated Government in Iraq will fulfil its interests. Firstly, Iraqi Shiites are nationalists to the core and they had defended their home country against Iran during Iran-Iraq war. Secondly, the leading Iraqi clerics, including Grand Ayatollah Ali-al-Sistani, strongly rejected Khomeini's state model of Velayat-e-Faqih (Rule of the Faqih). Iran also does not want to see of a rival Shiite Islamic Republic in Iraq. No doubt the major faultline between the *Shias* and the *Sunnis* in the Gulf region is receiving greater attention because of the sectarian violence/politics taking place in Iraq at the moment. The Sunni Arab minority, including Saddam Hussain and most of the Baath party members spent the past decades suppressing the Shiites. Even today, with the Baath party dissolved, and Saddam gone, majority Shiites group (65%) in Iraq are assuming power and replacing the Sunnis. The resultant sectarian conflict has engulfed Iraq and attracted the attention of the world to the sectarian divide in a major way.

In the light of prevailing situation in Iraq, the US now distinguishes more between extremists and moderates than between dictators and democrats. Both Washington and Riyadh are keenly interested in containing Iran's influence in the region, especially in Iraq. To curtail the influence of Iran, recently, US signed a deal with Saudi Arabia for the transfer of 900 of the precision-guided bomb kits worth $ 123 million that would give Saudi forces highly accurate targeting abilities. The US also proposed an arms package worth $ 20 billion to Saudi Arabia; the UAE and Kuwait, which included Patriot missiles.

Iran's Relations with the Gulf Countries and Sectarian Divide

In the West Asian region particularly Saudi Arabia and Iran have differing approaches to regional issues, which is often being projected as *Shia-Sunni* divide by many observers. In fact, it is true that there is a perceptible divide in the region. Some commentators even argue that Saudi mediation for effecting the Mecca agreement between the two main Palestinian factions was a product of Riyadh's desire to reassert Sunni influence in the region. The Saudis are indeed concerned about the growing influence of the *Shias* in the region, which they ascribe to the assertive policies of Iran.

Over the last couple of years, there have been also arguments about the re-emergence of *Shia-Sunni* divide in the region. Shia-Sunni conflicts, along the lines of those seen in Iraq, will constitute a major faultline in the region. Viewed from this perspective, the political conduct of Iran or Hezbollah could be interpreted as a reawakening of *Shia* identity. But this view is questionable.

Saudi Arabia and other Gulf Countries, with predominant Sunni populations, harbour deep suspicions about Iran's rising power. But at the same time, Arab allies are also worried about the world economy suffers badly if the US-Iran dispute turns into military action due to Iranian stands on nuclear enrichment programme. Saudi Arabia is worried about the prospect of a nuclear Iran. The Saudi regime is also fearful about the unrest Tehran could foster and support in the *Shia* Muslim population, which is in a majority in eastern Saudi Arabia. Saudis have expressed their concerns in recent years. For example, Mohammad Abdullah al-Zulfa, Member of Saudi Shura Council, has warned Iran as saying that "as a Gulf area, we don't want to see Iran as the major power in the region. And we do not want to see Iran having a nuclear weapon, where it will be a major threat to the stability of the Gulf region and Arab world altogether". [17]

Jordan's King Abdullah II also warned that a *Shia*-dominated power in Iraq could build a special relationship with Iran, Syria, the Lebanese Hezbollah and the Hamas in Palestine. This will create a "crescent …that will be very destabilizing for the Gulf countries and for the whole region." [18] The age-old enmity between Shiites and Sunnis and mutual antipathy between Arabs and Iranians are powerful obstacles to Iran's ambitions in the West Asia where religiously and culturally it remains isolated as ever. Tehran is upset that the Gulf Cooperation Council (GCC) states were looking for a counter-weight to Iran's growing power, rather than trying to develop a strategy of cooperation and collective effort to counter the US and western forces in the region.

Beyond the Sectarian Divide in the Gulf

Despite the US efforts to cultivate Arabs support against Iran, Saudi Arabia and Iran came together after sectarian violence in Iraq inflamed the region. Lebanon became the first state in which both countries agreed to coordinate their activities in order to alleviate its growing sectarian and religious divide. Iran and Saudi Arabia also worked with some success in Iraq, where the Saudi intelligence could exercise its influence over some of the Al Qaeda tribal groups. Iranian influence among Iraqis particularly the Shias and Kurds is well known. The Arab League, comprising of 22-nations, recently adopted a resolution, assigned the Saudi monarch, Abdullah bin Abdul Aziz, the task of undertaking efforts to resolve the Israel-Palestine dispute. Saudi Arabia hosted the Mecca peace summit in February 2007 to resolve the dispute between the two rival Palestinian factions. Subsequently, both Hamas and Fatah agreed to form a unity government to Israel's dismay. The two factions also realised that the goal of their unity government was to stop inter-Palestinian fighting that claimed dozens of Palestinian lives. Iran has also adopted a positive posture over the issue.

For further boost up the relations between the GCC and Iran, in an interesting development, the GCC invited Iran for the first time in December 2007 to attend its summit meeting held in Doha. The GCC groups Bahrain, Kuwait, Oman, Qatar, Saudi Arabia and the United Arab Emirates (UAE). The GCC was established in 1981 to foster multilateral co-operation in the Persian Gulf, but had adopted an exclusionary policy vis-à-vis Iran though the latter was an important actor in regional politics and economy. The invitation to Iran seems to point to a GCC initiative to overcome differences and act together for the larger good of the region. This is especially significant in the context of the GCC's serious contemplation to work towards regional economic integration. Iran's entry into such a group would only add to the organisation's strength and significance.

The two-day GCC summit kicked off with regional security and economic integration at the top of its agenda. In his opening remarks, Qatar's Emir Sheikh Hamad bin Khalifah Al-Thani, urged the adoption of measures to prevent existing regional tensions from spinning out of control. [19] He made particular reference to the Iranian nuclear programme, the military build-up in the Gulf, the situation in Iraq, Palestine and Lebanon as well as the growing threat of terrorism in the region. Iran, for the first time, had an opportunity to participate in the gathering and put across its views to its neighbours. Till now, revolutionary Iran has had rocky ties with GCC states, particularly because of the threat it perceivably posed to the political status quo in the Gulf States. For its part, the Iranian leadership looked at the GCC as an instrument of US policy in the region.

Be that as it may, Ahmadinejad's remarks at the opening session of the 28th GCC summit suggested support for the idea of closer economic co-operation among Gulf countries. He advocated that the six oil-rich Gulf Arab states and Iran work together to establish 'regional security and economic pacts' without foreign interference. He put forward a string of proposals including the abolition of visas between Iran and Gulf states to facilitate free movement of people, protection of the regional environment, the establishment of a free trade zone and common investments in the petroleum sector. Ahmadinejad also indicated readiness to enhance co-operation in the fields of commerce, tourism, cultural exchanges and collaboration in science and technology. In addition, he expressed his inclination to offer the GCC a free corridor from North to South for the transportation of goods across its territory.

While the West might be seeking to manipulate the Shia-Sunni divide, moves seem to be afoot to bridge the sectarian gap. The Arab League has called for a high-level dialogue between the Arabs and Iran. The GCC initiative to host Iran at its annual summit can also be seen from this perspective. The

GCC invitation also has to be seen in the context of apprehensions about an US attack on Iran and consequently the need to engage Tehran and prevent the region hurtling into a fresh crisis. These regional efforts also aim to bring peace to Iraq and the entire region. At the same time, Iran has also shown its desire to join these efforts. Iran's interest in improving ties with GCC countries seem to stem from the need to avoid international isolation because of its nuclear programme.

However, some GCC member states have expressed their concerns regarding a nuclear Iran, which they articulated at the summit. Bahrain's crown prince, Sheikh Salman bin al-Khalifa, accused the Islamic Republic of Iran of seeking to acquire nuclear weapons. The UAE Foreign Minister also expressed his concerns on the issue. At the same time, the GCC states made it clear that their criticism was not directed at the Iranian nuclear programme per se but at the Iranian conduct on the issue. In any event, this is undoubtedly a welcome departure from past trends in regional politics.

Following this, Saudi King Abdullah gave the special invitation to Iranian President Ahmadinejad to visit Mecca and met him again during his Haj visit. Iranian ambassador to Saudi Arabia said on the occasion that "Iran and Saudi Arabia, were two leading countries in the region and in the Islamic world" and had "a heavy responsibility on their shoulders". [20]

The relations between Gulf countries and Iran are poised for an unprecedented growth. In fact, the UAE Prime Minister Sheikh Mohammad bin Rashid Al-Maktoum visited Tehran with high ranking politico-economic delegation recently in February 2008. It was the first highest UAE official visit to Iran after the 1979 Islamic Revolution. The two countries signed MoUs related to joint investment, export of electricity and avenues to boost trade. This is not to deny that Iran and the UAE have had sound diplomatic relations in recent years. The visit has boosted the relations further. However, the dispute between the UAE and Iran over the three islands Abu Musa and the Greater and Lesser Tunbs created more gaps between the two countries.

There is also suspicion in the Islamic world that the US and its Western allies are making use of the Saudis to widen the gulf between the two sects. However, the Saudis seem to have realised Iran's importance as a regional power and appear willing to tolerate Iranian influence in the region. Both the GCC and Iran do not want to antagonise each other at this juncture when American forces began to withdraw its troops from Iraq.

Impact on India

India's foreign policy stance in recent years, particularly towards the region of West Asia in general and Iran in particular has been a subject of passionate debate. India's growing relationship with the US and Iran's arch-rival Israel, and its stand on Iran's nuclear programme has been seen as a basic shift in the Indian foreign policy exercise. India and Iran articulate frequently regarding the civilization cultural and historical ties that have bound the two countries for more than a millennium. Both nations enjoyed strong bilateral relations following India's independence, overcoming such obstacles as Cold War politics and Iran's relationship with Pakistan.

Iran's pursuing a nuclear programme has impacted bilateral relations between India and Iran. Despite official statements reiterating the important position Iran holds, India has been adopting an ambiguous position on Iran of late. New Delhi has repeatedly voted in favour of the International Atomic Energy Agency's (IAEA) resolutions against Iran, the recent one was in November 2009 on grounds that a nuclear Iran is not in India's interests. However, it also emphasizes that it favours dialogue and diplomacy as a means of resolving the Iranian nuclear crisis. However, India explained regarding its vote 'the IAEA's safeguards system is the bedrock of the international community's confidence that peaceful uses of nuclear energy and non-proliferation objectives can be pursued in a balanced manner. The integrity of this system should be preserved.' [21]

The continuity of India's official position on Iran's nuclear programme was also reflected in Prime Minister Manmohan Singh statement during the Ninth India-EU Summit on September 29, 2008, making it clear that India will not support Iran's nuclear weapon ambitions. However, in a balancing act, Manmohan Singh also mentioned that "Iran as a signatory of the NPT was entitled to all that is needed to develop its civil nuclear programme for which it must undertake all the obligations". [22] Despite New Delhi's repeated explanations, this issue remains a major challenge between India and Iran.

On the issue of energy relations, India claims that Iran is an important partner as well as an important source for hydrocarbon resources and that it is keen to further strengthen existing ties. Iran is also one of India's largest suppliers of crude oil, and India in turn is also a major supplier of refined petroleum products for Iran. However, the recent and forth UNSC resolution does not affect India's oil trade with Iran, though, the US sanctions have had an impact on Indian oil companies. The US has been applying pressure against Indian companies which have energy relations with Iran. RIL's refined products exports as the company has large investment interests in the US which could be impacted by US sanctions. As a result, after the House and Senate had passed the bills, RIL had announced the termination of all contracts, though Iran claimed that it was still getting supplies from India, although without specifying whether the sales were being conducted through third country or not. According to reports, Reliance's decision to cease exports to Iran came after several US lawmakers advised the Export-Import Bank to suspend the extension of $900 million [23] worth of financial guarantees to RIL to help it to expand its Jamnagar refinery on the grounds that it was assisting Iran's economy with the gas sales.

This is true that Indo-Iran relation is by no means at a satisfactory level at present, however, this short-term phase would shortly be ended and it will be enhanced. Due to historical linkages and geo-political situation, the two countries cannot remain far from each other for long time. There is unanimous strategic understanding between India and Iran on promoting stability in Afghanistan and managing great power relationship in South Asia and Central Asia. India and Iran can also contribute to a stable political and economic order in Afghanistan. It is important to take note of the fact that today both countries are equally threatened by the hazards of terrorism, drug trafficking, smuggling of arms, and organized crime.

Conclusion

Finally it can be argued that the nature of conflict in the region has widened its scope, which includes political, security, military, economy and ideological dimensions. It would require a radical shift in approach for the Western world and the Gulf Arab neighbours to engage Iran diplomatically to address the issue of nuclearisation of the region as well as other issue of regional interest. Analysts articulated that 30 years of Western ruthless policy toward Iran has showed to be counterproductive and futile. It believes that the combination of security guarantee, economic benefits, and direct diplomatic negotiation between Iran and the US can pave the way for non-violent, sustainable cooperation.

After the Islamic Revolution, Iran has faced lot of crises. These include the eight year war with Iraq (1980-88), the assassination of important revolutionary leaders, the death of Imam Khomeini, and the international embargo led by the US and other western countries. But Iranian has showed its capability to survive all these crises. The US should engage Iran more in multilateral talks on Afghanistan, Iraq and future Gulf security issues. Though, Iran and US officials met on numbers of occasions on Iraq issues. Not only this, for the first time, Iran also attended The Hague meeting on Afghan issue in April 2009 on the US invitation where Iran said it would help rebuild Afghanistan but condemned the Obama's administration proposed troop increases. US Secretary of State, Hillary Clinton pointed out that there was rare high-level meeting between Richard Holbrooke, US special representative for Afghanistan and Pakistan, and Iran's Deputy Foreign Minister, Mohamed Mehdi Akhundzadeh. But Iran's foreign ministry denied that any meeting took place. Undoubtedly, it will give some transparency as to US intentions in all these areas thereby easing Iranian concerns of "strategic encirclement", it will give a platform that facilitates Iran's interests to be considered, and it will also acknowledge Iran's desire to be recognized as a major player in its region. The geopolitical and geo-economics characteristic of Iran have a special situation that it cannot form regional alliance without maintaining its relations and communication with the global power centres.

Notes

1. Akbar Aghajanian, "A New Direction in Population Policy and Family Planning in the Islamic Republic of Iran", *Asia-Pacific Population Journal*, Vol. 10, No. 1, United Nations, 1995, pp. 3-20.
2. Reza Simbar, "The Prospect for Crisis Management and Non-Violent Sustainable Cooperation," *Alternatives: Turkish Journal of International Relations*, Vol. 4, No. 4, Winter 2005.
3. issinger, Henry, "Does America Need a Foreign Policy? Toward a Diplomacy for the Twenty-First Century", Free Press, 2002, p. 197.
4. Kenneth Katzman, "Iran: US Concerns and Policy Responses", CRS Report for Congress, June 27, 2005.
5. "Obama troubled by Iran post-election violence", *Reuters*, June 16, 2009, at http://www.reuters.com/article/politicsNews/idUSTRE55F0IL20090616.

6. "Iran's top leader warns West over alleged meddling," *Khaleej Times*, July 6, 2009 at http://www.khaleejtimes.com/DisplayArticle08.asp?xfile=data/middleeast/2009/July/middleeast_July148.xml&section=middleeast.
7. "Sarkozy stands by UK in Iran row", *Aljazeera*, July 6, 2009, at http://english.aljazeera.net/news/europe/2009/07/20097614759499498.html.
8. Cordesman, H Anthony, "Iran and the United States: The Nuclear Issue", *Middle East Policy,* Vol. XV, No. 1, Spring 2008.
9. "Implementation of the NPT safeguards agreement in the Islamic Republic of Iran", *IAEA*, November 26, 2003, at http://www.iaea.org/Publications/Documents/Board/2003/gov2003-75.pdf (accessed on February 19, 2008).
10. "Background Note: Iran", at http://state.gov/r/pa/ei/bgn/5314.htm
11. "Implementation of the NPT Safeguards Agreement and relevant provisions of Security Council resolutions 1737 (2006) and 1747 (2007) in the Islamic Republic of Iran", *IAEA*, at http://www.iaea.org/Publications/Documents/Board/2008/gov2008-4.pdf.
12. In addition, in resolution 1737 (2006) the Council called upon all States to prevent specialized teaching or training of Iranian nationals in disciplines which would contribute to Iran's proliferation-sensitive nuclear activities and development of nuclear weapon delivery systems. In resolution 1747 (2007) the Council called upon all States to exercise vigilance and restraint in the provision of heavy weapons and related services to Iran, and called upon all States and international financial institutions not to enter into new commitments for grants, financial assistance and concessional loans to the Government of Iran, except for humanitarian and developmental purposes, at http://www.iaea.org/NewsCenter/Focus/IaeaIran/unsc_res1803-2008.pdf (Accessed on January 2, 2009).
13. M. Mahtab Alam Rizvi, "Obama's Overtures to Iran", *IDSA Strategic Comments*, March 30, 2009, at www.idsa.in/publications/.../MahtabAlamRizvi300309.html.
14. "Ayatollah Ali Khamenei dismisses Barack Obama's overtures to Iran", *Guardian*, March 21, 2009, at http://www.guardian.co.uk/world/2009/mar/21/ali-khamenei-barack-obama-iran.

15. "Analysis: SOFA, the View From Parliament", *New York Times*, November 27, 2008, at http://baghdadbureau.blogs.nytimes.com/2008/11/27/analysis-sofa-the-view-from-parliament/(accessed on November 27, 2008.
16. "Iran Urges Closer Defense ties with Iraq", *Washington Post*, June 9, 2008, at http://www.washingtonpost.com/wp-dyn/content/article/2008/06/08/AR2008060801897.html (accessed on October 24, 2008).
17. Michael Slackman, "Iran the Great Unifier? The Arab World Is Wary", *New York Times*, February 5, 2006, at http://www.nytimes.com/2006/02/05/weekinreview/05slackman.html.
18. By Robert Satloff, "King Abdullah II: Iraq is the Battleground - the West against Iran", *Middle East Quarterly*, Spring 2005, Washington DC. Also see The Business Online, February 12, 2006.
19. "GCC Aims for Greater Integration", *Arab News*, December 4, 2007, at http://www.arabnews.com/?page=4&section=0&article=104278&d=4&m=12&y=2007.
20. "Ahmadinejad Invited for Haj," *Iran Daily*, December 13, 2007, at http://www.iran-daily.com/1386/3015/html/index.htm.
21. 'IAEA Resolution on Iran's 'non compliance' with NPT Safeguards,' *Acronym Report*. September 24, 2005, at http://www.acronym.org.uk/docs/0509/doc14.htm (accessed on 5 November, 2009).
22. "India won't support Iran's N-Weapon ambition: PM," *Sify.com*, 2006, at http://sify.com/news/fullstory.php?d=14768467 (accessed on 28 December 2009). Also see Ministry of External Affairs, Government of India, Question no. 450, 'India's Stand on Nuclear Issue of Iran', in Parliament (Lok Sabha), February 22, 2006, at http://meaindia.nic.in/ (accessed on 6 November 2009).
23. Shebonti Ray Dadwal and M. Mahtab Alam Rizvi, "US Sanctions on Iran and their Impact on India," *IDSA Issue Brief*, June 21, 2010, at http://www.idsa.in/system/files/IB_USSanctionsonIran.pdf.

10

Containment and Competition between US and Iran in the Caspian Sea Region: Implications for India

Pankaj Kumar

America is worse than Britain; Britain is worse than America. The Soviet Union is worse than both of them. They are all worse and more unclean than each other! But today it is America that we are concerned with.

-*Ayatollah Khomeini,* October 1964 [1]

Introduction

When the United States of America was supporting the Shah regime as bulwarks against the Soviet Union in 1970s, they had never dreamed that their pawn (Iran) in the Middle East would become hostile so much that for the next three decades their relationship would go in a deep freeze. The 1979 Iranian revolution and subsequent events including hostage crisis was a shock for the United States. The power taken by Ayatollah Khomeini and the US reaction over the developments in Iran marked with unprecedented animosity and hostility in US-Iran relations. Since then US and Iran have been on collision course and their bilateral relations have been non-existent. The 1988 shooting down of Iranian commercial flight over the Persian Gulf by USS Vincennes killing 290 Iranians made them mortal enemies who had crossed the rubicon.

The collapse of the Soviet Union provided some hope of repair in US-Iran relations but the successive administrations' tough and confrontational policy towards the Islamic Republic inhibited any improvement. The 'duel containment' policy of Washington against Iran and Iraq in the post Cold War era has been motivated by strengthening of American influence in the Middle East and denying any substantial role of Iran and Iraq in the West Asian politics (Takeyh, 2002: 27-30).

The September 11, 2001 event drew Iranian support and Iran condemned the tragic event. Iran also tacitly supported the US bombing of Afghanistan after 9/11 incident (Mahapatra, 2005: 14). But President Bush's State of the Union address in January 2002 categorizing Iran as a part of 'Axis of Evil' and an 'Outpost of Tyranny' ended any hope for rapprochement in the US-Iran relations. Several factors which inhibit improvement in US-Iran relations are Iranian anti Israel policy; historic mutual grievances; terrorism; the US military presence in the Persian Gulf; Iranian nuclear programme; sanctions and pipeline policies (Kemp, 2000: 157-58, Palit, 2004: 103-05). This paper explores the dynamics of US-Iran competition in Caspian Sea region and its implications for India's interest in the region.

Importance of Iran

Iran has second largest oil reserve after Saudi Arabia and second largest natural gas reserves after Russia in the world. The strategic location of Iran with the coastline longer than any other country in the Persian Gulf through which about one half of the world's oil is transported and its closeness to Azerbaijan, Kazakhstan and Turkmenistan who possess billions of barrel oil and trillions of cubic feet natural gas make Iran as a crucial factor for world energy security (Ar-Rahmani). The strategic advantageous position of Iran for transportation of Caspian hydrocarbon to the world market and extensive pipeline system for oil and natural gas make the country more convenient for landlocked Caucasus and Central Asian states to provide outlet to the international market. Further in view of continuing violence, bloodshed and political upheaval in Afghanistan the Iranian route attracts additional importance. For a long term exploitation of Caspian hydrocarbon reserves Iranian routes are more viable from security point of view as there are no war zones along the proposed pipeline through Iran. Moreover, Iran is also interested in making use of its geopolitical importance by seeking to expand its political, economic and cultural influence in the new republics.

The vacuum created after the collapse of the Soviet Union led to rush for extending influence by global and regional powers. For the West, particularly the United States Iran appeared as the greatest threat to the sovereignty and territorial integrity of the Central Asian states. The United States was apprehensive about Tehran effort to promote Iranian model of Islamic democracy in Central Asian countries. The United States therefore encouraged Turkey to play active role in Central Asia both to act as a bulwark against Islamic radical force and to promote a secular model of governance. Since then Tehran has been apprehensive about Turkey's growing activities in the Caspian Sea region. Tehran eyed with suspicion Ankara's contact with Turkmenistan and Azerbaijan as the population of both of those republics being ethnically close to Turkey (Swietochowski, 1998: 125-26). This has created an atmosphere of rivalry between Turkey and Iran with the US is playing invisible role of backing Turkey to push back Iran within its limit. For the United States any role of Iran in this region is absolutely unacceptable (Olcott, 2005: 53). The United States which follows the principle of containment has restricted Tehran and has been toiling hard to isolate her in the region. In view of persistent US hostility and antipathy, Iran has been very cautious of its role in Caspian Sea region and wants to cooperate with Russia to nullify western influence in the region (Bakshi, 1998: 136). Iran has provided rail and road links to the Central Asian Republics through neighbouring Turkmenistan and an outlet to the sea through its part of Bandar Abbas. A tripartite agreement has also been done among Iran, Turkmenistan and India to provide surface transportation linking India to Central Asia (Ibid).

US Policy in Caspian Sea Region

The United States pursues both strategic and commercial interests in Caspian Sea region. It views three aspects of the Caspian Sea region as crucial:

- Increasing the supply of energy to the world market,
- Excluding Iran from influencing the exploration, shipment development and marketing of energy products, and
- Preventing neighbouring states especially Russia from obtaining a monopoly over the local energy supply.

In order to achieve the above goals the US policy aims to enhance local states' capability to produce and ship oil abroad, to obtain equal access for US energy firms and other business who want to invest in these republics, to use US diplomatic auspices to negotiate settlements of local wars, and to create stable democratic government as an ultimate outcome of these processes.

The US involvement across the entire Caspian Sea region has exploded since 1994-1995, when Washington conclusively rejected Russia's claims for an energy monopoly. In September 1995, US experts on Central Asia met at NATO headquarter and cited the extensive US interests in Caspian energy deposits as a reason why Washington might have to extend its Persian Gulf security guarantees in this region (Bogmolov, 1995: 21). US involvement has only taken off since then. While US officials projected their visions of a win-win situation for everyone, where everyone has shared interests in developing these energy markets, they have actually aimed to deny Russian and Iranian role in the Caspian Sea region (Washington Post, 1997).

In May 1995, Under Secretary of Energy, William White, toured Central Asia, urging the republics to regard themselves as important producer of oil and natural gas and to treat Russia and Iran as competitors (Rumer, 1996: 10). Also in 1995,

Glen Rase, head of the State Department's energy policy section, bluntly rejected Russian efforts to dominate the Caspian, stating that Russian talk of condominium there was "a guarantee of inaction" (Bogmolov, 1995: 21). He further said "the Russian position must not be imposed on the states that prefer a more normal division of the Caspian [Since Washington] does not recognize any sphere of influence"(Ibid).

Due to increasing interest in preserving the area as 'a zone of free competition' and denying either Russia or Iran any lasting influence in the region, Washington is now becoming the arbiter or leader on virtually every inter-state and international issue in the area. The consuming interest in pipeline routes has led the US government to take public position as well on questions such as the legal status of the Caspian sea, to arbitrate or mediate competing claims between Azerbaijan and Turkmenistan and to take the lead in organizing' or guaranteeing regional investment projects.

Caspian Sea Legal Status

The status of Caspian Sea is still under dispute among Caspian riparian states. The two treaties of 1921 and 1940 between USSR and Iran provide the basis of negotiation and set the principles of right to use and exploit Caspian Sea resources by two states. [2] The two important principles: firstly the two countries have equal access to the sea and its use and secondly the sea is closed to all countries not located on the shore were underlined in this treaty. However, the emergence of three new littoral states in 1991- Azerbaijan, Kazakhstan and Turkmenistan- with a combined length of Caspian coastline which exceeded that of Russia and Iran- led these new states to demand a redefinition of the Caspian's legal status as a sea rather than a lake. Regarding the rights over sea or lake the international laws provide partition of sea among littoral states while lakes are treated as legal condominiums.

Applying the law of sea, full maritime boundaries for the five littoral states would be established.

The 1921 and 1940 treaties had some limitations and it left the issue of exploitation of mineral resources under the seabed of different interpretation. Iranian perception is that the agreement of 1940 refers neither to the exploitation of seabed resources nor the benefit accruing from these resources. Rather the common property clause indicates that two countries cannot claim sovereignty over the same part of the Caspian seabed. Iran is also of the view that the riparian states of Caucasus and Central Asia while signing agreement with oil companies violate these principles (Mohsenin).

The major actors of the Caspian riparian states have shifted their position time and again on the issue which has created more complexities in solving the problem. Their views have been guided by economic, political and international considerations with the extended interests of the western oil companies in the Caspian Sea region.

Russia considers Caspian as a lake rather than a sea and therefore it should be subject to the joint exploration effort of all five countries bordering the Caspian. Russia claims that the treaties concluded between Russia and Persia in 1921 and between the Soviet Union and Iran in 1940 were still in force as the collapse of the Soviet Union did not affect the validity of the treaty under international laws. Thus, Caspian Sea should remain divided into two zones, regardless of the existence of Azerbaijan, Kazakhstan and Turkmenistan around sea. Russia regards that the resource development of Caspian Sea is the responsibility of all littoral states and it favours division of the seabed but not the surface of the water (Jean-Christophe, 2001: 171).

The three newly independent countries - Azerbaijan, Kazakhstan and Turkmenistan- maintain that division of the Caspian Sea among riparian states is the only fair solution to the problem. The stand taken by these countries aimed at stalling the development of hydrocarbon fields in the respective area of the sea. However, Kazakhstan has been willing to cooperate with Russia in the Caspian Sea region and has adopted Russian stand on the status of the sea (Mohsenin).

The Iranian view on Caspian Sea status was expressed by Iranian Deputy Foreign Minister, Morteza Sarmadi, at the Eighth International Conference on Central Asia and Caucasus at the Institute for Political and International Studies, Tehran, in June 2000. He acknowledged the need to solve the problem on the basis of 1921 and 1940 treaties. He also expressed that Iran was supportive of demilitarized states of Caspian Sea and concerned for environment in laying of gas and oil pipeline on the seabed. Iran stand reflects her intention to be more closer to Russia as well as a sign of Iranian willingness to thwart growing western influence into the Caspian region. The United States is in support of declaring Caspian water body as 'sea' rather than as a lake against the Russian view due to its economic and energy interests and to preclude Russia to dominate it (Rutledge, 2005: 105-7, Dekmeijian and Honovann, 2003).

Oil Companies in Caspian Sea Region

The discovery of oil and natural gas in Central Asia and Caspian Sea region led to a scramble by western oil and gas companies to carve a niche and get some share in the pie. The recovery in hydrocarbon production was entirely the result of the influx of major foreign oil companies, mainly American into the region after 1993. It was a small Aberdeen-based oil services company, Ramco which arrived in Baku in 1989 and rediscovered a giant group of oilfield- in Southern Caspian.

Five years later, on 20th September 1994 Azerbaijan signed an oil agreement in Baku, a production-sharing agreement with the newly formed Azerbaijan International Operating Company (AIOC) to exploit the 4.3 billion barrels of estimated oil reserves in the Azeri-Chirag-Gunashli.

The Azerbaijani oil agreement was hailed as the 'contract of the century' (Swietochowski, 1998: 126). The deal, covering thirty years and valued at more than $7 billion, was concluded with an enlarged consortium of foreign companies including four American (Amoco, Unocal, Pennzoil, and McDermott), one British (British Petroleum), one Norwegian (Stat oil), one Turkish (TPAO), and Russia's Lukoil. Since then approximately twenty private sectors oil companies are involved in Caspian Sea oil and gas exploration and development. These companies control almost 60 per cent of the oil and natural gas reserve. Four US companies (Chevron Texaco, Exxon Mobil, Phillips Petroleum and Unocal) had the largest 'national' share of private sector reserves (36%). It is estimated that by 2020, these twenty companies will have invested between $ 237 billion and $314 in the Caspian oil and gas fields (McCutcheon and Obson, 2001: 26).

The US share of total Caspian oil and gas investment would therefore be between $85 billion and $113 billion. By far the largest single private sector holder of Caspian oil and gas reserves was Chevron-Texaco with 11 percent of the total oil and gas reserves and a putative investment requirement of somewhere between $ 26 billion and $ 35 billion over the lifetime of its production-sharing contracts.

Such an important investment by US companies required the assurance of US military support. The US adopted 'forward' energy and national security strategy to protect its economic interest by militarily engaging Central Asian States. NATO has played an increasing role in the Caspian Sea region by not just conducting Partnership for Peace (PfP) programme with local states but also holding military exercises in the region. For the implementation of US agenda in the Caspian Sea region the Pentagon allocated areas of responsibility to US commands for the Transcaspian; the US European Command (USEUCOM) got the Caucasus, and the Central Command (USCENTCOM) received Central Asia. Although this is as much an administrative devise to supervise the ongoing programs of military cooperation that are now underway bilaterally and through NATO, it also represents a major step for contingency planning (Bhatty and Broson, 2000).

The vested interests of the involved countries in Caucasus and Central Asian region have complicated the determination of oil and gas pipeline route to tap the vast hydrocarbon of Caspian Sea basin. The countries, which are in fray exercise its maximum diplomacy to sideline the rival country using her political, economic, technical, military might. The US favours to sideline Russia and Iran for political as well as geo-strategic consideration and support Turkey to play active role in the region. The winners of the pipeline game will gain strategic benefit while losers will be marginalized strategically. "The victory in the struggle will receive not only billions of dollars in the form of transit fee. The real gain will be control over the pipelines which will be the most important factor of geopolitical influence in the Transcaucasus and in Central Asia..." (Ebel, 1997: 37-38).

Pipeline Routes

The lack of adequate export infrastructure is probably the most difficult problem facing investors in the oil and gas sector of Caspian Sea region. The construction of new export pipeline has become a priority. However, most routing options are fraught with technical, financial, legal and political difficulties.

By 2010, Central Asia and Trans Caucasian could have over 100 Mt. of oil and 100 BCM of gas available for export. Even if there were no other limitation on exports from the region, existing oil and gas pipeline capacity would not meet future export needs. Additional oil and gas export pipelines are being proposed and in some cases are already under construction or constructed to serve the region. The projects are mainly for the transport of oil particularly Baku-Tibilsi-Ceyhan (BTC) from Azerbaijan, and the Caspian Pipeline Consortium (CPC) from Kazakhstan.

Table 10.1: Capacities of Selected Oil Pipelines from Caspian Sea Region, 2001-2015

Pipeline	Route	Length (Miles)	Capacity (bbls/day) 2001/2002	2010/2015
		Operating		
Atyrau-Samara	Atyrau, Kazakhstan, to Samara, Russia	432	310,000	310,000
Baku-Novorossiisk	Baku, Azerbaijan, to Novorossiisk, Russia/Black Sea (northern route)	868	100,000	300,000 (planned)
Baku-Novorossiisk	Baku to Novorossiisk via Dagestan, Russia	204	120,000	360,000 (planned)
Baku- Supsa	Baku to Supsa, Georgia/Black Sea	515	100,000	100,000
Caspian Pipeline Consortium	Tengiz oil field, Kazakhstan, to Novorossiisk Russia/Black Sea	990	565,000	1,340,000 (planned)
		Under Construction, Planned, or Proposed		
Iran Oil Swap (under construction)	Neka, Iran, to Tehran, Iran, where oil will be swapped for equivalent amount at	208	105,000	150,000

	Persian Gulf coast.			
Baku-Ceyhan	Baku to Tbilisi, Georgia, to Ceyhan, Turkey/Black Sea	1,040	1,000,000	1,000,000
Kazakhstan-Turkmenistan-Iran (proposed)	Kazakhstan to Kharg Island, Iran, on Persian Gulf, via Turkmenistan	930	1,000,000	1,000,000

Sources: Pennwell Publishing Company, Oil and Gas Journal, February 4, 2002; U.S. Department of Energy, Energy Information Administration (EIA), *Caspian Sea Region Country Analysis Brief,* February 2002; (EIA). *Caspian Sea Region: Tables and Graphs*, February 2002; (EIA). *Russia: Oil and Gas Export Pipelines*, October 2001.

Western Routes

The United States, Turkey, Azerbaijan and Georgia prefer western routes. These routes are intended to bypass the Russian territories and Iran. The less expensive alternative ($ 1.5 billion) is to build an upgraded pipeline to the Georgian port of Supsa on the Black Sea; from their oil will have to be taken by tankers through the Bosporus strait to Europe. But due to separatist movement in Abkhazia and rebellion in South Ossetia of Georgian territory the route is not secured (Joshi, 1999).

The other problem is Nagarno-Karabakh conflict. Baku Supsa pipeline passes through Nagarno – Karabakh enclave of Azerbaijan, but inhabited largely by Armenians. The rebel forces have established control over Nagarno-Karabkh tacitly supported by Armenia and is a source of security concern for the passing pipeline. Environmental problem of Bosporus strait is another impediment for the free movement of oil. Turkey has raised concerns that higher oil export level will increase congestion in Bosporus straits. Turkey has stated that as a result of increased traffic there may be possible collisions ensuing oil spills in the strait (Tevzade, 2004: 96-99, EIA, Central Asia, 2005).

With the support of Turkey and Israel, United States has promoted East-West pipeline consisting Baku-Tbilisi-Ceyhan and the Tran-Caspian line. The United States' attraction to the Ceyhan route and the Trans-Caspian line emanates from its desire to build an East-West axis of influence and commerce in the Eurasian region and curtail Russian and Iranian influence. Baku-Tbilisi-Ceyhan (BTC) pipeline was the long favoured East-West 1750 km route emanating from Azerbaijan through Georgia and ending in Turkish Mediterranean port of Ceyhan. This will allow oil to bypass the Bosporus strait. The United States waged an impressive and sustained diplomatic campaign, investing enormous political capital in order to make Baku Ceyhan the Main Export Route (MER) to mould the region in its image. The strategic point about BTC is that it would skip both Russia and Iran, while reinforcing Turkey's economy and role as an oil entrepot (Aliriza, 2000).

The American support for the proposal had several merits:

1. It would benefit its NATO ally Turkey which would earn considerable income from the fees charged for oil transit. Turkey also had concerns about the alternative to the BTC pipeline. BTC pipeline would mitigate Turkey's environmental concern for Bosporus strait.
2. BTC pipeline would bypass both Russia and Iran.
3. The construction of BTC, at a total project cost of $3.6 billion would offer lucrative contracts for US companies, opportunities which would be unlikely to materialize if alternative major pipelines were built through Russia or Iran.
4. The port of Ceyhan on Turkey's Mediterranean coast would not only be a safe outlet for western oil supplies, but if

would only be 403 km by sea from the Israel port of Haifa, providing a bonus of secure oil supplies to America's Middle East-ally.

5. A major energy infrastructure in the region would bind former Soviet republic to a NATO ally in the west, offering a promising geo-strategic platform on which to build further economic and political linkages to the East, while at the same time frustrating any tendency of Russia and Iran to form a North-South economic and political axis (Hill, 2001,Georgian, 2002).

The construction of Transcaspian pipeline was envisaged by the US to feed Kazakh oil and Turkmen gas to Baku-Ceyhan route. The United State lobbied in the Kazakh and Turkmen government to support the pipeline. USA also urged Kazakhstan to commit towards building the 'under–the-sea' Caspian oil pipeline, so that Kazakh oil could be pumped along the Baku-Ceyhan corridor. At the same time US pressurized Kazakhstan to exclude Iran from Transcaspian pipeline plan. In a joint statement in December 2001 US President Bush and Kazakh President Nazarbaev backed the idea of 'multiple pipeline' for Caspian oil export gave a joint statement. Bush added Aktau port of Kazakhstan in the BTC corridor to bring Kazakhstan into the frame of energy chain. Aktau, in Kazakhstan, is on the eastern shore of the Caspian and the addition of this link would require undersea transcaspian pipeline"(EIA, Caspian Sea, 2005). However Russia and Iran argued ardently against construction of an underwater pipeline across Caspian, pointing out that such a project would prove hazardous to the Caspian sea ecosystem. They also stressed the high cost of building such pipeline (DeLay, 1999: 62-63).

Southern Route

The Southern routes are the shortest, quickest and cheapest. Iran and various oil companies favour these routes. They are cheaper to build (under $ 1 billion), pass through relatively safer territories and pose no serious environmental hazard. It is to be noted that significant pipeline and port facilities also exist as discussed above. Iran has also constructed a gas pipeline from Turkmenistan to Iran which will be further extended to Turkey for the export of Turkmen gas to the European market. Iran is already tendering to build its own pipeline so as to bring Caspian oil shipped by tanker to a Caspian Sea port inland to reach refineries in northern Iran. Iran has also built at its own expense, a natural gas pipeline for transporting Turkmen gas to Iranian industries near Iran - Turkmen border. Iranian officials continue to pursue the possibility of a major export pipeline from the Caspian to the Persian Gulf (Kalicki, 2001: 125-26).

Despite all the merit of Southern routes United States oppose any pipeline traversing through Iran due to estranged relation with the latter. President Bill Clinton's Executive Orders in 1995 and Iran Libya Sanction Act (ILSA) enacted by US Congress in August 1996 and renewed in 2001 prohibited all national firms from supervising, managing, or financing projects relating to the development of Iran's energy resources and imposing penalties on non-American companies that invest over US $ 20 million (now it has raised to $ 40 million after 2001) in the energy industries of Iran. In April 2010, Washington stepped up its efforts to impose a new round of sanctions on Iran over its nuclear program. In June 2010, expressing deep concern about Iran's lack of compliance with its previous resolutions on ensuring the peaceful nature of its nuclear programme, the UN Security Council imposed additional sanctions on Iran, expanding an arms embargo and tightening restrictions on financial and shipping enterprises related to "proliferation-sensitive activities". The real motive behind imposing sanction on Iran was to alter Iranian foreign policy of what US consider it as promoter of terrorism and nuclear proliferation as well as undermining Middle East peace process. However, the trade sanctions imposed by the US on Iran specifically exempt the swap of Caspian oil for Iranian oil delivered in the Persian Gulf (Mojtahed-Zadeh, 2000: 180). Despite growing pressure from US oil companies to lift the embargo upon Tehran, the US is still reluctant to soften its stance towards Tehran. In a conference on oil and gas in Almaty Kazakhstan, US presidential advisor John wolf affirmed that his country would not support the construction of pipeline via Iran. Wolfe said that the transfer of control over the transport of oil to Iran 'would only have negative consequences' (The Economist, 1999).

In 1997, Turkmenistan and Iran completed the $ 190 million Korpezhe-Kurd-Kuy pipeline linking the two countries, thereby making it the first natural gas export pipeline from Central Asia, that bypass Russia. The US government backed away from applying sanction on Ashgabat under ILSA saying that Turkmenistan rather than Iran would be the main beneficiary of the project (DeLay, 1999: 64-65).

ILSA has cost heavily to the US oil companies in clinching lucrative deals in oil and gas sector in Iran. Instead European and Asian firms invest heavily in Iranian hydrocarbon sector(Karagiannis, 2003: 151-52). The US oil barons are lobbying hard to get permission to invest in the Iranian oil and gas sector which has been available to Russian, French and Malaysian firms (Manning, 2000: 52). The waiver given by Clinton Administration to France's TotalFinaElf, Russia's Gazprom and Malaysia's Petronas was in order to avoid a clash with its European allies as European government were livid about the extraterritorial provisions of the ILSA, which they regard as unacceptable in principle, irrespective of its aim. Major US oil companies especially Anadarko, Bechtel and BP are engaged in lobbying against US sanction on Iran as it cost heavily in terms of loss of profit and investment to the US economy. That lobbying has mitigated the anti-Iranian feeling among the policy makers resulting a new added provision in ILSA which allow periodical review of sanctions to assess their 'effectiveness and continued stability'(The White House, 2001). Former National Security Advisor Zbigniew Brzezinski advocated "to promote multi-pipeline strategy and US must adopt a position which does not exclude the pipeline through Iran. Moreover the pipeline through Iran is not something that would be implemented instantly in any case. And one has to anticipate some evolution in Iranian attitudes including the possibility eventually, of an Iranian-American accommodation. We ought to be willing to encourage that. Therefore, it is not wise for the United States to be opposing the possibility of international financing of a pipeline through Iran." (Karagiannis,2003:160).

The Southern routes also offer the swap option of oil that no other route has offered as yet. Turkmenistan and Kazakhstan have initiated low-volume oil 'swap' deal with Iran. Under this arrangement, the Iranian side would take delivery of Caspian oil, send it to Teheran and/or Tabriz refineries for processing and distribution, and then make an equivalent amount of crude available in the producer's name at the Kharg island terminal in the Persian Gulf. Tehran likes swap because they offer a relatively easy way both to supply the northern, more heavily populated region of the country – which are far from the big oil fields in the South- with crude oil and refined products and to put more Iranian oil on the world market, even if it is being sold on another's behalf (DeLay, 1999: 64-65).

In 1996, despite US opposition Iran and Kazakhstan signed a swap agreement whereby Kazakhstan would deliver 2 million tons of crude oil to Iranian port of Neka and in exchange Iran would allocate an equivalent amount of its own oil on world market to Kazakhstan. The deal foundered in 1997, when the refineries in Northern Iran refused to accept Kazakh oil on account of its high sulphur content. However, Iran subsequently upgraded its refineries and the swaps agreement was reinstated in 2002. By early 2003 Iran was importing about 50,000 b/d from Kazakhstan (Ehteshami, 2004: 67-68). The upgraded pipeline linking the port of Neka on the Caspian to the Rey (near Tehran) and Tabriz refineries was completed in September 2003. In the late 2003 the Canadian company PetroKazakhstan started sending approximately 1 million tones of crude per year by rail via Uzbekistan and Turkmenistan to the Tehran refinery, which boosted the Iranian- Kazakh swap deal (Jafar, 2004: 204-5). A second larger pipeline from Neka to the northern refineries was also due for completion. Further Turkmenistan, Kazakhstan and Iran were exploring the viability of laying a pipeline running from western Kazakhstan via Turkmenistan to Iranian coast of Persian Gulf (Ibid).

The oil swap arrangement between Turkmenistan and Iran began in July 1998. As per this agreement, Turkmen oil is shipped from the Turkmenbashi refinery to the Teheran port of Neka. Turkmenistan's quest for export through Iran has drawn disapproval from the US government. Washington has repeatedly urged Ashgabat not to partner up with Tehran, but Iranian routes-and swap- have geography on their side. Turkmenistan cannot ignore its southern neighbour, but neither can ignore the United States as such. Turkmen President Niyazov has taken some steps towards the construction of an oil export pipeline in a direction more to Washington's liking Westward, across the Caspian Sea, and towards the oil export routes leading out of Baku through Georgia and Turkey (DeLay, 1999: 72).

South Eastern Route

The South-Eastern Route caters to the expanding Asian market by linking Turkmenistan to Pakistan and India through Afghanistan. This route is favored by Pakistan, Afghanistan, Saudi Arabia, Delta oil and the US Unocal corporation led by US Unocal, the CentGas consortium of a 1271 km pipeline from the Daulatabad Gas field in south-eastern Turkmenistan to Karachi and Multan in Pakistan, with a possible extension to Fazilka (India) on the Pakistan-India border (EIA, Central Asia, 2005).

Immediately after the Independence, Turkmenistan started working with an Argentinean oil company Bridas to sell its hydrocarbon to the outside world. Bridas offered to build the gas pipeline for about $2.5 billion and oil pipeline $ 3 billion. On March 16, 1995 Pakistan and Turkmenistan signed a memorandum allowing Bridas to prepare a pre-feasibility study of the proposed pipeline (Rashid, 2000: 159). However, Bridas and Ashgabat relation soured on the issue of revenue sharing and US oil company Unocal was engaged in the project. Turkmen President Niyazov saw that Unocal could become the means to engage a major US company and US in Turkmenistan's development. The Americans also needed to support Turkmenistan if they were to prevent Niyazov from becoming dependent on Iran. An agreement was signed in October 1994 between Turkmenistan and Unocal along with its partner, the Saudi Arabia owned Delta Oil Company, to built a gas pipeline through Afghanistan (Olcott, 2005: 38). Unocal set up the CentGas consortium holding a 70% stake, giving Delta 15%, Russia's state owned gas company Gazprom got 10% and the state-owned company Turkmenirosgaz 5%. Unocal signed a second project (Central Asian Oil Pipeline Project-CAOPP), a 1050 mile oil pipeline from chardzhou in Turkmenistan to an oil terminal on Pakistan coast, delivering one million barrel/day of oil export (Rashid, 2000).

However, the major problem regarding both pipelines is the lack of political stability in Afghanistan, through which both pipelines would pass. The country has been riddled by in fighting between numerous factions since Soviet invasion of 1979. Pakistan supported Taliban militia captured Kabul in 1996. Many of those involved with the pipeline projects welcomed the Taliban victory. Unocal was accused of helping along with Delta oil, to finance the Taliban's seizure of Kabul in 1996. The respected French observer Oliver Roy charged that "when the Taliban took power in Afghanistan, it was largely orchestrated by the Pakistani secret service (ISI) and the oil company Unocal, with its Saudi ally Delta" (Labeviere, 2000: 280). Unocal executive John Maresca then testified in 1998 to the House Committee on International Relations on the benefits of a proposed oil pipeline through Afghanistan to the coast of Pakistan (Rashid, 2000: 166).

The US government saw Taliban regime "as a source of stability in Central Asia that would enable the construction of an oil pipeline across Central Asia," from the oil field in Turkmenistan, Uzbekistan, and Kazakhstan, through Afghanistan and Pakistan, to the Indian Ocean (Godoy, 2001). September 11, 2001 event changed the whole dynamics in Central Asia. Taliban regime was exterminated by the US and hopes emerged for peace in Afghanistan. A stable Afghanistan revived the interest of foreign countries and companies to invest in pipeline route. A feasibility study commissioned by Asian Development Bank was completed in 2005 for the proposed pipeline. By completion of this pipeline attraction to Iranian route and Russia monopoly over Caspian oil and gas transportation would be decimated.

Implications for India

The Caspian region represents an area of great strategic significance for India. India considers Central Asia and the Caspian region as important for a multitude of geopolitical, economic, commercial, and strategic reasons. The potential of Central Asia in providing transportation corridors between India and other countries in the region, particularly Iran, is of great value to India, especially in view of Indian needs for energy security. Hence, India is carving its niche in the Caspian Sea region through development of various infrastructure projects in Afghanistan and Iran. Iran is the only Caspian state from which India gets energy supply from the Southern energy field. In 2005, India signed a US $ 40 billion deal with Iran to import 7.5 million tons of Liquefied Natural Gas (LNG) annually over a period of 25 years. It also obtained 20% stakes in the development of Iran's onshore oilfield,

Yadavaran, as well as the Jufeir oilfield. In exchange for Iranian gas, India is investing in Iran's ports and energy infrastructure (Bajpaee, 2005).

India is developing Chabahar port of Iran, which will serve as India's entry point to Afghanistan, Central Asia and beyond, bypassing Pakistan. India has already built the Zaranj-Delaram road in Afghanistan's Nimroz province, which will connect to the Chabahar port via Milak. Significantly, the Chabahar-Milak-Zaranj-Delaram highway will open up the Indian market to Afghan agricultural products and other exports. This is significant because Pakistan has been denying transit facility to India for Afghanistan through its territory. It will also help in combating the scourge of illicit drugs production and export, and assist the trade, transport and transit network of Iran. At this juncture cooperation with Iran turns out to be crucial to gain strategic depth in the Caspian Sea region.

The competition between United States and Iran in Caspian Sea region and American attempt to isolate Iran has been detrimental to India's energy security. The bottom line is that Iran is a major source of energy supplies for the expanding Indian economy. If the United States maintain its stronghold in the Caspian Sea region it will affect all the main traditional regional players as well as India. Moreover, US control over the oil and energy resources of Central Asia will make it neither cheap nor accessible to others. If the US succeeds in controlling most of the energy resources by excluding traditional guardian of the region, Russia and regional power, Iran, it will use this as an instrument of its external policy. Consequently it would make emerging powers like India most vulnerable (Bedi: 2002). Indeed, the US has used the energy issue as a tool of its foreign policy in the Caspian region. For instance, the US has been consistently opposing India from pursuing the IPI gas pipeline project. Expressing US view over India's involvement in IPI pipeline Condoleezza Rice once stated "if India is buying Iranian gas my country will get upset"(BBC News Persian: 2006). Hence, India in no way benefits out of the US-Iran competition and, in fact, has a great deal to lose as United States vehemently oppose cooperation with Iran which forms India's extended neighborhood.

The Iran nuclear issue potentially can complicate the US-India strategic partnership as New Delhi firmly oppose to any use of force in the resolution of the problem. India's vote against Iran in the International Atomic Energy Agency (IAEA) Board of Directors meeting grievously damaged long-term Indo-Iranian relations. As a result Indian energy security in the Caspian Sea region came under severe risk. Iran is the only country that offers entry point to tap Caspian hydrocarbon for India. Reconsidering the importance of Iran, India has ventured into coarse correction with Iran and opposed the United States for its June 2010 sanctions against Iran. India argued that US pressed sanctions against Iran adversely affect Indian companies and India's energy security. In a speech at an India-Iran strategic dialogue in New Delhi, Indian Foreign Secretary Nirupama Rao said, "We are justifiably concerned that the extra-territorial nature of certain unilateral sanctions recently imposed by individual countries, with their restrictions on investment by third countries in Iran's energy sector, can have a direct and adverse impact on Indian companies and more importantly, on our energy security and our attempts to meet the development needs of our people" (Gilani: 2010).

India and Iran has "civilizational ties". In 2003 two countries signed the "New Delhi Declaration" which set forth a vision of a bilateral "strategic partnership". Both New Delhi and Tehran have sought to strengthen their bilateral relationship. India has multidimensional interests in Iran. The steep rise in demand of energy in India due to rapid economic growth in the last two decades have added new quest for energy security in Indian diplomacy. Iran being a close neighbour endowed with vast energy resources offers low cost and long-term source of India's energy requirements. A $ 7 billon ambitious Iran-Pakistan-India pipeline was mooted long back in 1993 to supply natural gas to Indian market. However, it has not yet materialised significantly because of India's skepticism about security of pipeline traversing through Pakistan territory and disagreement over gas price between New Delhi and Tehran. In fact, such a project would tie India into long-term economic relationship with Iran which Washington would hardly prefer. Millions of dollar payment by India in return of import of Iranian gas would be seen in the American Congress and State Department as financing Iran's nuclear ambitions (Iran or the US? India's Delicate Balancing Act: 2008).

India has long term strategic interests in Afghanistan. India see presence of Taliban in Afghanistan as manifestation of Islamic extremism that India is battling in Kashmir and success of Taliban in Afghanistan has spillover effect on Kashmir and rest of the country. Hence, for India a good relationship with Tehran is useful in helping to stabilise Afghanistan and contain Pakistan. At the same time Iranian concern in Afghanistan is two-fold. Firstly, the presence of American troops and Secondly, Iran fears the Sunni Islamic extremism espoused by Taliban regime as a threat to Iran's Shiite sect. Both factors heavily undermine Iranian security in the region. Consequently, both India and Iran have been cooperating to secure their respective interests in Afghanistan.

India and United States are strategic partner. In June 2010 both countries concluded their strategic dialogue, in which they committed themselves to sustaining and deepening their cooperation on numerous issues of socio-economic, security and environmental significance. The deepening tie between Washington and New Delhi especially in the field of nuclear technology, security, defence and economic has reached at a level where two countries cannot disregard each other interests (Lakshman: 2010). Nevertheless, the growing partnership between United States and India in the new millennium sometimes eclipsed by New Delhi friendship with Tehran. It was speculated time and again both in Washington and New

Delhi that Indian strategic partnership with Iran would significantly create obstacles to derail further development of a US-India global partnership (Kronstadt: 2006). However, US-India relations have remained unaffected by Iranian factor essentially because India has acted on expected line of the United States at crucial juncture in IAEA. So far Indian voting in favour of the IAEA resolution at the Board of Governors meeting was guided by two significant factors: firstly, India does not want another nuclear capable state in its neighbour. Secondly, India is deeply concerned with the way international non-proliferation order has been ineffective in preventing the illicit nuclear and missile related transfers to North Korea, Libya and Iran by Pakistan and China. For India the immediate concern is to maintain a balance in the policy approaches towards its international commitments for non-proliferation and the international nuclear energy cooperation arrangements.

At the same time by adopting a clear cut stand towards Iranian nuclear programme India has sent strong message to the West that it is a responsible nuclear power of the world. However, India wants to solve Iranian nuclear standoff through amicable way and consistently oppose use of force against Iran. The United States die hard endeavour to isolate Iran and exerting pressure on New Delhi to restrain herself in deepening tie with Tehran has not yielded much desired outcome. Moreover, positive and potentially strengthening India-Iran relations present a challenge to the US policymakers. At the same time India is bringing its Iran policy into closer alignment with that of the United States. In fact, India has range of interest in strengthening tie with Iran.

Indeed, India would like to preserve its healthy relationship with both Iran and the US. India has been busy on diplomatic front to do a careful balancing act to make sure that its relationship with Iran does not impinge upon its relationship with the United States. Few suggestions are recommended to ensure that New Delhi must not be caught in the zero-sum game between Washington and Tehran:

- India should make it clear to the United States that it will continue to support American efforts to bring Iran into legal compliance over its nuclear programme.
- India must convince the United States that it should see India-Iran relations the same way as India sees US-Pakistan relations. India must persuade US to De-hyphenate US-Iran-India relations with the illustration of US relations with India and Pakistan. As India's External Affair Ministry former spokesperson Navtej Sarna stated "the United States has its relationship with Pakistan, which is separate from our own relationship with them" (Ramachandran: 2005).
- The United States can use India as a mediator to win over Iran to abandon its nuclear programme for military purpose.
- For the United States India–Iran cooperation will promote stabilisation and development in Afghanistan which is in accordance with Washington long term interest in the region.

India's need to counter Pakistan influence, diversification of partners in the Islamic world and the engagement of Central Asia are responsible for growing convergence in Indo-Iran relations based on mutual and shared interests have reached on advanced state. Just how close can New Delhi afford to be to Tehran before it seriously anger Washington is a question for debate in the foreign policy circles in both US and India but for now it seems that over the time New Delhi relations with Tehran continue to excel irrespective of Washington pressure.

Conclusion

At the broadest level, irrespective of Iran's troubled relationship with the United States, Iran is and will remain an energy competitor of the Caspian producer. The Americans and Iranian both obviously expect the importance of the energy resources from this key region to grow in the face of the expected long-term increase in global demand. Notwithstanding the fact that their political, economic and strategic interests no longer coincide. Successive US administrations have recognized that Iran's regime poses a profound threat to US interests in the Middle East and more broadly across the globe. The Iranian aspiration to become nuclear power and the United States exaggerated hostility to the Islamic Republic has diminished any hope for further reconciliation between the two enemy countries. In fact Washington's attitude towards Tehran is influenced more by domestic politics rather than strategic interests. The power struggle of conservative and reformist at domestic front in Iran has made Iranian foreign policy towards United States more complex and contradictory. The deteriorating relationship between United States and Iran has posed a challenge to the Indian diplomacy to maintain balanced relationship with the two foes. It is apparent that India can reach Kazakh, Uzbek and Turkmen oil and gas through Iran. The United States should realise the importance of Iran for India for numerous interests which it cannot relegate. Interestingly, for the United States Iranian cooperation becomes inevitable to tackle menace of global terrorism, especially in Afghanistan and to solve Arab-Israel conflict. Hence, the course of West Asian politics and thickness of Indo-US relations would be determined by the chemistry between United States and Iran.

Notes

1. Imam Khomeini, Islam and Revolution, trans. Hamid Algar, Berkeley, Calif.: Mizan Press, 1981, p. 185.
2. Treaty of Friendship between the Russian Soviet Federal Socialist Republic and Iran (Persia), 1920, and the Soviet-Iranian Trade and Navigation Agreement, 1940.

References

Aliriza, Bulent, (2000), "US Caspian Pipeline Policy: Substance or Spio? Centre for Strategic and International Studies, 24 August 2000, URL: www.csis.org/turkey/CEU00024. htm.

Ar-Rahmani, Bijan Mossav, "*Oil in US Iran Relations*," URL: www.worlddialogue.org/ pdf/speech8.pdf.

Bajpaee, Chietigj, (2005), "India, China locked in Energy game", *Asian Times online*, 2005, URL: www.atimes.com.

Bakshi, Jyotsna (1998), "No Single power or Power Centre can have Exclusive Sway Over Central Asia: A Geopoliical Analysis," *Strategic Analysis*, pp. 119-141.

BBC News Persian, 4 February 2006, URL : www.bbc.co.uk.

Bedi, Rahul, (2002), *Frontline*, September 14-27, 2002).

Bhatty, Robin and Rachel Broson (2000), "NATO's Mixed Signals in the Caucasus and Central Asia, *Survival*, 42(3): 129-45.

Bogmolov, Pavel (1995), 'If we Clash It'll be on the Caspian," *Current Digest of Post Soviet Press*, 21: pp. 21.

Dekmeijian , R Hrair and Honovann H Simonian (2003), *Troubled Water: The Geopolitics of Caspian Region* , London: IB Tauris.

DeLay, Jennifer (1999), "The Caspian Oil Pipeline Tangle: A Steel Web of Confusion" in Michael P. Croissant and Bulent Aras; (eds), *Oil and Geopolitics in the Caspian Sea Region,* London: Praeger.

Department of Energy (2005), EIA, Caspian Sea, Country Analysis brief, URL: www.eia.doe.gov.

Department of Energy, EIA (2005) Central Asia, Country Analysis Brief, URL: www.eia.doe.gov.

Ebel, Robert (1997/98), *Energy Choices in the Near Abroad, and International Institute of Strategic Studies, Strategy Survey*, London: Oxford University Press.

Ehteshami, Anoushiravan (2004) "Geopolitics of Hydrocarbons in Central and Western Asia," in Shirin Akiner, (eds), *The Caspian Politics , Energy and Security*, London , NY: Routledge Curzon.

Gilani, Iftikhar, (2010) "US Sanction on Iran a Threat to India's Energy Security: Rao", *Daily Times,* 6 July, 2010, URL: http://alethonews.wordpress.com)

Georgian, Armen (2002), "*US Eyes Caspian Oil in 'War on Terror'*" Armenian National Committee, 1 May 2002, URL: www.ancsf.org/essays_analysis/caspian-oil.htm.

Godoy, Julio (2001), "*US Policy Towards Taliban Influenced by Oil*", 15 Nov. 2001, URL:
http://www.truthout.org/docs_01/11.17A.oil.Taliban.htm.

Hill, Fiona (2001), "*A Not So Grand Strategy: United States Policy in the Caucasus and Central Asia since 1991*"; URL: www.brook.edu/dybdocroot /views/articles /fhill/2001 politique.htm.

Iran Libya Sanction Act, (1996),
URL: http://www.jewishvirtuallibrary.org/jsource/US-

Israel/iran_libya_sanctions_act_sum.html.

Iran or the US? India's Delicate Balancing Act", May 6, 2008, URL: http://blogs.reuters.com/india/2008/05/06.

Jafar, Majid (2004), Kazakhstan: Oil, Politics and the new 'Great Game', in Shirin Akiner (eds), *The Caspian: Politics Energy and Security,* London , New York: Rouledge Curzon.

Jean-Christophe, Peuch (2001), Private and National Interests in the Caspian Region, in Bulent Gokey (eds,), *The Politics of Caspian Oil*, New York: Palgrave.

Joshi, Nirmala (1999), Russian Security Interests in the Transcaucasia, in Shamsuddin (eds), *Nationalism in Russia and Central Asian Republic; Unfinished Democratic Revolution*, New Delhi: Lancer Book.

Kalicki, Jan H (2001), "Caspian Energy at the Crossroad," *Foreign Affairs*, 80(5): 120-34.

Karagiannis, Emmanuel (2003), "The US-Iranian Relationship after 11 September 2001 and the Transportation of Caspian Energy," *Central Asian Survey*, 22(2/3), June/Sept 2003, pp. 151-52.

Kemp, Geoffery, US Iranian Relations: Competition or Cooperation in the Caspian Sea Basin, in Robert Ebel and Rajan Menon (eds), *Energy and Conflict in Central Asia and the Caucasus*, Lanham: Rowman and Littlefield Pub. Inc.

Kronstadt, K Alan and others (2006), "India-Iran Relations and US Interests", August 2, 2006, CRS Report RS 22486.

Labeviere, Richard (2000), *Dollars for Terror: the United States and Islam*, NY: Algora.

Lakshman, Narayan (2010), Hillary: US-India relationship 'an affair of the heart', *The Hindu*, 5 June 2010, p. 14.

Levine, Steve (1995), "High Stakes," *Newsweek,* 17 April 1995, p. 10.

Mahapatra, Chintamani (2005), "US Policy Towards Caspian Region," *Contemporary Central Asia*, IX(1): 1-26.

Manning, Robert A (2000), *The Asian Energy Factor: Myth and Dilemmas of Energy, Security and the Pacific Future*, New York: Palgrave.

McCutcheon, Milary, Richard Obson (2001), "Risk Temper Caspian Rewards Potential", *Oil and Gas Journal* , 24 December, 2001 , pp. 26.

Mohsenin, Mehrdad M, "*The Evoluion of Security Role of Iran in the Caspian Region*," URL:

books.sipri.org/files/books/SIPRI01Chufrin/SIPRI01.

Mojtahed-Zadeh, Pirouz (2000), The Geo-politics of the Caspian Region, in Hooshang Amirahmadi (eds), *The Caspian Region at the Crossroad*, London: Macmillan Press Ltd.

Olcott, Martha Brill (2005), *Central Asia Second Chance*, Washington D.C.: The Brooking Institution Press.

Palit, Parama Sinha (2004), "US-Iran: The Changing dynamics and the Likelihood of a Conflict", *Strategic Analysis*, 28(1): 102-116

Ramachandran, Sudha (2005), The Glue that Bonds India, Iran, 12 January 2005, URL: www.atimes.com/atimes/south_Asia.

Rashid, Ahmed (2000). *Taliban, Islam, Oil and the New Great Game in Central Asia,* London, New York: IB Tauris Publisher.

Rumer, Boris (1996), "Disintegration and Reintegration in Central Asia: Dynamics and Prospects," in Boris Rumer, (eds)., *Central Asia in Transition: Dilemmas of Political and Economic Development*, New York: M.E. Sharpe and Co. Inc

Rutledge, Ian (2005), *Addicted to Oil: America's Relentless Drive for Energy Security*, London, New York: IB Tauris.

Swietochowski, Tadeusz (1998), The Politics of Oil and the Quest for Stability : The Caspian Sea," in Tauraj Atabaki and John O' Kane, (eds), *Post Soviet Central Asia*, London, New York: Tauris Academic Studies.

Takeyh, Ray (2002), "Re-imagining US-Iranian Relations", *Survival*, 44(3): 23-36.

Tevzade, Zurab (2004), "Caspian Oil: Its Export Routes and transportation Problems," *Central Asia and the Caucasus*, 1(25): 88-100.

The White House, Office of the Press Secretary, Statement by the President, 3 August 2001.

Washington Post, 15 September 1997.

Map 1

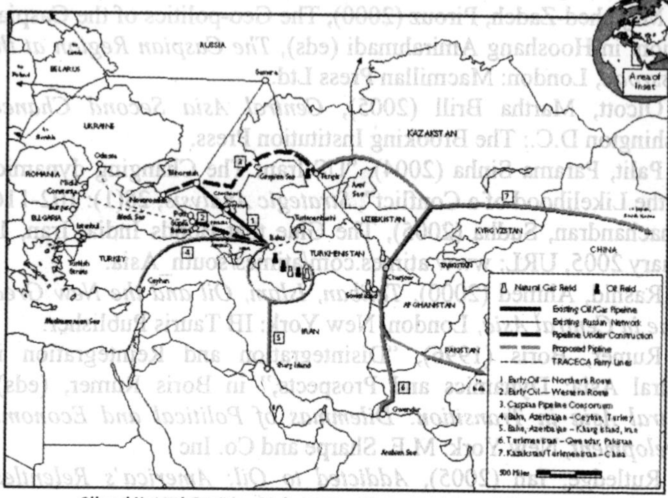

Oil and Natural Gas Export Infrastructure in Central Asia and the Caucasus

Sources: US Department of State.

Table 2

Current and Future Pipelines in the Greater Caspian Region

Name	Type	Route	Capacity (Barrels/Day)	Length	Status
AIOC* Early oil (South-North)	Oil	Baku-Novorossiisk via Groznyi	120,000+	1000 mi.	Russian side inoperative
AIOC Early oil (East-West)	Oil	Baku-Supsa via Tbilisi	120,000+	550 mi.	Under construction
AIOC Main export pipeline (MEP)	Oil	Undecided; preferable via Turkey	1,000,000	2,000+ mi.	Decision pending
Caspian Pipeline Consortium (CPC)	Oil	Kazakstan/Tengiz-Novorossiisk	1,340,000	1,500 mi.	Contracts signed
Turkmenistan-Afghanistan-Pakistan pipelines	Gas	Dauletabad gas field to central Pakistan	2 billion cubic feet/day	872 mi.	The civil war in Afghanistan is stalling construction
	Oil	Chardzhou, Turkmenistan to Gwadar, Pakistan	1,000,000	800+ mi.	
Kazakstan-China	Oil	Western Kazakstan to China	TBA	Approx. 3,700 mi.	Feasibility study pending
Turkmenistan-China	Oil	Chardzhou to China	TBA	Approx. 3,700 mi.	Feasibility study pending
Central Asia-Turkey	Gas	Kazakstan, Turkmenistan, Azerbaijan	TBA	Approx. 1,300 mi.	Pending decision on the status of the Caspian Sea
Iran-Turkey	Gas	Northern Iran to eastern Turkey	10 bcm/yr.** over 23 years	600 mi.	Contract signed; financing unclear

Notes: *AIOC = Azerbaijan International Operating Company, **bcm/yr. = Billions of cubic meters per year.
Source: US. Department of State, *Caspian Region Energy Development Report (As Required by HR 3610)*, undated report attached to letter from Barbara Larkin, Assistant Secretary for Legislative Affairs, to Senator Robert Byrd, April 15, 1997, p. 3.

Index

Index